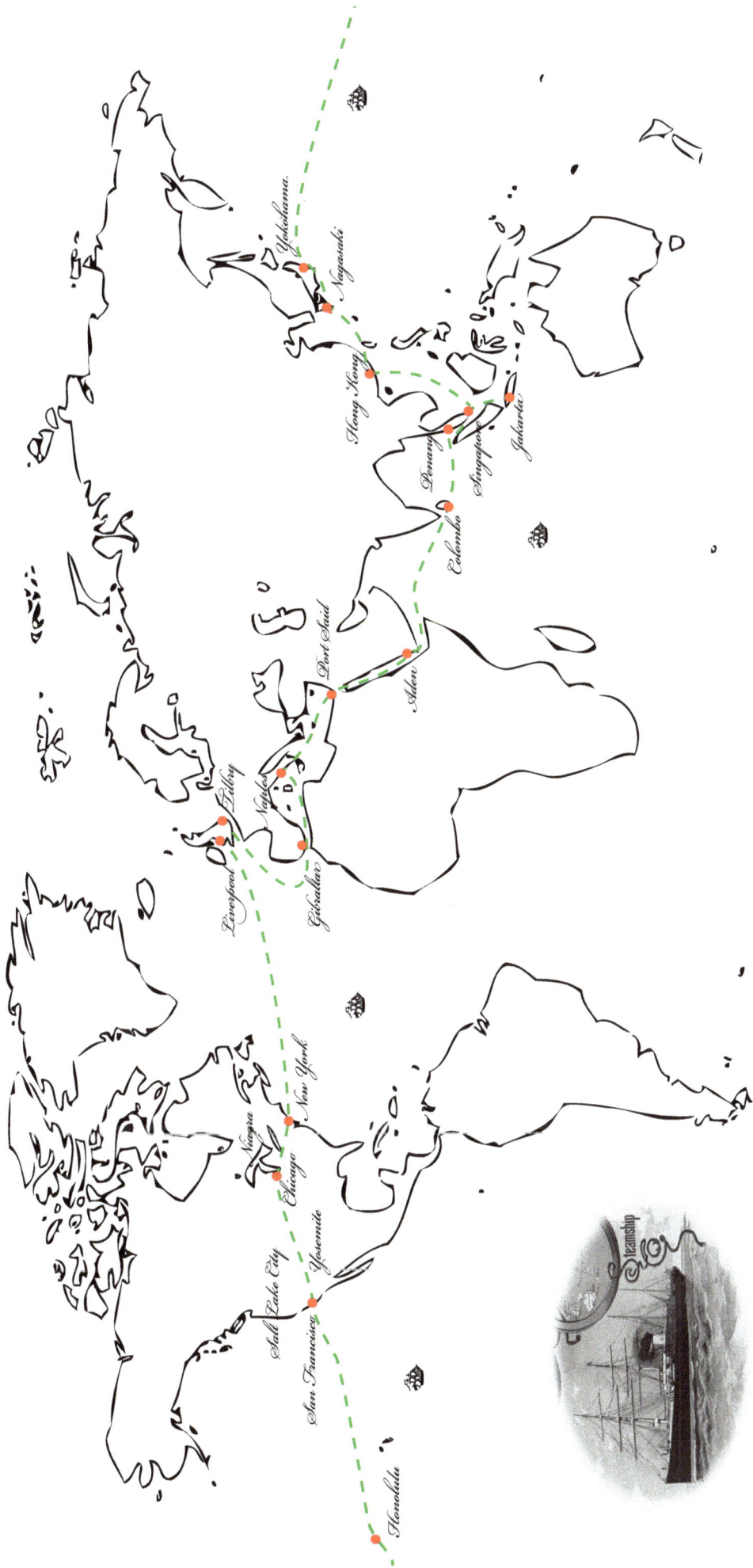

Bertie Bristowe's Voyage   Around the World, 1896-1897

Cover design by Philip Goldfinch, Lime Creative, London

The cover illustration is of the *SS Victoria*, the flag ship of the P&O Line
(from the P&O Pocket Book 1887)

Design and typesetting by Richenda Goldfinch

Published through Linellen Press

Travels in the Realms of Gold

The Revolution in Travel Empowered by Steam

*"Much have I travell'd in the realms of gold,
And many goodly states and kingdoms seen."*

John Keats

Bertram Arthur Bristowe, 1890 aged 26

Travels in the Realms of Gold
Published by Virginia Bristowe, 2019

ISBN 978-0-9872072-8-9

Contents

1896-1897 Bertie Bristowe, A Round the World Journey

Date	Place	Ship	Land days	Sea days
27 Nov – 22 Dec	At sea	SS Orient (Orient Line)		24
	Gibraltar, Naples, Suez Canal ports			
22 Dec – 7 Feb	Ceylon		40	
8 – 13 Feb	At sea	SS Kaiser i Hind (P & O)		7
13 Feb	Penang			1
14 Feb	At sea	SS Kaiser i Hind (P & O)		1
15 – 20 Feb	Singapore			
21 – 22 Feb	At sea	SS Telamon (Holt Line)		2
23 – 11 March	Java		16	
12 – 13 March	At sea	SS Van Dieman (K P Mij)		2
14 – 16 March	Singapore		3	
17 – 21 March	At sea	SS Thames (P & O)		5
22 March	Hong Kong		1	
23 March	At sea	SS Fatshan and Canton		1
24 March	At sea	SS Kian Tung, Macau, SS Heung Shan		1
25 March	Hong Kong		1	
26 – 29 March	At Sea	SS Verona (P & O)		4
30 – 9 June	Japan		72	
10 – 19 June	At sea	SS Gaelic (O & O SS Co.)		9
20 June	Honolulu		1	
21 – 26 June	At sea	SS Gaelic (O & O SS Co.)		5
27 June – 8 July	San Francisco, USA		11	
9 – 18 July	Train, Salt Lake City, Chicago, Niagara		8	
July – 20 July	New York City		2	
21 – 30 July	At sea	SS Adriatic (White Star Line		9
30 July	Arrival at Liverpool			
		Total	161	70

Travels in the Realms of Gold
The Revolution in Travel, Empwered by Steam

Much have I travell'd in the realms of gold,
And many goodly states and kingdoms seen.
John Keats

The brown leather bound book I spotted in my late father's bookshelf sat looking conspicuously out of place amongst the dusty collection of paperbacks. It had the air of a venerable old gentleman being jostled by brash youngsters all competing for my attention. The book had no visible title, but when I opened it, the next page beyond the beautiful marbled end papers was inscribed *B.A.Bristowe.* This I knew to be the name of my paternal grandfather, and on the next page, was the hand written title;

' *Notes taken during my journey round world* '

' *I left Tilbury on 27th Nov 1896. Before we passed Margate I was seasick & I did not get over it till we got to Gibraltar....* '

As I read on I realised to my excitement that I had stumbled on the journal my grandfather had kept when he escaped from his job at the London Stock Exchange to explore the world for nearly eight months.

My early childhood was spent living in the house of my maternal grandparents, with whom I very close, so I have always felt that grandparents were special people. I regretted I never knew my paternal grandparents, as both had died long before I was born: my grandfather, Bertram Arthur Bristowe, in 1926 and my grandmother, in 1930. My grandfather was always known by his family and friends as Bertie and that is the name he will be referred to in this narrative.

I know my father was deeply attached to his parents, but as a child I don't remember him talking about them often, so I grew up thinking of them as rather shadowy figures. We were told our grandmother had been a beauty, but little about what they were like as people. The discovery of this journal enabled me to make a vicarious journey round the world myself, with the grandfather I had never met and make his acquaintance for the first time. As I read his day-to-day account, I gained the impression we had much in common; both of us had a keen interest in people, natural history, travel and beautiful things. I also admired his energy and enjoyed his droll sense of humour.

In his journal Bertie described the places he visited, the people he met, and wrote, sometimes with lively amusement, of the adventures and misadventures he had along the way. He sometimes recorded the prices of items he bought, hotels he stayed at and fares for the vessels on which he travelled. It is interesting to compare these with today's prices.

As a dedicated naturalist, he was keen to obtain new butterflies and moths for his collection and he also shot many small beautiful birds. These he skinned, to take home as specimens. This practise may shock modern conservationists, but Victorian scientists at that time felt justified in doing so. Also, he wrote from the viewpoint of a middle class Victorian gentleman, using terms that sound somewhat patronising these days. The workers were universally known as 'coolies', or a bad guide might be referred to as a 'lazy rascal' or other disparaging epithets, but we have to accept he was a man of his time, and this was how many people spoke or acted in those days. It is obvious that he thoroughly enjoyed the strange experiences he would never have come across before. He was willing to rise before dawn and climb for miles to see bubbling mud pools and volcanoes on Java Island, or eat gut-wrenchingly disgusting food in Canton. He even sampled durian for a second time while holding his nose, to see if it was quite as disgusting as he found it the first time (it was, he resolved never again!). However, he was enchanted by the beautiful landscapes, the temples and the flowers, especially in Japan as springtime unfolded and touched the landscape with fresh green leaves and colourful blossoms.

Luckily the journal was written in a clear hand which was easy to read, except sometimes the place names were difficult to decipher, especially as some names had changed since 1896. He may have spelled some phonetically, as occasionally places are spelt differently from one entry to the next. It The account was obviously not written for general publication, but more for himself to read later, or possibly family members..

In addition to the journal, there are some letters Bertie wrote to his family while travelling. These were to his father, whom he addressed as 'Governor', his mother, 'Mater' and his sisters, Kathleen and Ethel, who were still living in the family home. Many of the descriptions were similar to the observations in his journal, but written with a more personal slant, which gave a slightly different perspective. There is also a large photo album with images of many of the places he visited on his journey. We see Singapore as a picturesque place of palm trees and wooden houses, Hong Kong with sailing ships in the harbour and not a sky-scraper in sight, and Japan, with beautiful traditional buildings that look delightfully rural.

He visited exotic places where he wandered amongst ruins, temples and other cultural sites. As an avid lepidopterist, he spent many happy hours wielding his butterfly net in hot pursuit of beautiful tropical butterflies and moths. He obviously enjoyed making friends with people wherever he went. He met some on board ship. (There is even a hint of a ship-board romance on the SS Gaelic sailing between Yokohama and Hawaii). Others he encountered at the various places he visited, some of whom joined him on his excursions. Besides sea travel, he used the local train service, and in a few places mentioned electric tramcars. He rode on horseback and in a variety of horse-drawn vehicles, rickshaws pulled by men, and bullock carts, but at no time was there mention of motor vehicles, as in the 1890's these were still a rarity. It is hard, nowadays, to imagine the cities he visited without the noise and pollution caused by cars, bikes, trucks and other traffic. He walked many miles during his explorations, so he became an extremely fit man by the time he returned home to his family.

Bertie embarked on his journey on 27 November 1896 and in total, he spent sixty-nine days at sea on eleven different vessels. All of these were coal-fired steamers, some of which also relied on sail-power to save on coal consumption. He often mentioned sea-sickness in his journal, but did not record much about his life on board ship. He spent 161 days on land visiting twelve different countries: some places for only one day, such as Naples, Penang, Canton, Macau and Honolulu, others for much longer. He spent forty days in Ceylon (Sri Lanka as it is now called), sixteen days on the island of Java, nine days at Singapore and three days in Hong Kong. He lingered for seventy -two days in Japan, and just twenty-one days in North America, which included eight days travelling by train from San Francisco to New York City. Finally, from New York he boarded the SS Adriatic for the eight day Atlantic crossing, to arrive at Liverpool on 30 July 1897.

By the time he returned home, Bertie had acquired many beautiful things to remind him of all the countries he visited. Not only his extensive collection of butterflies, but also a huge quantity of exquisite art works he purchased and arranged to have shipped back. He spent many happy hours seeking out 'curios' as he called them as presents for his family and friends, or to preserve for himself. Most of these have been passed on to his descendants who treasure these lovely Asian art works to this day.

It was a courageous act for a young man, who had never previously travelled further than France, to set off alone on such an epic journey. He was not, however, particularly unusual in undertaking such a venture. By the second half of the 19th century steam power had revolutionised travel by train and ships, to make it more affordable for people to reach almost anywhere in the world. The Victorians became enthusiastic travellers and many wrote books about their explorations. These became best sellers, which spurred others on to experience the pleasures of visiting foreign countries.

This book may have started as a chronical of one man's journey around the world, but while Bertie, his journal and letters may be regarded as the core of this narrative, the book has expanded, almost of its own volition, to cover transportation and travel in general in the 1890s. It includes sections from other nineteenth century travellers' writings who visited the same places as Bertie. There are also interesting stories to be told about the magnificent steam ships on which he was a passenger, the places he visited and the hotels he patronised.

Chapter One

Bertie's Family Background

In August 1748 great excitement was caused in the scientific world by the capture of two strange and handsome butterflies. These were seen flitting among the willow trees lining Cool Arbour Lane, just outside the small village of Camberwell Green, a few miles south of London. This was the first time they had been recorded in England and were named the 'Grand Surprize' or 'Camberwell Beauty'. For years people travelled to Camberwell in the hope of sighting, or even capturing, an elusive Camberwell Beauty (Nymphalis antiopia), and consequently this obscure little village became famous.

It was at Camberwell, in the county of Surrey, that Bertie's grandfather practised as a doctor and where his father, William Bristowe and his new wife, Sarah Jane, purchased an imposing Georgian house set in extensive grounds on Champion Hill, named 'Durlstone'. They had enough land to keep a cow, and for a large orchard and later, a tennis court. It was in this house that Bertie and his nine brothers and sisters spent a very happy childhood.

An old postcard of Camberwell Beauty butterflies Nymphalis antiopa, also known as Mourning Cloak butterflies in the USA.

"Durlstone" Champion Hill.
1893

In the early 19th century, Camberwell was still a rural village. It did not become incorporated as part of the London County Council until 1889. It was, however, connected to London by a good train service. This resulted in a rapid growth in population and enabled William to travel up to his business in the City of London easily. He was a member of the London Stock Exchange (LSE) in partnership with his brother, Thomas Lynn, in their firm, Bristowe Brothers.

An old postcard of Camberwell Green, showing the horse-drawn tram cars - and the exact same view in 2019

Thomas Lynn, or Sir Thomas as he became, entered politics in 1885 as a Conservative Member of Parliament representing the constituency of Herne Hill. He was active in social issues and supported a campaign for the preservation of Brockwell Hall and its extensive parkland in Herne Hill. There had been plans to divide this beautiful area into building plots, but, due largely to his efforts, it was preserved for the use of all the people. It was a great shock when Sir Thomas collapsed and died of a heart attack on the steps of Brockwell Hall, just after Lord Rosebery had made his speech at the formal opening of the park in 1892.

William Bristowe, Bertie's father, was a large and athletic man, but he also had artistic ability and would draw funny cartoons and caricatures to amuse his family and friends. Unlike many Victorian fathers, he was particularly kind and indulgent with his children and loved to play with them and read stories to them. He delighted in taking his large family on holidays to the seaside in Britain and Europe. Bertie's mother, whilst being fond of all her children, tended to be more of a disciplinarian than her husband. They were, however, a close and loving family.

During the 19th Century, the LSE was divided into two categories of operators. These were Stock Brokers and Stock Jobbers, or Jobbers, as they were usually known. Brokers earned a commission from their clients when they arranged to buy or sell shares for them.

Brokers did not own the shares and would buy them from the Jobbers.

Jobbers were known as 'market makers'. They usually specialised in certain securities and relied on detailed knowledge of them. They made their money from buying shares with the aim of promoting the stocks and then selling them at a higher price, which was known as a 'turn'. Bristowe Brothers were a highly respected firm of Stock Jobbers. The LSE motto was Dictum Meum Pactum (my word is my bond). Since deals were often made informally on a handshake, integrity was essential. Dress code at the LSE was formal with the seniors wearing top hats and tailcoats, whereas the juniors and clerks might sport a bowler hat.

William Bristowe, Bertie's father, a popular member of the London Stock Exchange

Bertie was born in 1864. Photographs of him as a child show him as a stocky little boy and he grew into an attractive young man with an impressive moustache which he retained all his life. In his youth, he always had plenty of children to play with, for in addition to his eight surviving brothers and sisters, he had dozens of cousins living nearby, all of whom were his extended family. Especially close were the five sons of his uncle Thomas, who were about the same age as him. They attended the same school and later became his closest friends at work when they joined their fathers on the Stock Exchange.

Bertie, like his father, was athletic and while at Radley College, represented the school in cricket and rugby. He won trophies for boxing,

Sarah Jane Bristowe (nee Mason) Bertie's Mother; her dress is in the fashion of 1860's, so perhaps this photo was taken at the time of her marriage in 1862.

Bertie aged seven years old

tennis, diving and fives (a game similar to squash, but using padded gloves instead of a racquet). He was artistic and throughout his life produced some lovely landscape paintings, some of which were exhibited and won awards. Even though he worked in the City of London, Bertie was, at heart, a country loving man. He developed a keen interest in natural history and built up an extensive collection of butterflies, moths and beetles. He was also extremely knowledgeable about birds and wild flowers and enjoyed activities such as gardening, going for long cycle rides, fishing and shooting.

When he left school in 1881, it was taken for granted that Bertie would become a member of the family firm at the LSE. It was not to be a career that he particularly enjoyed, but in time he became a skilful Jobber in the new partnership formed by his father with his sons, Bertie, Alexander and Lewis. The LSE tended to be something of a 'boys' club'. To be accepted as a member, no formal qualifications were required, beyond being known to be honest and 'of the right sort' and with three existing members willing to sponsor the applicant. Not surprisingly there were quite a number of family firms, in which young men were recruited by their fathers, uncles, or other family members.

Bertie continued to live with his parents, as did his other siblings until their marriages. Walter, his older brother, married Mary Wright in 1890 and they had three children. His sister Amy, born two years after Bertie, married Herbert Bressey, a tea planter and went with him to Ceylon. Rose, seven years his junior, married Australian-born Guy Boothby in 1895 and they had four children. Guy was a successful author who wrote popular thrillers.

By 1896 Bertie was 32 years old, a bachelor living at home and working with his father on the Stock Exchange. Why was it at this time that he decided to take extended leave to explore the world? He was away for over eight months and it

Some illustrations of insects which demonstrates that at age 14, Bertie was a skilled artist with an interest in entomology

13

would have been a costly exercise. There have been two explanations suggested by family members. His son, William (Bill), wrote of his father in his memoirs:

The early strains of the Stock Exchange had caused some temporary upset which led to his going on a round-the-world journey in 1986-87, which had a great influence on his life.

To work on the Stock Exchange in the 1880s and 1890s would have been a high-pressure occupation. It was a time of extraordinary expansion and uncertainty, with fluctuations in the economy, which inevitably affected the stock market. The technological communication revolution had begun with the invention of the telegraphic methods of sending messages; ticker-tape was introduced to the LSE in 1872, and telephones in 1880. These allowed instant access to prices and opened up opportunities for investments far beyond the English domestic market. While this was a good time to make money if you read the market correctly, investments have always been a gamble and any time of rapid change is stressful.

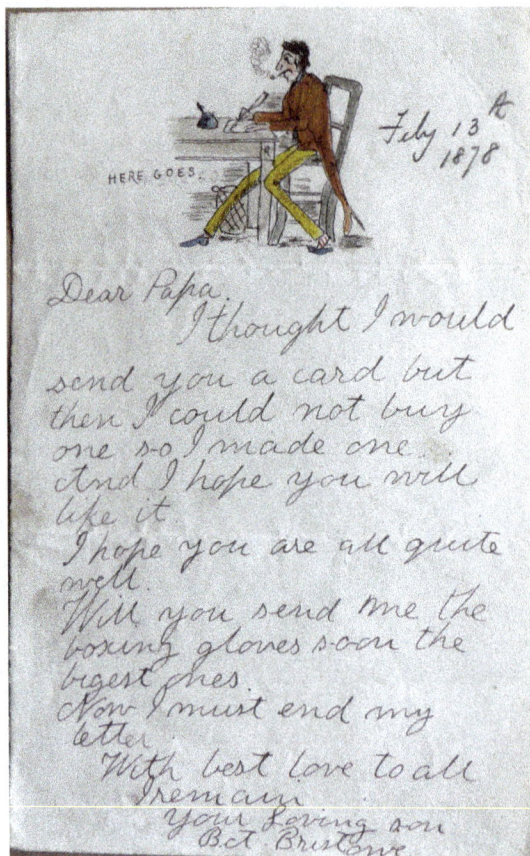

A letter Bertie sent to his father from school when he was twelve years old.

However, a romantic family legend suggests the real reason for his desire to travel was that he had fallen deeply in love with the beautiful Mary Rosa Johnston, and someone had informed him she had become engaged to Another Man. The story was that he was so devastated by this that he sailed away to forget her.

Contemporary photographs indicate that Miss Johnston was indeed an exceptionally pretty girl. She and her lively family lived close by in Camberwell and were all involved in the artistic and cultural world. According to Bill Bristowe's memoirs, poor Bertie had as his rivals such distinguished personalities as Sir Arthur Conan Doyle, Sir Robert Morant, (an eminent public servant) and the playwright, Rudolph Besier, later to be the author of the highly acclaimed production, The Barretts of Wimpole Street. All were admirers of Miss Mary Johnston; no wonder he found it hard to compete.

Another possibility may have been that Bertie's desire to marry Mary was viewed with disfavour by her father, John Johnston, because he was a younger son with only moderate prospects. Perhaps Mr. Johnston hoped for a more brilliant match for his daughter. Also the Johnston family belonged to an exclusive religious sect which discouraged social interaction with people with different beliefs.

Bertie's decision to sail away to explore the world for eight months was probably a combination of all these factors. After about fourteen years working with the stresses and strains of the Stock Exchange, he may have just felt the need for a break. He may even have questioned whether he should continue his employment in the family firm, or if he should consider a career change. Equally, the disheartening lack of progress in his courtship of Mary might have caused the desire to get away for a while; perhaps he hoped his absence would make her heart grow fonder. If this was the case, his strategy certainly worked, because when he returned as a sophisticated, worldly traveller with wonderful tales to tell, it seems she found him a more attractive prospect.

1894 Tennis party with Bristowe family and friends at Durlstone

An old photograph of the City of London, showing the various forms of horse transportation in the 1890's.

Britain in the 19th century experienced a time of extraordinary developments and changes. The Industrial Revolution produced new inventions, factories and the burgeoning of steam power. This was used extensively in industry and for transportation, with the development of the railways and steam driven ships. It was through the new railway service that over six million people were able to travel up to London from all over Britain to marvel at the wonders of British invention and industry, displayed at the Great Exhibition in 1851.

At the time of Bertie's birth in 1864, the British Empire was approaching its height, with colonies throughout the world to provide valuable raw materials such as minerals, cotton, wool, sugar, tea, coffee and other commodities. These were transported by steam ships and steam trains to Britain's manufacturing towns, and transformed into products that were then traded. The manufacturing Industry also provided employment to many people and this resulted in greater prosperity.

At the same time, there was a huge demographic shift of people from rural to urban living, caused by a downturn in agricultural employment, due to changes in agricultural methods and a depressed market. This led to a high unemployment rate among farm workers, but even if employed, their wages were woefully inadequate and fluctuated seasonally, so they scarcely earned enough to support themselves and their families. Many had no choice but to move to the towns in search of employment in the factories created by the Industrial Revolution. The 1801 census recorded that 20 per cent of the population lived in towns, but by 1881 urban dwellers had risen to nearly 70 per cent. The result was that towns become hugely over-crowded with many people living and working in appalling conditions, with low pay, child labour and long hours of work being the norm. This was a time of translocation and the development of transportation methods on a scale never experienced before.

As cities grew and new suburbs were built, there was a need for public transportation to increase, as people lived further away from their work places. While many of the poor could seldom afford the cost of public transport and had to walk many miles to and from work each day, others could travel on the various options that became available to people in the 19th century.

The urban well-off could afford to maintain their own carriages, with staff to drive and care for the horses. These were often housed in court yards, or small cobbled streets behind their residences with space for the horses and carriages downstairs and accommodation above for the coachmen and grooms. These were known as mews. This term originally meant the place where hunting hawks were housed, but since the royal horses had been kept at the site of the monarch's hawking mews in Charing Cross, it came to be a term used to describe stables.

For the majority of people, owning a carriage was impossible, but various new forms of horse drawn public transport became available. In London, there were short haul coaches, sometimes called hackneys. These had been in use since the 17th century, but tended to be too expensive for most people, so when George Shillibeer introduced the innovation of the horse drawn omnibus (meaning 'for everyone') in 1829, they became very popular. These conveyances were drawn by two or three horses and were double deckers. They may have been convenient, but they were not comfortable. The driver would pick up passengers anywhere along their route and the greater the number of people on the bus, the more he earned; it is not surprising, therefore, the buses were often over-crowded. In addition, there was little ventilation and the straw used to cover the floors was an excellent breeding ground for fleas. The passengers sitting downstairs were under cover, while those on the upper deck had no shelter from the weather and had to climb up a steep ladder to reach their seats. The first route ran between Paddington and the City, a distance of five miles. This took one hour and the fare was one shilling. The service was expanded to many other parts of London and in 1855 the London General Omnibus Company (LGOC) was formed, which took over the majority of the smaller bus companies. Mr. Shillibeer fell on hard times later in life, and spent some time in the debtor's prison. He eventually resurrected his business by running a fleet of horse-drawn funeral carriages.

In the 1860s some bus routes were converted to horse-drawn trams with wheels that ran on tramlines. This improved the speed and smoothness of the ride. Some routes were converted to electric trams at the end of the century, but horses continued to haul buses until the beginning of the 20th century when motorised buses replaced them.

In 1834 Joseph Hansom designed and patented a new form of horse carriage to be used for hire. These were first introduced in Paris, where they were known as hansom cabriolets, but in England, they were generally called hansom cabs. After trying out several types of carriages, two designs became the standard. One had four wheels which could carry up to four people and their luggage. These were popularly known as growlers because of the noise their wheels made. The other form had two wheels, designed to be swift and easy to manoeuvre in the traffic and to carry two passengers under cover. Both versions had a low centre of gravity which made them very stable and safe. The cabman, or cabbie as he became to be known, sat high up at the back of the cab, holding the reins over its roof. The passengers could communicate with the driver by a small trap door in the roof of the cab and also pass up their fare to him through it. The charges were generally 6d per mile. Hansom cabs became very popular in London and at their

A Handsome Cab from *Humorous Victorian Spot Illustrations Magazine*

peak, there were up to 11,000 seen on the streets, or waiting in cab ranks at such places as railway stations, outside hotels or theatres hoping to pick up a fare. Hansom cabs were featured frequently in literature by authors such as Robert Louis Stevenson and Sir Arthur Conan Doyle. Sherlock Holmes and Dr Watson often travelled by cab, valuing their speed and at times, their anonymity, when in pursuit of villains. Horse drawn cabs were eventually superseded by motor vehicles and when, in 1907, taximeters were made compulsory to measure accurately the distance travelled, the term taxi cab, or just taxi, came about.

Horses were also used in heavy haulage of goods and London streets could become extremely congested with horse drawn vehicles. It is not surprising that the amount of manure deposited became very unsavoury and hazardous, especially in wet weather, so

The development of steam power in the 19th century radically affected public transport. The Thames River had always been a thoroughfare for boats transporting people and goods. With the invention of steam boats, many people could travel to and from work on them, or use them for pleasure trips. Later in the century, as more bridges were built and other means of transportation became available, the use of river boats to transport people declined.

Most early steam boats had large paddle-wheels on the side of the vessel. These were efficient in the calm water of rivers and lakes, but less so in rough seas where the paddles may have been alternately deep into a rising wave or completely out of the water. Larger ocean going steam ships were developed more extensively with the invention of the central screw with propellers at the stern of the vessel. Ocean going vessels were used extensively for the carriage of freight and passengers throughout the world, cutting down transport costs and the time it took to travel between ports.

Land Transportation was revolutionised by the invention of the railways and steam trains. Since the introduction of the first trains at the start of the century, virtually all parts of the British Isles quickly became connected by rail lines. Rail transport within cities came later. In 1863 the first Underground Railway in the world was constructed between Paddington and Farringdon and named the Metropolitan Line. A deep trench was built, the rail lines were laid, and over them a brick tunnel was constructed, which was covered again by soil. The early locomotives were coal-burning steam engines, so air vents were also constructed to allow the smoke to escape, which prevented the lines being built too deeply underground.

When technology advanced to allow the powering of trains by electricity, it was possible to construct much deeper train lines underground, nicknamed The Tube. The first line in London, was the City and South London Railway in 1890. The underground railways enabled people to travel quickly and cheaply throughout the metropolitan area and they could live further away from their place of employment.

The bicycle was another form of transport that was invented and developed during the 19th century. This was to have a huge impact on society, allowing people to travel independently at a fair speed using the power of their own legs.

The first models were not efficient or comfortable, earning themselves the nickname of bone shakers and sometimes known as velocipedes. Later in France, the term bicycle was introduced. Throughout the century inventors and engineers worked on improving the design and in the 1870s, the high wheeler bicycle made its appearance. This model had a very large front wheel with pedals attached to its axis and a small rear wheel. It has become known as the Penny Farthing and could attain good speeds, but was difficult to ride safely especially for women with long skirts. John Woodforde, in his book, The Story of the Bicycle, estimated that there were around 50,000 high wheelers in Britain during the mid-1870s, manufactured by up to thirty firms. Bicycling was, however, almost exclusively a pastime for agile young men and as Woodforde observed:

The prime drawback, cheerfully accepted by the agile, was that the high-wheeler was unstable. Though it rolled smoothly over lesser bumps and dips, an angular obstruction such as a brick could check its progress alarmingly. The whole thing tipped over. Too hasty application of the brake, normally a spoon type clamping down on the top of the front tyre, could easily cause the same result.'

Ladies mostly preferred to use tricycles, which were also manufactured at this time. In *The Young Ladies' Treasure Book, (1889)* a guide for young ladies, it was stated:

'Of the advantages of tricycle riding from a physical point of view, little needs to be said. It is an eminently healthy amusement, if not begun too fiercely and continues too long. Moderation must be insisted on.'

From *Humorous Victorian Spot Illustrations*

It was in the 1880s that the bicycle was adapted into what became known as the safety bicycle. There were several designs, but eventually these machines became similar to modern bicycles with both wheels roughly the same size, pedals connected to the back wheels by a chain, pneumatic tyres and efficient brakes. Cycling became far more comfortable and less hazardous than it had been before, and in the 1890s became a worldwide craze among young men and women who could afford the high cost of a bicycle, which was equivalent to six months' wages for a working class man. It was in 1892 that Harry Dacre, who was a bicycle enthusiast, composed the song *Daisy Bell*. This was to become popular on the music hall stages in England and the USA. Its chorus ended with the words: *You'd look sweet upon the seat of a bicycle built for two.*

When manufacturers in the United States began the mass production of bicycles, this brought the cost down to an affordable level. For many, the bicycle became the preferred method of transport to work. Bicycle riding was also immensely popular as a form of recreation for young men and women too, in spite of the fact they were hampered by their long skirts and the need for decorum. They overcame this by fitting a skirt holder, which held their skirt down so that it would not blow up to reveal too much of their legs. Later, they adopted the more daring divided skirts and even the shocking Bloomers. In Punch Magazine in the late 1890s cycling, especially by ladies, became the frequent subject for humorous cartoons. However, it was claimed by many that the sense of greater freedom and independence provided by bicycles may have been a significant factor in the rise of demands for women's rights. In an interview with the investigative journalist, Nelly Bly, Susan B Anthony, a well- known American Civil Rights campaigner and feminist, said in 1896:

Let me tell you what I think of bicycling. I think it has done more to emancipate women than anything else in the world. I stand and rejoice every time I see a woman ride by on a wheel. It gives her a sense of self-reliance. It makes her feel as if she were independent. The moment she takes her seat ... away she goes, the picture of free, untrammelled womanhood.

From *Humorous Victorian Spot Illustrations*

The Safety Bicycle made bicycle riding a much safer and more pleasant occupation for everyone, young and old.

Bicycle racing soon became a serious sport, both on roads and race tracks. In 1896, at the first modern Olympic Games held in Athens, there were cycle races for men and not long after, the famous Tour de France race was founded in 1903 by Henri Desgrange.

There were even instances of the bicycle being used for world travel. The first person to circle the world by bicycle was Thomas Stevens, who set off on 22 April 1884 from San Francisco on a Penny Farthing, heading for New York and then on around the world. It took him over two years. His belongings consisted of some pairs of socks, a spare shirt, a rain coat which served as a tent at night and a revolver, which were all packed onto his handle bars. He peddled across America on roads that were so bad or non-existent, that he had to walk much of the way. He reached New York in August and spent the winter there. He then travelled by steamer to Liverpool, crossed England, Europe and Asia Minor to Persia (Iran), where he spent the winter months as a guest of the Shah. In the spring he travelled on through Asia to Japan where he caught a steamer to take him back to San Francisco in January 1887. He calculated that he had covered 13,500 miles. Everywhere he went he was hailed as a hero and greeted by bicycle enthusiasts, who helped him with advice and obtaining new equipment. He sent articles recording his progress and about his amazing adventures to the press and magazines. He later wrote a two volume book published in 1888: *Around the World on a Bicycle*.

In 1894, Annie Kopchovsky cycled around the world starting in New York. Annie was also known as Annie Londonderry, because her journey was sponsored by the Londonderry Lithia Spring Water Company. She carried a change of clothes and a pearl-handled revolver and her bicycle was decorated with Londonderry banners and ribbons. She changed her attire from skirts to bloomers when she decided to exchange her 42lb woman's bicycle for a lighter man's model. Her progress received much publicity and she returned fifteen months later, a celebrity. Like Stevens, she wrote colourful accounts of her epic journey.

Bertie had always taken pleasure in sporting and physical activities. He had enthusiastically taken up the hobby of bicycle riding and with his brothers, enjoyed going for long cycle rides through the English countryside. The roads had rough surfaces, but at that time very little traffic, and bicycle riding was relatively safe.

Movement in the Victorian populous was not only physical but also social. Traditionally the British people were divided into Upper, Middle and Lower, or working, classes. The Landed Gentry and aristocratic classes were those who owned large tracts of land and property, which had been acquired mainly through inheritance. The upper classes were active in politics and held other positions of power, but tended to shun commerce, or trade. In the 19th century, they wielded a disproportionate amount of political power because only landowners could vote.

At the other end of the spectrum were the working classes. They provided the labour for the mining, manufacturing, transportation, and service industries. They generally had limited, or no education, low wages and lived in substandard rental accommodation close to their place of employment. Their living conditions were often crowded and un-sanitary. Working class women and children were expected to work long hours, often in dreadful conditions, as well as the men. However, the standard of living slowly improved. Schooling became available to almost everyone; in 1886 free primary schools were introduced, and for the first time, improved wages allowed some money to spare for minor luxuries and leisure activities.

The poorest people had little time for leisure, as they worked up to twelve hours a day, six days a week. They were only allowed Sunday off as a day of rest, but gradually working hours were decreased when employers allowed their workers to have Saturday afternoons free for recreation. In 1871, a law was passed to create Bank Holidays. These enabled workers to enjoy four extra days a year to spend with their families and for outings.

The working class people became more politically active and aware of their rights, and there was intense pressure on the government to improve working conditions and give more people the right to vote. With improved educational opportunities, some 'blue collar' working class people were able to become upwardly mobile into the 'white collar' middle classes.

Industrialisation created an increasing need for large numbers of white collar workers in the retailing, financial, trading and communications industries. The people who filled these positions were generally classified as the lower middle classes. They would have had some education and often would travel to work by train, electric tram, or horse drawn omnibus and live in the new suburbs being built on the outskirts of the towns. *Diary of a Nobody,* the brothers George and Weedon Grossmith's book, gives a lively account of lower middle class life. This originally appeared in a serialised form in the satirical magazine, Punch, but was later published as a book in 1892. It is written in the form of a diary by a fictional character, Mr Charles Pooter, who worked as a senior clerk in the City of London. He recorded the day to day vicissitudes of his life very seriously, with wonderful and very funny accuracy. It begins with Mr Pooter's description of his house.

My dear wife Carrie and I have just been a week in our new house, 'The Laurels', Brickfield Terrace, Holloway – a nice six-roomed residence, not counting basement, with a breakfast parlour. We have a little front garden; and there is a flight of ten steps up to the front door, which, by-the-by, we keep locked with the chain up. Cummings, Gowings and our other intimate friends always come to the little side entrance, which saves the servant the trouble of going up to the front door, thereby taking her from her work. We have a nice little back garden which runs down to the railway. We were rather afraid of the noise of the trains at first, but the landlord said we would not notice them after a bit, and took 2 pounds off the rent … After my work at the City, I like to be at home.

Charles Pooter worked six days a week and earned the princely sum of £80 per annum, later increased to £100. This enabled him to employ a maid, take a week's annual holiday by the seaside and travel by horse omnibus to work, with occasional rides in hansom cabs when he and his wife went out in the evening on social occasions.

A further category of people were generally known as the propertied or upper middle class. They were reasonably well off and included those employed in the professions such as doctors, academics, lawyers, colonial administrators, or clergy, which required them to be well educated, possibly including a tertiary degree. Those who held a senior position in the manufacturing industries, or financial institutions such as banking, insurance and the Stock Exchange, also were regarded as upper middle class. Mostly, they could afford to send their sons to a so-called good school, often as boarders. These schools provided discipline and a classical education based on Ancient History, Greek and Latin, with plenty of character-forming corporal punishment, cold baths and sports such as cricket and rugby, to foster team spirit and competitiveness. The Duke of Wellington is reputed to have stated that: *The Battle of Waterloo was won on the playing fields of Eton.*

Middle class girls were provided with an education sufficient to become good wives. Some considered it undesirable for women to be too clever, or a blue stocking. Domestic and artistic accomplishments were deemed most suitable for the weaker sex. Gradually, this attitude began to change and some women demanded the right to be as well educated as the boys. Many girls' schools were founded to cater to these aspirations in the latter half of the nineteenth century, and, despite staunch opposition from male academics, even female colleges at Universities were founded; the first being Girton College at Cambridge in 1869. At first women were allowed to study, but were not granted degrees, but by 1880, the first three females graduated at the University of London and later, other universities followed suit. With better education, women and the population at large became more interested in expanding their horizons and developed a curiosity about the whole world and travel.

Bertie Bristowe aged three

Chapter Three

The Development of Travel in the 19th Century

Prior to the latter half of the nineteenth century, only the rich could afford to travel for pleasure. During the seventeenth and eighteenth centuries, it was considered desirable that aristocratic young men should travel to Europe on a Grand Tour. They were usually accompanied by a tutor and guide, sometimes referred to as a bear-leader who could instruct him about cultural matters, arrange accommodation and hopefully keep him out of trouble. In addition, depending on their means, the young tourists might take their own carriage, valet, cook and other staff to care for them and protect against the very real threat of bandits and robbers. The usual itinerary included Paris, where the young men could learn how to behave in polite society, often including how to conduct oneself in affairs of the heart. Italy was also considered essential, since its arts and culture were highly regarded and all wished to see, and hopefully acquire, art works and relics of the Roman Empire to grace their stately homes in Britain. Many were influenced by the architecture they observed and built houses in the Palladian, or Neoclassical style to mimic Roman or ancient Greek villas and temples. In Italy, the main cities visited were Rome, Florence, Venice and Naples, which would include visits to the excavations in Pompeii and Herculaneum. These tours might last several months, or even years, and some embarked on several tours and visited other countries such as Switzerland, Germany and Holland. The young British travellers acquired a reputation for eccentric and dissolute behaviour. Venice in particular was known for its lively courtesans who were happy to accommodate the needs of the young gentlemen, particularly at Carnevale time.

The Grand Tours ceased at the time of the French Revolution and then the Napoleonic wars, because during the later years of the eighteenth century and up to 1815, it was too dangerous for the British to travel on the continent.

Unlike their wealthy masters, the poor could only undertake travel for reasons of necessity, perhaps to move from the country into town to obtain work. Their means of locomotion was almost exclusively walking to their destination, but gradually conditions changed. While there were still deep inequalities between the different classes, in the second half of the nineteenth century, the less advantaged people were generally better off and better educated than their parents had been. They had more money in their pockets, since real wages had increased by 45 per cent between 1880 and 1896. They also had more leisure time to spend enjoying life. Gambling, soccer, greyhound racing and drinking beer or Gin at the pub were popular pastimes. For the first time, the lower classes were able to travel away from home for outings and holidays, using the railway services. In addition, sea travel by the new steam-driven vessels, or steamers, as they were known, was faster, safer, and more affordable than in the old sailing ships.

Why did people of the mid to late nineteenth century Britain become such passionate travellers of the world? Some of course, were travelling to seek a better life, or to escape intolerable conditions resulting from poverty, or for political, or religious reasons. These were the emigrants who flocked to the United States, Canada and also Australia, New Zealand and other British Empire countries, which offered the prospect of work and land for all.

Many travelled for a specific purpose. Some were known as Empire Builders. These were people who set out to explore, develop, protect or administer the vastly growing British Empire throughout the world. One such person was Sir Harry Johnston. He was employed by the Colonial Office in Africa and was later to be Bertie's brother-in-law. Many more went abroad for commercial reasons associated with the Empire such as Herbert Bressey, who was a tea planter married to Bertie's sister, with whom he would stay in Ceylon.

A significant number of Victorians travelled because they were inspired by their religious convictions to spread the word of God to the heathens living in foreign lands. The missionaries, both men and women, went with the best of intentions and the desire to help. Even though they were not always successful in persuading their flock to abandon their own religion and convert to Christianity, many also provided education and medical services which benefited the people. They also spoke out bravely against slavery and other cruel practices. Unfortunately, many had narrow ethnocentric attitudes that saw no value in the culture of the people they were proselytising, and tried to supress the customs the missionaries regarded as immoral, or indecorous.

Others travelled for scientific reasons such archaeology, zoology and botany. Charles Darwin and Alfred Russel Wallace both studied and collected vast numbers of scientific specimens and their theories of evolution were presented jointly to the Royal Geographical Society in 1858. Others focused on botany and collected or painted the flora of the world. Two examples of those were F.W. Burbidge who collected plants professionally for botanical gardens and commercial nurserymen, and Marianne North who travelled the world producing wonderful botanical paintings which are still on display at the Royal Botanic Gardens in Kew, London.

There were also people who chose to travel purely for travel's sake out of a keen sense of curiosity about the world. These were men and courageous women, who were prepared to venture alone into extremely wild places. Quotes from their written accounts have been used to supplement Bertie's sometimes sketchy descriptions, when he travelled to the same countries. It is possible he may have read their books, either before or after his journey. One was Marianne North who travelled the world extensively. Another, Isabella Bird, was widely travelled, and wrote several books about her adventures including one entitled *Unbeaten Tracks* in Japan covering the period she spent in Japan in 1878. Bertie may well have been inspired by the exploits of the US journalist, Nellie Bly, who in 1889, succeeded in travelling around the world in seventy-two days amid considerable publicity, in competition with her rival, Elizabeth Bisland. Another American travel writer was Eliza Ruhamah Scidmore.

She wrote several books about her travels. One book, which Bertie might have read was published in 1891, entitled *Jinricksha Days in Japan*. Another was published in 1897, called *Java: Garden of the East*. This book was extremely interesting for him to read after his return, as she visited many of the same places that he did, and her observations were often similar to his. They both found the Dutch colonists were not welcoming to tourists and were shocked at the scanty and casual dress of the Dutch ladies. Bertie may also have enjoyed Mark Twain's amusing accounts of his travels to Europe in *Innocents Abroad*, or *Following the Equator (1897)* which was his account of a trip around the world. An English explorer, Sir Samuel White Baker was best known for his books about exploration in Africa, but in his youth spent time in Ceylon, and wrote two books about his experiences there. One in particular, *Eight Years Wandering in Ceylon*, would have been relevant to Bertie as it contained an account of the founding of an agricultural settlement at Nuwara Eliya, a place he visited while in that country. Major Thomas Skinner's autobiography, *Fifty Years in Ceylon*, provides a fascinating account of the colony in the early days of British occupation, when Skinner was responsible for the building of most of the roads on the island.

Both Bertie and his father were keen collectors of books about the sciences and travel, some of which are still in the possession of family members.

In addition to books written by people relating their travel adventures, there was also a demand for travel guide books with practical information about accommodation, transportation, costs and excursions to notable sights. Bertie mentioned he used John Murray's *A Handbook for Travellers in Japan including the whole Empire from Saghalien to Formosa*. This was an English publication, but there were also Baedeker's guides from Germany and Frommer's, first written in the United States.

It was books such as these which must have inspired Bertie and other Victorians to escape from their boring, daily life and explore the world. By the end of the nineteenth century, it was becoming easier and less costly to see the world.

For English people, one of the first to promote the concept of travel as a recreational activity in organised groups escorted by guides, was Mr Thomas Cook. He ran his first excursion in 1841. This was a ten mile day trip from Leicester to Loughborough and back, which cost one shilling. On this significant occasion, 570 people in high spirits somehow managed to squeeze into nine open railway carriages. Upon arrival they were greeted by banners and were entertained by brass bands and a variety of games, dancing and general jollification. Tea was served, but absolutely no alcohol, as Thomas Cook was a keen supporter of the temperance movement. This day outing was deemed a huge success and from that first foray into travel, the great travel institution, Thomas Cook was launched.

With the willing co-operation of the railway companies who were keen to increase their passenger numbers, Cook arranged more excursions and holidays to places of interest and the seaside throughout the British Isles. Later he expanded to the European Continent, to the United States and the Middle East and Egypt. Cook arranged a special tour to mark the opening of the Suez Canal in 1869. In 1872 he embarked on his first round-the-world tour. This was the same year as the publication of *Round the World in Eighty Days* by Jules Verne, but Cook's tour took 222 days and his passengers travelled in comfort. Unlike Verne's fictional Mr Phileas Fogg and his faithful valet Passepartout, they did not have to resort to elephant or balloon travel and were safely escorted all the way home. Later Cook planned future around-the-world tours at a cost of 220 guineas.

Several factors made travel right round the world, an easier proposition in the latter half of the nineteenth century. In 1869 several significant developments occurred. Firstly, the Suez Canal was opened, also the rail line connecting the east coast to the west coast of North America was completed and regular steamer ship services commenced between the west coast of America and Asian ports. Steam ships which were already operating between Asia and Europe and on to the USA completed the circle.

As his business expanded, Cook was joined by members of his family, particularly his son John Mason, whereupon the company was re-named Thomas Cook and Son. The class of his customers broadened from its working class origins to cater for the respectable middle classes, upper classes and even royalty, who wished to travel to practically any part of the globe. Cook's Tours were a major factor in promoting world travel, which became so popular among British people of all walks of life in the late nineteenth century.

While Thomas Cook was encouraging people to explore the world, the shipping companies were expanding their businesses. Steam ships were becoming larger and faster. They still carried cargo, mail and provided a cheap means of transport for immigrants, but they also provided First Class luxury for those who could afford it. It is claimed that P&O was the first to promoted the idea of cruising for pleasure, rather than just using a ship as a means to transport passengers from one place to another. There was intense rivalry between the shipping lines, as to which could provide the fastest passage between ports, the best food, most luxurious accommodation and the most exotic locations visited to attract potential passengers. Their schedules were advertised widely in the national press and colourful posters were displayed showing the various exotic destinations on offer.

It appears that Bertie did not use the services of Thomas Cook for his journey in 1896. He makes no mention of the company in his journal or letters home and probably was able to make his bookings directly through the shipping companies, or their agents, however, he would have seen accounts of other peoples' journeys in the press and the many travellers' guide books written at the time which may well have inspired him to see the world. One example is a book he owned, called *The Malay Archipelago: the Land of the Orang-Utan and the Bird of Paradise. A Narrative of Travel, with Studies of Man and Nature.* The author, Alfred Russel Wallace, with Charles Darwin, was the originator of the idea of evolution. This great book was first published in 1869, but Bertie's copy was a later edition of 1890. He would have been fascinated to read of Wallace's discoveries in Asia and made a point of visiting some of the places mentioned in the book. He would have noted in the preface Wallace's account of the specimens he collected:

These comprised nearly three thousand bird-skins, of about a thousand species; and at least twenty thousand beetles and butterflies, of about seven thousand species; besides some quadrupeds and land shells.

Bertie also acquired specimens on his travels, which were mainly butterflies. They were not on the scale of Wallace's collection. Unlike Wallace, he did not take home an orangutan skeleton and its skin.

When Bertie embarked on his journey, he chose to travel on *SS Orient*, of the Orient Line, or to use its full name, The Orient Steam Navigation Co. Ltd. (OSNC). This shipping line was founded in 1878, resulting from the amalgamation of several companies which previously ran sailing ships carrying cargo and passengers to the West Indies, the Americas, Australia and New Zealand. The Orient line was headed by James Anderson, a visionary Scotsman, and also members of his family. They were able to lead the company through the tricky transmission from sail to steam.

SS Orient was a grand ship in many ways. At the time she was launched she was the

An early photograph of SS Orient in Sydney Harbour, Australia

vessel with the largest gross tonnage ever built by the Glasgow shipyards, and was the second largest ship in the world, only surpassed by Isambard Kingdom Brunel's monster, the 211 metre long and 19,000 gross ton, *Great Eastern*. She was also very modern, with state of the art features to her powerful engines, safety equipment and passenger comfort. With a 15-knot cruising speed, *SS Orient* was very fast and she broke existing records by steaming from London to Adelaide in 37 days 22 hours. At first, the OSNC ships travelled out to Australia via South Africa and returned via the Suez Canal, but later they used the canal in both directions.

SS Orient was built by John Elder & Co. in Glasgow. She was launched by Lady Gertrude Boyle, daughter of the Earl of Glasgow. This event was witnessed by thousands of people and reported widely in the press. The splendid ship was a 5,386 gross ton vessel and 460 feet (140,21metres) long. She had two funnels and four masts rigged for sail. It was normal for steam ships to use wind power when possible to save on their coal consumption. There was passenger accommodation for 120 first class passengers, 130 in second class, and 300 in steerage. The ship also carried cargo and had a contract to carry the mail between England and Australia. In 1881, refrigeration holds were fitted so Australian meat and fruit became a major cargo, and in 1884 electric lighting was installed. She also had government contracts to transport immigrants to Australia at a cost of £15 sterling per head. The fare to travel first class was £50.

On her first arrival at Tilbury from Glasgow, it was reported in an article in the Illustrated London News on 4th October, 1979:

This magnificent new vessel arrived at the South West India Dock from the Clyde, on the 13th ult. She has been visited by thousands of people desiring to see the finest and best-fitted ship, indeed the only full-powered steamer expressly built and equipped for the Australian trade, and the grandest vessel for the conveyance of passengers that has ever appeared in the Thames.

As he was to travel in First Class, no doubt Bertie would have been glad to read:

A great feature of the first-class accommodation is the splendid saloon forward, free from the engine room, free from berths, running through from side to side, 44 feet square and very lofty. It is fitted with electro-plated brass furniture, carpeted with a pattern by William Morris, and opening into the music saloon above, where amid ferns and dracaenas growing as plentifully as in the Sunbeam, a piano and an organ are to be placed. Here are elaborate wood carvings and ornamentation in patterns of the English Renaissance of the nineteen century.

When the ship was first launched, it was stated that: *Cattle enough to stock a farm are carried to provide fresh meat and milk on the voyage.* However, by 1896, when Bertie sailed on her, ample cold storage holds had been installed where meat could be stored, so carrying large numbers of live animals could be dispensed with.

In 1896 Bertie was preparing for his journey. He could have booked his passage by visiting the OSNC office at 5 Fenchurch Avenue, which was their headquarters for 80 years, until destroyed by a bomb in 1941. This was conveniently close to his place of work at the Stock Exchange. He needed to purchase a steamer cabin trunk, or possibly two to hold his clothes, his guns and butterfly hunting paraphernalia. As a first class passenger, he was allowed 40 cubit feet of luggage, with items 'not wanted on journey' being stowed in the hold.

In an 1888 P&O Pocket Book for future passengers, it was suggested their clothing should

include suits made of thin flannel, or specially-made, gossamer cloth for the tropics. Shirts to be made of flannel with studs, as buttons became damaged by frequent washing. Shoes of white canvas or buff leather were recommended, and that a Mackintosh and umbrella were essential items, as were a warm rug, an anti-cholera belt and a flannel money belt. A sun helmet or Terai hat with a chin strap, to avoid them being blown off in the wind, were suggested. The guide also stated that baggage should be packed in a tin trunk with an outer wooden box. This should be air and water tight, and insect proof.

To avoid embarrassment, passengers were advised that the Captains of P&O ships should be addressed as 'Commander', however Orient Line Masters should be referred to as 'Captain'.

Fire and boat drill would be held once every week, and the Captain would do his weekly rounds inspecting all parts of the vessel and the assembled crew and Divine service would be held every Sunday when at sea.

Bertie had to arrange through his bank for money to be made available to him at foreign banks, which he could request by telegraph, so as to avoid having to carry large amounts of cash. There is a clue that his father may have facilitated this, as Bertie wrote in one of his letters home from Japan, that he did not anticipate that he would require any more money to be sent out.

Passports, as we know them now, did not exist in 1896. The British passport books were not introduced until 1920, but there were passports in the nineteen century which consisted of one large sheet of paper on which there was a formal request on behalf of the reigning monarch, that the holder be accorded safe passage. Some people kept their passport safe and folded up in a special holder. In 1896 most European countries did not require passports, until 1914 when they were re-introduced for reasons of security and required a photo. Records show that Bertie applied for a passport in 1882, but he may have up-dated it to cover the countries he was to visit. He also mentioned in his journal that he had to apply for a passport from the police station in Batavia to allow him to travel around Java.

Part of Bertie's preparations would have been the purchase of light weight clothing suitable for the tropics, as suggested in the P&O Pocket Book. These would be readily available in the London department stores that catered for travellers and Empire builders. One example was Harrods which had been in business since 1834. There were plenty of advertisements for tropical clothing, trunks and other goods required by travellers in periodicals such as the Illustrated London News.

Bertie packed up his cabin trunks, his shot guns and butterfly nets and travelled to Tilbury on the boat train to embark on his great adventure. It is possible that at least some of his family accompanied him to the ship and may have gone aboard the *Orient* to see him to his cabin. The first section of his journey, taking twenty-five days, was the longest sea voyage he was to undertake. This was from London to the port of Colombo in Ceylon (Sri Lanka), where he would be staying with his sister Amy and her husband Herbert Bressey at their tea estate, not far from Kandy. He planned to spend Christmas with them and then explore places of interest in Ceylon. He was also to meet up with his younger brother, Douglas who worked on the estate. It was several years since they had seen each other, so they all must have been eagerly anticipating this family reunion.

'In the River', an illustration from P & O Pencillings by W.W. Lloyd showing passengers embarking at Tilbury [P&O Heritage]

"On Deck" from P&O Pencillings, WW Lloyd, (P&O Heritage)

This was the first time Bertie had been separated from his close and loving family and may have had mixed feelings about his venture: certainly excited, but probably apprehensive about sailing off into the unknown. Unfortunately, things did not start well for him. The first entry in his journal reads:

Nov. 27th 1896 SS Orient
I left Tilbury on the 27th Nov. 1896. Before we passed Margate I was seasick & did not get over it till we got to Gibraltar. It was raining hard when we got to Gib. So I did not land.

He was not a good sailor and frequently mentioned suffering from seasickness in the first few days of most of his sea voyages. Ships had no stabilisers in those days, and in rough weather would pitch and roll excessively, which caused great discomfort to passengers.

Seasickness is a malady which causes intense distress to the sufferer and Bertie might even have wished fervently that he could return to England and the safety of his family. He was not alone in feeling the effects of motion sickness. It is a universal problem to humans and also some animals. It may occur in land vehicles, at sea, in the air and even including space travel. Lawrence of Arabia even reported that he suffered from it while riding camels in the desert. The writers of ancient Greece, Rome and China mentioned the condition and ginger was suggested as one of the earliest remedies. Columbus and his sailors suffered from it and the acute seasickness of the Duke of Medina Sidona, Spanish commander of the supposedly invincible Armada fleet in 1588, may have affected the outcome of that great sea battle. Other famous sufferers were Admiral Lord Nelson and Charles Darwin. The causes of motion sickness are believed to be the conflict registered between what a person sees and what is being experienced by the vestibular balance senses in the ears and the kinetic, or positions sensors of the body. A sufferer may become dizzy, feel nauseous and sometimes vomit. At sea the symptoms are most acute at the start of the journey, but may lessen as the passenger becomes more accustomed to the movement of the vessel. Remedies in the nineteenth century included chloroform and tincture of belladonna, opium, creosote, or strychnine, but one of the most popular was Bullard and Shedd's Wine of Coca, which contained alcohol and cocaine. This was marketed as a cure for seasickness, but a wide variety of Wine of Coca drinks were available and used as stimulating health tonics.

Medical services were provided in the all the larger passenger ships, but would have been limited or non-existent in some of the smaller vessels Bertie travelled on, so he would have depended on the cabin stewards, who would have been used to caring for seasick passengers. The doctors on board ships were usually referred to as the Surgeon and according to P&O policy, stated in the 1888 P&O Pocket book, their services were free to passengers.

Surgeons – Although the Directors do not object to Surgeons accepting any compensation which may be voluntarily offered by passengers for professional attendance upon them, it must be distinctly understood that Passengers are entitled to medical attention without fee and Surgeons are strictly prohibited from making any demand for such service rendered.

Ships' surgeons were often kept very busy. They had to cope with the seasickness and usual ills and accidents of the passengers and crew. In addition, it was quite common for Victorian doctors to prescribe a long sea voyage to cure various illnesses, so some passengers may have embarked on their journey in bad health, hoping that the sea air and relaxation might cure them. Bertie, himself may have been advised by his doctor to travel following the stresses he had experienced from his work at the Stock Exchange. As was pointed out in the P & O 1888 Pocket book:

To the brain worker of our large cities, a voyage at sea offers a form of holiday which is probably unequalled ... To such a man, the rest which a voyage offers to the nervous system can hardly be over-estimated. The restoration of his exhausted energies begins with the first day at sea, as soon as he realises the intense relief of knowing for a time he has escaped the post-office and telegraph wire.

The passage from Tilbury to Colombo via the Suez Canal almost always followed a fixed schedule. The following passage comes from a description of the entire journey by a retired P&O ship's officer who knew the route well and had preserved all his log books.

The SS Orient would have sailed from Tilbury Landing Stage on high water making her departure from Ovens buoy just over a mile down-stream from Gravesend. Taking the ebb tide with her down the Thames Estuary, she would have rounded North Foreland into the Downs passing inside the Goodwin Sands, disembarking the pilot off Dungeness. She would have then proceeded down the English Channel, passing north of the Channel Islands to Ushant, entering the infamous Bay of Biscay the following day. Once past Finisterre, the weather would have improved while running down the Spanish and Portuguese Atlantic seaboard passing Cape Rocca and Lisbon to Cape St Vincent. Rounding Cape Sagres, course would have been set direct for the Straits of Gibraltar, the gateway to the Mediterranean and the port of Gibraltar where the ship would anchor off the Royal Navy Base. Having left Gibraltar and rounded Europa Point, SS Orient would have sailed along the Spanish coast to Cape Gata and thence south of Sardinia to reach Naples three days later.

Shortly after leaving Naples the volcanic island of Stromboli would be passed on the starboard side before entering the narrow Straits of Messina between Italy and Sicily. Having passed through the Straits, course would have been laid to pick up Damette lighthouse two days later on the Nile Delta near Port Said. Having embarked a pilot, SS Orient would have entered Port Said harbour with its long breakwater and impressive statue of Ferdinand de Lesseps. The vessel would be moored to buoys and its bunkers loaded with steam coal from barges. Sailing from Port Said SS Orient would have entered the Suez Canal along with other southbound vessels. Between Port Said and Ismailia the southbound convoy would have stopped temporarily and moored to the east bank to allow the north bound vessels to pass. Continuing down the Canal, SS Orient would then enter the Great Bitter Lake and may have anchored briefly, to enable other north bound vessels to pass. Leaving the Lake she would again enter the Canal and proceed to Suez where the pilot would disembark.

Sailing down the narrow Gulf of Suez against a stiff southerly breeze, Mount Sinai could be sighted on the portside before entering the Red Sea at Shadwan Island. The temperature by now would be much higher and the vessel's ventilators continually trimmed to any breeze to make conditions on board comfortable. At the southern end of the Red Sea, the vessel would pass through the Straits of Mandeb leaving Perim Island to port, and so entering the Gulf of Aden. At the port of Aden, she would have been moored to buoys.

Sailing from Aden, after rounding Steamer Point, SS Orient would enter the Arabian Sea and have set course direct for Minicoy Island Light which lay some way south of India's Cape Corim. December is the time of the NE Monsoon, so the conditions would have been good with gentle breezes, calm blue seas and fair weather, with cumulus clouds drifting across the sky. Crossing the Indian Ocean, Socotra Island would have been sighted on the starboard side two days out from Aden. This remote island has many rare plants found nowhere else in the world. One day before reaching Colombo, Minicoy Island could be seen, a coconut palm-clad atoll, which was a leper colony.

On reaching Colombo, vessels were moored to buoys within the harbour and passengers and their luggage taken ashore by boats. (Michael Vale, personal communication)

Perhaps because he was suffering the misery of sea sickness, Bertie did not record anything in his journal about embarkation, or his experiences on the journey, nor did he go ashore at Gibraltar, but we can refer to other first-hand accounts by travellers who wrote more fully of their impressions.

William Mawson and his new wife, Esther, also embarked from Tilbury on an Orient Line ship, the *SS Liguria* in 1888. William was a Methodist lay preacher from Yorkshire, and he and his wife were bound for a new life in Albany, Western Australia. In the unpublished account of his journey, he wrote:

'Arrived on board. We were very much interested in looking around at the various new and strange things which met our gaze on every hand, which need not to be wondered at when you remember that we were real bred and born Yorkshire land-lubbers who understood just about as much about the floating monster as it knew about us. We had not been on board long when we were called upon to part with our last relative who had accompanied us to the ship. The warning was given and our sister Lizzie...had to leave us. It was rather different to the parting we read of. Instead of the handkerchief being used pretty freely to wipe away the falling tear, everyone seemed to be in good spirits, and when the last good-bye had been uttered, and the tender was leaving the ship, the handkerchief was waved as a last means of showing good will and expressing our hearty sympathy and love.
After the tender left us, we were not long before we too were on the move. Clang, clang went the massive cable as it passed around the drum and so the anchor was weighed...We enjoyed it immensely until we got into the English Channel and it became rather rough, and then there was soon an alteration on board, a great part of the passengers began to be sick...

We entered the Bay of Biscay about seven o'clock on Sunday morning and had a tolerably good passage, that is to say we got a good rocking and nothing worse. The ship rolled from one side to the other so much so that one side was down to the water's edge, while the other was about 30 feet above it, and we had to hold on by the bulwarks to prevent ourselves falling while she rolled from side to side. We got out of the Bay of Biscay into calmer water about two o'clock pm. By that time we had got a little more used to the sea and began to enjoy the voyage...

After sunset the sky was really lovely, its colours were of green, crimson, yellow, grey, blue and dark purple, all of which harmonized in such a manner as only God Himself could arrange them. On Wednesday I rose pretty early and we sighted the coast of Africa about seven o'clock, and we beheld the rising sun which looked magnificent, as he rose in his silent glory. The African coast line was bounded with rugged rocks, rising one above the other in splendid variety and the clouds lit up with the rising sun's rays made the rocks appear as though they were crowned with caps of fire.
We entered Gibraltar harbour about nine o'clock am and this historic town presented a most lovely aspect with its terraced houses rising terrace above terrace along its rocky ascent. There is something very attractive in the view of Gibraltar from the sea. The blue sky, the still bluer sea

and an exquisite landscape with its fold after fold of giant mountains fading away insensibly in the distance is most fascinating. As we steam up to an anchorage we can identify the chief sights of interest. At the southern extremity mentioned on a low spit of land is the lighthouse marking Europa Point. Then rising up the hill are endless rows of barracks interspersed with a few private houses until the eye reaches the little tract of woodland which stands above the end of the town. Above all rises the bare rock to a height of 1361 feet crowned by a lightning struck tower known as O'Hara's Folly.

We left Gibraltar at 1 o'clock and proceeded on our way along the Mediterranean Sea. At night the phosphorous in the spray looked lovely and could be seen around the ship for miles. It broke away from the ship's side and assumed all kinds of shapes as it ran along the water like liquid fire, and in the distance looked like some hideous sea monster riding along the crest of the waves.'

Obviously, William Mawson and his wife had good weather and were able to appreciate the beauty of Gibraltar and the passing scenery, though they did not go ashore there.

In 1869 Mark Twain was a young journalist who managed to persuade several New York newspapers to pay his fare for an excursion to Europe and the Holy Land with a large group of 'pilgrims.' His account of the trip was published in the papers; later to be the book, *Innocents Abroad*. He and his companions enjoyed their time ashore at Gibraltar.

We rode on asses and mules up the steep, narrow streets and entered the subterranean galleries the English have blasted out of the rock. These galleries are like spacious railway tunnels, and at short intervals in them great guns frown out upon the sea and town through portholes five or six hundred feet above the ocean. There is a mile or so of this subterranean work, and it must have cost a vast deal of money and labour. The gallery guns command the peninsular and the harbours of both oceans, but they might just as well not be there, I should think, for an army could hardly climb the perpendicular wall of the rock anyway. Those lofty portholes afford superb views of the sea, though. On the topmost pinnacle of Gibraltar we halted a good while, and no doubt the mules were tired. They had a right to be. The military road was good, but rather steep … There is an English garrison at Gibraltar of 6,000 or 7,000 men, and so uniforms of flaming red are plenty; and blue, and underdress costumes of snowy white, and also queer uniform of bare-kneed Highlander; and one sees soft-eyed Spanish girls from San Roque, and veiled Moorish beauties (I suppose they are beauties) from Tarifa, and turbaned, sashed, and trousered Moorish merchants from Fez, and long-robed, bare-legged, ragged Muhammadan vagabonds from Tetuan and Tangier, some brown, some yellow and some as black as virgin ink.

Things improved for Bertie by the time he reached Naples, his next port of call. His journal records:

I went ashore at Naples with a party, taking young White with me. We spent a most interesting day at Pompeii.

The photos Bertie purchased of Naples showed a busy port city, with the volcano, Vesuvius emitting a lazy plume of smoke in the background. There had been an eruption in 1872, and another major one occurred just ten years after Bertie's visit, in 1906. This devastated the city to such a degree that the Italian government had to cancel the Olympic Games, scheduled to be held in Rome in 1908, so funds could be diverted

Naples -- photograph from Bertie's album

to the restoration of Naples (the Games were held in London at White City Stadium instead). Fortunately the mountain was quiet while he was there.

Naples had a population of around 600,000 in 1896, and had been part of the unified country of Italy since 1861, when Garibaldi was greeted with acclamation by the citizens who enthusiastically supported the idea of unification. This port is one of the oldest, continuously inhabited cities in Italy, having first been settled by the Greeks then the Romans, and lastly the Goths. Later still it was ruled by various European powers and for a time, by Napoleon Bonaparte, but when Bertie visited, the people were proud to be Italian citizens.

William Mawson, the Methodist lay preacher, also landed at Naples and he wrote:

We found Naples to be a very attractive place. It surrounds the Bay of Naples in a semicircle. As soon as the ship was at anchor in the Bay there was a perfect babel around the ship caused by the people who had come in their boats with various articles for sale ... and although it was Sunday they seemed to do a good business amongst the passengers ... We could see Mount Vesuvius ... during the day smoke could be seen rising out of the mountain and it travelled so slowly and was so thick that if you did not observe it closely, you might very easily mistake it for a passing cloud.

The mountain tapers off almost to a point and at night the blaze is of a deep red colour which does not appear to flicker, but burns steadily on in a tongue like flame and can be seen for miles around.

Bertie was able to catch a train to Pompeii at Naples' Statione Centrale, which was situated conveniently close to the docks on the Piazza Garibaldi. The Circumvesuviana train line had been constructed in 1890 and was popular with Victorian tourists, many of whom wanted to visit the Roman cities of Pompeii and Herculaneum.

Pompeii - photograph from Bertie's album

Since the eruption in 79 AD, which buried the city, Pompeii had remained forgotten under its deep covering of volcanic ash until 1599, when it was discovered accidentally, but not excavated. In the eighteenth century some excavations were undertaken, but their methods were somewhat unscientific since they concentrated on extracting the best art works, the rest being destroyed. The buildings were then reburied. These destructive practices were discontinued following strong protests by experts. Excavations continued when Naples came under the rule of Bonaparte of France from 1806 - 08, but it was in the late nineteenth century that archaeologists really began to uncover the city in earnest and in a systematic manner. Between 1863 and 1873 Giuseppe Fiorelli was Director of Excavations. He brought order to the digging: on discovering ash-encrusted human remains, he developed the technique of filling the cavities with plaster, so the shapes of the sad victims, and other decayed organic substances, could be revealed. Some art works that were uncovered were considered to be too pornographic and shocking, so were hastily reburied. Others were displayed in the museum, but when King Francis I of Naples inspected them, he was so shocked by their decadence, he decreed they should be made accessible only to *'people of mature age and respected morals.'*

Mark Twain and his fellow pilgrims visited Pompeii; like Bertie, travelling there by train. He was obviously entranced by the place and wrote a wonderful description about what he saw:

Fully one half of the buried city, perhaps is completely exhumed and thrown open freely to the light of day; and there stand the long rows of solidly built brick houses (roofless) just as they stood eighteen hundred years ago, hot with the flaming sun; and there lie their floors, clean-swept, and not a bright fragment tarnished or wanting of the laboured mosaics that pictured them with the beasts, and birds, and flowers which we copy in perishable carpets today; and here are the Venuses and Bacchuses, and Adonises, making love and getting drunk in many hued frescoes on the walls of saloon and bedchamber; and there are narrow streets and narrower sidewalks, paved with flags of good hard lava, the one deeply rutted with chariot-wheels, and the other with the passing feet of Pompeiians of bygone centuries; and there are the bake-shops, the temples, the halls of justice, the baths, the theatres – all clean-scraped and neat … And so, I turned away and went through shop after shop and store after store, far down the long street of the merchants, and called for the wares of Rome and the East, but the tradesmen are gone, the marts are silent, and nothing was left but the broken jars all set in cement of cinders and ashes; the wine and oil that once had filled them were gone with their owners.

In a bake-shop was a mill for grinding the grain, and the furnaces for baking the bread; and they say that here, in the same furnaces, the exhumers of Pompeii found nice, well baked loaves which the baker had not found time to remove from the ovens the last time he left the shop, because circumstances compelled him to leave in such a hurry.

In one house (the only building in Pompeii which no woman is now allowed to enter) were the small rooms and short beds of solid masonry, just as they were in the old times, and on the walls were pictures which looked almost as fresh as if they were painted yesterday, but which no pen could have the hardihood to describe; and here and there were Latin inscriptions – obscene scintillations of wit, scratched by hands that possibly were uplifted to Heaven for succour in the midst of a driving storm of fire before the night was done …

In one of these long Pompeiian halls the skeleton of a man was found, with ten pieces of gold in one hand and a large key in the other. He had seized his money and started towards the door, but the fiery tempest caught him at the very threshold, and he sank down and died. One more minute of precious time would have saved him. I saw the skeletons of a man, a woman and two young girls. The woman had her hands spread wide apart, as if in mortal terror, and I imagined I could still trace upon her shapeless face something of the expression of wild despair that distorted it when the heavens rained fire in these streets, so many ages ago …

But perhaps the most poetical thing Pompeii has yielded to modern research, was the grand figure of a Roman soldier, clad in complete armour; who true to his duty, true to his proud name of a soldier of Rome, and full of stern courage that had given that name its glory, stood to his post by the city gate, erect and unflinching, till the hell that raged around him, burned out the dauntless spirit it could not conquer...

We came out from under the solemn mysteries of this city of the Venerable Past and went dreaming among the trees that grow over acres and acres of its still buried streets and squares, till a shrill whistle and a cry of 'All aboard – last train for Naples!' woke me up and reminded me that I belonged in the nineteenth century, and was not a dusty mummy, caked with ashes and cinders, eighteen hundred years old. The transition was startling. The idea of a railroad train actually running to old dead Pompeii, and whistling irreverently, and calling for passengers in the most bustling and businesslike way, was as strange a thing as one can imagine, and as un-poetical and disagreeable as it was strange.

After his visit to Pompeii and Naples, Bertie re-joined the ship and the voyage continued. *Orient* was scheduled to visit Port Said, Ismailia and Suez. She would have also passed through the Suez Canal and the Red Sea before crossing the Indian Ocean to Colombo. Once again, Bertie did not write anything in his journal about this part of his journey, so we have no record of his impressions of these places, nor of life on board ship.

Another traveller, who wrote of her journey from Europe to Colombo, was Miss Gertrude Bindloss. She was an English governess, who was employed to be in sole charge of three small children escorting them in 1887 from Pau, France, to Bangkok. They travelled with the French Line, Messageries Maritimes, and even though the passage was nine years earlier than Bertie's, many of the experiences she recorded in her journal would have been similar to his.

Miss Bindloss describes her fellow passengers, many of whom were not English. They included several priests, a group of Sisters of Mercy nuns, and also a large French theatrical company who were travelling to Saigon. She also wrote of aspects of life on board, the ports they visited and about the passage through the Suez Canal. She joined her ship at Marseilles:

At length we made our way to the Messageries Maritimes Company's Steamer "Iraouddy" bound for Singapore. What a scene it was. The bustling, the shouting, the hurrying to & fro – it is one which must be seen to be imagined. At length the passengers were all on board, the luggage stowed away, the last goodbyes said…& at 10.30 off we started…

I was much amused by the Chinese waiters in their long white garments & heads closely shaved except for the pigtails which they often wore twisted round their heads. These men used to run along the passages at a great rate. During meals the punkahs were always worked by Chinese…

The food on board, I thought very good; the meals consisted of tea or coffee early, dejeuner at 9. (about 7 courses) tiffin about 12 (soup, cold meat, & fruit) an excellent dinner of 9 courses at 6, & a cup of tea in the evening….

The vessel was lighted by electricity – a most convenient & delightful arrangement & a large

Old postcard of a French Messageries Maritimes ship passing through the Suez Canal

awning covered the whole of the decks. So that sunshades were never necessary....

We had plenty of animals on board to be killed for food... and the crowing of the cocks could often be heard even in the middle of the night.

The nights were very hot...Later on we very often slept on deck. Sometimes on mattresses, sometimes on the long deck chairs, but always covered ourselves up well with cloaks & rugs. It would have been impossible in the Red Sea to remain in the cabins for the heat was truly awful. One poor lady in very delicate health, nearly died & had to be kept constantly under the influence of ether...On Sept. 2nd we arrived at Alexandria,...

Early in the morning Arabs came on board bringing merchandize to sell, & it was most amusing to watch the bargaining for that and the hire of boats ...At one o'clock we left Alexandria, & the following night reached Port Said, where we coaled, & some of the passengers went ashore to escape the noise & dirt. The former was frightful & every sound I could hear through the thin partition which divided our cabin from the saloon... From what I heard those who went ashore were not profitably employed, rumours of gambling, especially among the "artistes" met my ears...

'Punkas' are a type of fan suspended from the ceiling that required a servant, (punka walla) to pull a rope which activated the fan which flapped to and fro. 'Tiffin' is a word meaning a light meal, usually eaten at mid-day. In British India, it was often used to describe a meal which supplanted afternoon tea.

Miss Bindloss was not interested in watching the dirty and noisy activity of coaling the ship, but William Mawson found it quite entertaining. He wrote:

'I stayed up to see the ship enter the mouth of the Suez Canal which we reached about midnight. It was a very interesting experience, there were the lights of Port Said glowing away in the distance, and the revolving lights in the lighthouse which is 175 feet, along with the white, red and green lights of ships moored in the harbour of the historical town and the large fire lights on the coal boats. It did not look much like midnight. The various shops in the town were open, and the harbour was full of coal boats conveying coal to the various ships moored in the harbour. It was a sight I shall never forget. The Arabs who were coaling the ships made a perfect babel with their jab jabbering. I dare say it will be interesting to you, so I will tell you how the coaling business is done. One of the coal boats was got alongside the ship and then the others were placed one against the other so that they could get from one to the other without any trouble. When these had been brought into position, the next thing was to raise a tremendous plank or gangway which reached from the coal boat to the opening in the ship's side. It was very amusing to see them raise the plank. Before they could touch it they must receive the word of command from their foreman and then jabber something back at him and then they condescended to first move the plank a little, after which came another command followed by another jabbering from the coalers and so on until they got the plank into proper position. This was a very tedious piece of business I can tell you, but once they got this done they were running up and down like wild fire, with great buckets of coal upon their heads and in the dim light they presented a very curious appearance.. We got all done and away again at 7 o'clock the next morning.'

Old Postcard of Port Said, in the days when coal was carried on board ships on the backs of men

Nelly Bly, the American investigative newspaper reporter arrived in Port Said in 1889 on her journey attempting to travel around the world in less than eighty days. Her lively accounts of her progress were being widely reported by the American press and later the articles were collected into a book: *Around the World in Seventy-two Days*.

When they arrived at Port Said, she wrote of the chaotic rivalry between the Arab boatmen as they fought to snare the passengers who wished to go ashore:

Our party were about the first to go down the ladder to the boats. It had been our desire and intention to go ashore together, but when we stepped into the first boat some were caught by rival boatmen and literally dragged across to other boats ... Having our party divided there was nothing to do under the circumstances but to land and reunited on shore, so we ordered the Arabs to pull away. Midway between the Victoria and the shore the boatmen stopped and demanded their money in very plain and forcible English. We were completely at their mercy, as they would not land us either way until we paid what they asked ... Walking up the beach, sinking ankle-deep in the sand at every step, we came to the main street. Almost instantly we were surrounded by Arab boys who besought us to take a ride on the burros that stood patiently beside them. There were burros of all colours, sizes and shapes ... I knew all about burros, having lived for some time in Mexico, but they proved to be quite a novelty to many passengers, almost all of whom were anxious to take a ride before returning to the boat. So as many as could find animals to ride, mounted and went flying through that quaint sleeping town, yelling with laughter, bouncing like rubber balls on their saddles, while half naked Arab boys goaded the burros on by short, urgent hisses, and prodding them from behind with a sharp stick.

After seeing about fifty of our passengers started off in this happy manner, a smaller number of us went to a gambling house, and in a short time were deep in the sport of placing our English gold on colours and numbers and waiting anxiously for the wheel to go 'round to see the money at last swept in by the man at the table. I do not think that any one of us knew anything about the game, but we recklessly put our money on the table and laughed to see it taken by the man who gave a turn to the wheel.

There was another attraction in this place which helped to win a number of young men from that very expensive table. It was an orchestra composed of young women, some of whom were quite pleasing both in looks and manners.

Miss Bly and her friends strolled around town looking at the old houses and the activities of the locals until it was time to return to the ship:

Darkness came on us very suddenly and sent us rushing off for our ship. This time we found the boatmen would not permit us even to enter their boats until we had paid them to take us across to the Victoria. Their price now was just double what they charged to bring us to land. We protested, but they said it was the law to double the price after sunset.

Elizabeth Bisland was also travelling around the world, but in the opposite direction to Miss Bly. They had both left New York on 14 November 1889, and were rivals attempting to beat Jules Verne's fictional record of eighty days. She was not impressed with the delights of Port Said. She wrote in her book: *A Flying Trip Round the World*, (1891).

A dim lurid sunset ends the day, and when night comes we are anchored of the town of Port Said – a wretched little place, dusty, dirty, and flaring with cheap vice – all the flotsam of four nations whirling about in an eddy of coarse pleasures. The shopkeepers are wolfish-looking, and bargain vociferously. Almost every other door opens into a gambling-hell and concert-hall. One of these gambling-places boasts an opera ...In the concert-hall, Traviata is being sung by a fourth-rate French troupe, and the audience sit about at little tables, drinking and eating ices. I ask for something native – Turkish – to drink, and they bring me stuff that to all the evidence of sight, taste, and smell cries out that it is a mixture of paregoric [a camphorated tincture of opium] and water, and one sip contents me. We are glad to go away.

After passing through the canal, both William Mawson and Gertrude Bindloss observed Mt. Sinai as they passed into the Red Sea. Miss Bindloss records in her journal:

'Sept 4th We saw Mt. Sinai in the distance & passed some wrecks. On the 5th my diary says "In the Red Sea, very hot." On the 6th the Operatic Company gave a concert in aid of the Mariners, tickets 10, 5, & 3 francs. The deck was most prettily decorated & lighted by the sailors & some of the "artistes" sang extremely well. It lasted from 9 till 11 when ices & other light refreshments were served & there was some dancing in the stern, but we retired to rest... On the morning of the 8th the Iraouddy arrived at Aden, & nearly everybody went ashore, ... But we had to content ourselves with watching the numerous little boats filled by Arabs & negroes & at first it was very amusing to see the boys swimming about & diving for money: Sometimes, from the awning of the vessel. Their agility was admirable, but the monotony of their cry, "Heave for a dive, Heave for a dive", which continued the whole day, soon became an intolerable nuisance. The bargaining with the Arab merchants was more entertaining, and as everyone who has been in the East knows, it is impossible to buy anything from Arabs without bargaining, for they always expect it, & begin by asking about 3 0r 4 times the price they mean to take. Ostrich feathers are the chief things for sale....

We left Aden at 6.30 & the following day got into the monsoon, so experienced some very rough weather. Such a night I hope never to spend again – We were advised to sleep on deck & our chairs were all lashed to the sides of the vessel which rolled about all night, with the waves occasionally breaking over the deck...I did not sleep at all & for the first time that voyage indulged in mal de mer....

On the 13th another concert was given on deck, but this time for the benefit of the artistes themselves. A rope was fastened across the improvised platform & it was very comical to see the singers holding on to this rope in order to save themselves from toppling over each time the "Iraouddy" gave a lurch....

Sept. 15th We reached Colombo about 8.30 am & were very thankful to get some clothes washed by the native dhotees who came on board in crowds to fetch linen or to sell curios. They brought it back the next morning...The charge is always 2/- per dozen... They are very fond of getting

English gold & prefer an English sovereign to an Australian one, though my friend explained he knew they were worth the same amount.

After breakfast … We went ashore in a small tug & drove to the Oriental Hotel. A very fine building with a splendid dining room & pleasant verandah where a few Singhalese sell "curios" chiefly silver, ivory, tortoise shell and precious stones…We then did some shopping at Cargill's, a large English store. From there we drove to the Galle Face Hotel where we dined & I bought some silver bangles, thimbles, & a buckle. After dinner we engaged three jinrickshaws … and were rapidly drawn along in these curious little carriages by men. I cannot say I liked the feeling, for it seemed so unnatural for human beings to be doing the work of animals…. We arrived at the station only to find the train to Mt Lavinia had just gone. So we decided to drive there, the distance only being 7 miles, and for this we had two carriages, each drawn by one horse…. It was a lovely drive & I was not sorry we missed the train for we were thus enabled to see more of the country and the people.

Old postcard of the Grand Oriental Hotel, Colombo

All was so novel to me that I thoroughly enjoyed it. The huts by the side of the road were most picturesque, in many fruit and vegetables were for sale & I felt a strong wish to get out & explore a little & have some conversation (by signs) with some of the natives. We saw a great many little naked Singhalese & Malays playing about, nearly all wore bracelets & anklets, their faces as a rule were bright & intelligent & they looked happy, but some of the bigger children ran after us calling out a few English words & begging. One boy was quite pathetic repeating "Me very poor boy, Me very hungry boy." Till we felt impelled to throw him a Sinale coin. Some of them cast flowers into the carriage evidently in hopes of reward for the kind attention. The tropical plants were splendid, such varied & brilliant colours.

We reached Mt Lavinia soon after 4 o'clock & sat on the terrace of the Hotel which is beautifully situated facing the sea, & built very high. Here we had tea… then we wandered about the grounds & adjacent cocoanut grove & watched a Scotch regiment play football. The sunset was a most glorious one. At 6.30 we left by train for Colombo.

No. 11 Mount Lavinia, **Colombo.**

Old postcard of Mount Lavinia Hotel, Colombo

After her time in Colombo, Miss Bindloss and her young charges returned to the *SS Irraouddy* and travelled on to Singapore, before changing to another ship which carried them to Bangkok.

It is likely that Bertie also had encounters with rapacious Arab traders and the heat crossing the Red sea, but not perhaps quite as excessively hot as Miss Binloss experienced, since he was there in December, whereas she crossed it in August. Hopefully his sea sickness abated so he was able to enjoy the journey and ship board life.

On 22nd December 1896, Bertie arrived at the colourful port of Colombo. Ships, at that time could not tie up at the dock, but had to anchor off-shore and passengers had to be ferried ashore in small boats. Elizabeth Bisland, a passenger on the P & O ship *Thames*, wrote of their arrival:

'. . . It is eight o'clock in the morning. The ship is anchored off the coast of Ceylon.

We arrived late last night; sailing into the harbour by the light of great tropical stars and the planet gleams of a Pharos shining from the tall clock-tower of Colombo. Already many ships lie in the narrow roadstead, and it requires the fine art of navigation to slip our boat's huge bulk into her berth between two of these and make her fast to her own particular buoy. The pilot came aboard just outside, and it is his firm hand that jams her nose up to within three hairs' breath of the vessel in front, holds her there with a grip of iron, and with cautious screw-revolutions swings her into line with her heels in the very face of the Australian mail-ship - arrived a few hours earlier.

Then the entire passenger list – on deck for the last half hour, aiding the pilot by holding its breath – sighs relievedly and joyously, and goes below in a body to recuperate on brandy and soda.

Bertie's ship arrived in port in the morning. He knew he was to be met by his brother in law, Herbert Bressey, so he needed to assemble his cabin trunk and other luggage, ready to be taken ashore. He would have been eager to get off the ship and start the first leg of his travels.

Bertie's brother in law, Herbert Bressey
Photo by Skeen and Co, Colombo & Kandy

Chapter Five

Ceylon

*Old postcard of Colombo harbour showing Steam ships at anchor
and the Grand Oriental Hotel*

Twenty five days after leaving Tilbury, *Orient* arrived at the port of Colombo, the capital of Ceylon.

The island of Ceylon, or Sri Lanka as it is now known, has been the subject of invasions throughout its long history. Powerful kings came from southern India and established their kingdoms mainly in the northern part of the island. Arabs came to trade and settle in coastal areas and then, in 1505, the Portuguese arrived attracted mainly by the rich spices which grew on the island. The remnants of their forts can still be seen in Galle and other places where they settled. The next European maritime power to arrive was the Dutch in 1658. They were also attracted by the rich resources of the island, so they took over control of the coastal regions in addition to their colonies in Indonesia. In 1796, Britain was at war with Napoleonic France and since France had annexed Holland, the Dutch colonies in Java and Ceylon came under French control. This posed a potential threat to British interests in India, so for strategic reasons, British forces took control over the Dutch colonies. In 1802 the Dutch ceded Ceylon to Britain and most of the island became part of the British Empire. It was not until 1815 that the British finally ruled the whole of the island, when the powerful Kingdom of Kandy was conquered. This came

49

about, not by open warfare, but by encouraging internal disputes within the Kingdom, so the last King, Sri Vikrama Rajasinha, lost the support of his powerful chiefs and was deposed without much resistance. One major reason it had been so difficult to conquer, and later control, the mountainous regions of the island's interior, was that there were no roads or bridges along which armies could travel, especially in the monsoon months.

The British retained control over the whole island, in spite of bitter rebellions and resistance by many people who found their rule offensive. It was decided that to retain control, a network of roads were needed. At first, they were required for military purposes, but later to transport the valuable commercial crops and products from the interior to the ports to be exported world-wide. In the first instance these were spices such as cinnamon, pepper, cloves and cardamom valued for medicinal and culinary purposes, also precious gems, pearls and timber. Later plantations of coffee, cocoa, rubber and tea were developed and became valuable exports. By the time of Bertie's arrival in 1896, the country was prosperous and largely without disputes to disrupt his visit.

A vivid description of Colombo in the 1890s is contained in Mark Twain's book, *Following the Equator*, which describes a thirteen-month journey he took around the world in 1895. Though he did not stay long in Ceylon, he was enchanted by the colourful and exotic environment that assaulted his senses in Colombo. He wrote:

Dear me, it is beautiful! And most sumptuously tropical, as to character of foliage and opulence of it. 'What though the spicy breezes blow soft o'er Ceylon's isle' – an eloquent line, an incomparable line; it says little, but conveys whole libraries of sentiment, and Oriental charm and mystery, and tropic deliciousness - a line that quivers and tingles with a thousand unexpressed and inexpressible things, things that haunt one and find no articulate voice … Colombo, the capital. An Oriental town, most manifestly; and fascinating … Ceylon was Oriental in the last measure of completeness – utterly Oriental; also utterly tropical; and indeed to one's unreasoning spiritual sense the two things belong together. All the requisites were present. The costumes were right; the black and brown exposures, unconscious of immodesty, were right … in sight were plants and flowers familiar to one in books but in no other way – celebrated, desirable, strange, but in production restricted to the hot belt of the equator; and a little way in the country were the proper deadly snakes, and fierce beasts of prey, and wild elephant and the monkey. And there was that swoon in the air which one associates with the tropics, and that smother of heat, heavy with odours of unknown flowers, and that sudden invasion of purple gloom fissured with lightnings- then the tumult of crashing thunder and the downpour – and presently all sunny and smiling again; all these things were there; the conditions were complete, nothing was lacking. And away off in the deep of the jungle and in the remoteness of the mountains were ruined cities and mouldering temples, mysterious relics of the pomps of a forgotten time and a vanished race – and this is as it should be, also, for nothing is quite satisfyingly Oriental that lacks the sombre and impressive qualities of mystery and antiquity.

The drive through the town and out to the Galle Face by the seashore, what a dream it was of tropical splendours of bloom and blossom, and oriental conflagrations of costume! The walking groups of men, women, boys, girls, babies – each individual was a flame, each group a house afire for colour. And such stunning colours, such intensely vivid colours, such rich and exquisite minglings and fusings of rainbows and lightnings ... The stuffs were silk – thin, soft, clinging; and as a rule, each piece a solid colour; a splendid green, a splendid blue, a splendid yellow, a splendid purple, a splendid ruby, deep and rich with smouldering fires – they swept continuously by in crowds and legions and multitudes, glowing, flashing, burning radiant; and every five seconds came a burst of blinding red that made a body catch his breath, and filled his heart with joy ...

I can see it to this day, that radiant panorama, that wilderness of rich colour, that incomparable dissolving-view of harmonious tints, and the lithe half-covered forms, and beautiful brown faces, and gracious and graceful gestures and attitudes and movements, free, unstudied, barren of stiffness and restraint.

When *Orient* dropped anchor in Colombo harbour, Bertie was welcomed by his brother-in-law, Herbert Bressey. His journal records nothing quite as flamboyantly as Mark Twain's purple prose, but he was obviously happy to have arrived on dry land and interested in what he saw in Colombo:

22 December

Arrived at Colombo 9.30. Herbert came off to meet me in a boat. Nothing to pay on my guns as I am only staying a short time in Ceylon. We went to the Grand Oriental Hotel to lunch. In the afternoon I watched a Polo match at the Galle Face. There were many passengers from S.S. Orient dining at the GOH. Dr Power had a large party with him, also Bloomfield. There is a fine veranda with lots of lounge chairs.

The Grand Oriental Hotel (GOH) was something of an institution in Colombo. In 1896 it was situated right by the sea front, so guests could watch the arrival and departure of the ships while listening to the hotel's band. Nowadays, the GOH still operates as a hotel, but the dock area is not considered a smart part of town. However, present-day hotel guests can still enjoy excellent views of port activities from the fourth floor restaurant windows. The building still retains vestiges of its former grandeur.

It was first built as a residence for one of the Dutch Governors and later used as a military barracks, and in 1875 it was converted into a splendid hotel with 154 luxury and semi-luxury rooms. There was electric lighting and cooling fans, and the hotel's logo GOH was displayed on all the cutlery and chairs. They were proud of the fact that this was the only hotel in the East owned and managed by Europeans. There was even a stirring poem written about it in one of their promotional brochures:

Solid Roots and Bright Future
Where soldiers marched and sailors once waved,
Where life's best moments are most often cheered,
Where style and stature stays top grade,
The GOH looks forward, staying well geared.

The Grand Oriental hotel was the first place visited by Nellie Bly on her arrival in Colombo in 1889 whilst on her round-the-world trip. She wrote:

A nearer view of the hotel, the Grand Oriental, did not tend to lessen its attractiveness – in fact it increased it. It was a fine, large hotel, with tiled arcades, corridors airy and comfortable, furnished with easy chairs and small marble-topped tables which stood close enough to the broad arm-rests, for one to sip the cooling lime squashes or the exquisite native tea, or eat of the delicious fruit while resting in an attitude of ease and laziness. I found no place away from America where smoking was prohibited, and in this lovely promenade the men smoked, consumed gallons of whisky and soda and perused the newspapers, while the women read their novels or bargained with the pretty little copper-coloured women who came to sell dainty hand-made lace, or with the clever high-turbaned merchants who would snap open little velvet boxes and expose, to the admiring gaze of the charmed tourists, the most bewildering gems. There were deeply-dark emeralds, fire-lit diamonds, exquisite pearls, rubies like pure drops of blood and the lucky cat's-eye with its moving line ... Most of the jewellery bought and sold in Colombo is sold in the corridor of the Grand Oriental Hotel. Merchants bring their wares with them and tourists find it pleasanter than visiting the shops. Leading off the corridor, pleasant in its coolness, interesting in its peculiarities, is the dining-hall, matching the other parts of the hotel with its stateliness. The small tables are daintily set and are richly decorated daily with the native flowers of Colombo, rich in colour, exquisite in form, but void of perfume. From the ceiling were suspended embroidered punkas that invention of the East which brings comfort during the hottest part of the day ... They send a lazy cooling air through the building, contributing much to the ease and comfort of the guests.

The other hotel that Bertie referred to, the Galle Face Hotel was founded even earlier than the GOH. It was originally a grand Dutch villa named Galle Face House and in 1864, was converted into a beautiful hotel with magnificent views overlooking the sea and the parkland, known as Galle Face Green. This may have been where Bertie witnessed the Polo match.

Nellie Bly was a guest at the Galle Face Hotel during her time in Colombo. She enjoyed her stay there, even when a cheeky crow invaded her bedroom and stole her early morning slice of toast. She enjoyed relaxing in the evenings soaking up the atmosphere:

'Lounging on long-bottomed, easy chairs, on the stone floored and stone-pillared verandah, one can see through the forest of tall palms where the ocean kisses the sandy beach, and while listening to the music of the wave, the deep, mellow roar, can drift – drift on dreams. ... Or when the dreams fade away, one can drown the sigh with the cooling lime squash ... at the same time lazily watching the jinrickshas come silently in through the gas-lit gate, the naked black runners coming to a sudden stop, letting the shafts drop so the passenger can step out.'

Bertie and Herbert only stayed one night in Colombo, as the aim was to celebrate Christmas at the tea estate with Herbert, Amy and brother, Douglas. They were to travel up into the hills by train. He was lucky not to have visited the island earlier in the century before the advent of roads and railways.

In ancient times when Ceylon was divided into separate kingdoms, the chiefs realised that not having distinct thoroughfares connecting their territories was an effective defence against invading armies. Thomas Skinner arrived in Ceylon as a fifteen-year-old in 1830. He joined the British army and his main assignment was to build roads throughout the island for strategic purposes. In his autobiography, *Fifty Years in Ceylon*, is included a letter written in 1864 on behalf of the Native Chiefs which congratulated him on his achievements as Commissioner of Roads, Ceylon. This stated:

As regards roads, the main cause for the growing prosperity of this island - Where fifty years ago a man from Colombo had to trudge six weeks before he could reach Kandy, and that, too, with great personal inconvenience, over scraggy rocks, precipices and ravines, he is now able to make the same distance in less than ten hours. A country that had no roads in 1807, and where wheeled carriages could only be used in the neighbourhood of the large European settlements on the sea-coasts, is now intersected with carriage roads in every direction ... Where ten years ago the line of travelling led over natural meadows, sometimes over rugged strata of clay, sometimes through beds of deep and heavy sand, there are now upwards of 2,550 miles of road, highly finished and well maintained, over which 800 miles have been opened during the last 15 years. And the means of conveyance in the Colony is about to be made to keep pace with the immense development of its producing powers by the opening of a railroad.

Galle Face Hotel, Colombo, Ceylon

Old postcard of Galle Face Hotel, Colombo

Later train travel was to reduce the time it took to reach Kandy from Colombo to only about two to four hours, depending on how many stations the train stops at. Road travel times can be extremely variable depending on the time of day and traffic. A delightful description of train travel in Ceylon is provided by one of the island's early Governors. Sir William Gregory was appointed Governor of Ceylon in 1872 and on arrival, he and Lady Gregory travelled to Kandy by train. He wrote in his autobiography:

Immensely interesting and even the low flat country which we traversed to the foot of the hills, with its bare paddy fields, clumps of trees, plants of gigantic foliage and herds of wallowing buffaloes and little humped cattle, uttering an extraordinary noise, more resembling an eructation than the loud, bold lowing of our domestic oxen was not without enjoyment. The distance from Colombo to Kandy was about seventy-four miles, and at the station of Rambakkan we all at once went up the ascent from the flat plain to the mountainous region of the Kandy kingdom ... The city of Kandy is about 1700 feet above the sea-level, and we rose that height in a few miles. The engine grunted and creaked as it dragged us up over alarmingly sharp curves and gradients; but the scenery was of entrancing beauty and grandeur. On each side of us were bold peaks, clothed with vegetation almost to the summit ... Below us we looked down immense depths, with only a foot or two between the rails and the precipice ... It is a fearful place for a nervous novice ... if they are awful to look down, still they were most beautiful, the mountain-side was generally clothed with trees of remarkable beauty ... and parrots and strange birds of many hues darting among them to and fro. And all about us huge and gorgeous butterflies, so there was not for an instant repose for the eyes.

Bertie also commented on the beautiful scenery in his journal and noticed the 'fine butterflies':

Tea Gardens

December 23rd ' 96

Caught the 7.30 train to Kandy. The scenery on this part of the railway is beautiful. I saw plenty of fine butterflies. We changed carriages & had lunch before we got to Kandy. At Kandy we got into another train for Wattigamma. (Wattegama) It was raining hard when we got there. 16 miles to drive to Nillo Mally. (Nillomally, or Nillumally) Herbert rode and we gave a Mrs.Hardy a lift. The road was washed away in places by the rain. Got to Nillo Mally about 3.30. Douglas was busy in one of the tea gardens.

The extensive tea plantations of Ceylon were developed after 1878 when the spread of a fungal disease decimated the coffee crops. Tea, made from the leaves of Camellia *sinensis* bushes, has become a major export for Ceylon, with many acres of hill country being cleared for the plantations.

Tea was first esteemed as a drink in China. Containers with tea in them were discovered in tombs from as early as 206BC. The first Europeans to sample and export this valuable commodity were the Portuguese, and later the Dutch. In England, it was popularised among the elite by Catherine of Braganza, a Portuguese princess who married Charles II in 1662. She enjoyed her cup of tea at breakfast. Later, high born ladies would sip tea out of elegant cups in the afternoons. It was also sold in coffee houses, but always at high cost. It was expensive, partly because it had to be transported so far from China by way of sailing ships, known as Tea Clippers, but also because the government imposed a tax of up to 119% on it. This led to widespread smuggling and other criminal activities. These included the frequent adulteration of tea with other cheaper and sometimes harmful substances.

Early in the nineteenth century, traders of the British East India Company conceived the idea of growing tea in the cool hill country in British India. They imported seed from China, but found that tea bushes grew wild in the mountains of India, and this form of Indian tea from the local bushes became as acceptable to British tea drinkers as China tea. Well known varieties of Indian tea are Assam tea and Darjeeling.

One of the major tea industry pioneers in Ceylon was a Scotsman, James Taylor. He had come to the country at the age of seventeen in 1852. In 1866, he trialled tea seeds he brought from India on a nineteen acre plot. These flourished and he later established a tea processing factory on the Loolecondera Estate which previously had grown coffee.

In 1890 Thomas Lipton, a self-made Glasgow grocer, visited Ceylon and went into partnership with James Taylor. He bought five ailing coffee estates, on which they planted tea. Thus began the great Lipton Tea tradition, with the slogan 'From tea gardens to the teapot'. Lipton was able to harvest tea from his own estates, package it and sell directly to the public, cutting out any middlemen. His products were also advertised widely. This enabled him to sell tea to vast numbers of working class people, who had never been able to afford this luxury item before. Tea became immensely popular, and was exported all over the world by Lipton, including the United States. It became the national drink of the British people from all walks of life.

There was a need of an efficient means of transporting the rubber, coffee, tea and other goods from the hill country to the port at Colombo, so the construction of the Ceylon (Sri Lanka) railways began in 1864. The first line ran between Colombo and Ambepussa, about 45 km north-east of Colombo. Between 1864 and 1926 the railway network was expanded throughout the island. The first steam locomotives were imported from Britain. Sir Guilford Lindsey Molesworth was the first engineer, later to be Director General, of the railways. To build rail lines through mountainous jungle was a great feat of engineering and required the construction of many viaducts, tunnels and bridges. The network of railway lines in operation by 1896, enabled Bertie to travel with comparative ease to many parts of the island.

Many of the labourers used in the construction of the railways and on the tea plantations were Tamils, thousands of whom were brought over from Southern India as indentured servants. This meant they were contracted to work for their masters and many were essentially slaves, even though slavery had been abolished in 1844. The working and living conditions were extremely harsh, with long hours and pitifully low pay. The women in particular were doubly disadvantaged. Their job was to 'pluck' the tea and they were paid by the amount they picked, but they were also expected to care for their husbands and families as well. The men were employed to cut trees, and do the planting and weeding and were paid a weekly wage. This usually came to a little more than the women could earn, but still barely enough to live on, or for any extras. Basic education for their children was sometimes provided, but they often had to walk a long way to the schools. Many of the children were employed by the tea estates from a young age.

The owners and managers of the tea gardens, such as Bertie's family members, lived in comfortable houses known as bungalows, with lush tropical gardens.

Nillo Mally, or Nilloomally as it is now known, still exists. All the tea estates were nationalised by the Sri Lankan Government in 1972, and Nilloomally was amalgamated with other estates in the area. The gracious bungalow is now occupied by the present manager of the tea estates. It still has a lovely garden surrounded by mature trees, which were probably planted about the time of Bertie's visit. There are extensive views from the bungalow of the valley below and of hillsides covered in sculptured tea bushes, and the misty blue Knuckles Mountain Range in the distance. The road to the house has probably not changed much since 1896. It is still extremely narrow, snaking its way between the hills and at times with a surface deeply pitted and washed away by the rains. There is also one extremely rickety bridge over a little river which has to be crossed with great caution.

It was Christmas time when Bertie arrived and there was plenty going on. During the next ten days he obviously enjoyed the lively social life among the tea planters with his family and their friends. He explored the jungle around Nilloomally and pursued elusive butterflies to add to his collection. With an estimated 245 species to be found in Ceylon, many unique to the island, it is not surprising that he was so enthusiastic:

Dec.24th
Got up a little before 6 after a splendid sleep, the best I have had since I left England. Early tea 6.30. Had a look round the estate with Herbert & caught a few butterflies. Saw one "Kallima" and one "Ornithoptera." Called on Mr Gordon at Watakelly. (Wattekelle)

The *Kallima* butterfly mentioned was probably the Beautiful Oak Leaf butterfly, this has iridescent blue upper wings, but the under wing is mottled brown, so when the wings are closed, it resembles a dead leaf and is almost impossible to see. According to present day classification there are no Ornithoptera species in Ceylon, but Bertie was probably referring to the large and brightly coloured Bird Wing and Swallow tail butterflies, which in the nineteenth century were classified as Ornithoptera.

Bertie's journal continues:

Dec. 25th 96. Xmas Day
Got up at 5.30 & went after pig with Douglas. Apps came with us & 10 coolies; one had a spear, one an axe, one a sword & three had guns of various antiquated patterns. We had a jolly day in the jungle but no sport. Saw some fine butterflies. A species of balsam was in full flower in the jungle & looked very pretty. Got back to Nillo Mally at 2pm, very tired. Nine came to dinner - 2 Woods, 2 Gordons, B. Bressey.

Splendid feed but I was too tired to enjoy it & went to bed at 9 o'clock. The rest of the party set up till 11 o'clock.

Dec 26 - 96
Mooched round after butterflies but it was too dull for them. Lost my watch among the tea. It rained hard in the afternoon so I did no more collecting. Blare came to dinner.

Sunday. Dec 27th
It was too wet & misty this morning to go after pig. In the afternoon

Oak Leaf butterfly, Kalima philarchus. Showing its contrasting wing colours [from a painting by Sally Birch]

I went with Herbert to call on the Foxes. Met a young "creeper" (Paul) who was in the Jameson raid. It is the prettiest bungalow I have seen up to now. A splendid view down the valley, in the distance you can see Adam's Peak & Petrogalle. Lovely sunset on our way home. The colours on the hills & in the river were beautiful. Bed 8.45.

Amy Bressey

Douglas Bristowe

This part of Sri Lanka is extremely beautiful and many of the tea planters' bungalows were built at superb vantage points. In modern times, some of them have been converted into up-market boutique hotels where guests can enjoy the experience of living amongst the tea gardens. The term 'Creeper' is the name in Sri Lanka for young men who work on tea plantations similar to apprentices, learning the intricacies of running a tea estate. They hoped, in time, to be promoted to assistant manager and later, manager. In the past, fathers would sometimes pay the manager handsomely to teach their son the trade.

The two mountains Bertie mentioned are the two highest peaks in Ceylon. Adam's Peak, or Sri Pada, at 2388 metres, has always been venerated as a holy place and visited by many pilgrims at certain times of the year. An interesting account of his experiences on Sri Pada was written by a John Still, who was obviously awed by the spirituality of the mountain. He arrived in Ceylon as a young man in 1897 to work in tea plantations. but was later to join the Archaeology Department. Still always had an abiding passion for the wild places of Ceylon and his book, *Jungle Tide*, he wrote:

In the middle of the hills of Ceylon, now sacred to tea, there towers a mountain so famous that the literature of two thousand years in several languages would have to be searched if all references to it were to be assembled in one book. Hindus and Buddhist, Mahomedans [Muslims] and Eastern Christians alike revere the mountain as a holy place, and there is some evidence that the jungle people who came before all these did likewise ... Holy in the past, at present day it is so sacred that rich men, accustomed to wear European clothes and socks and boots, will toil barefoot up its rough and stony way to the shrine of the footprint upon the summit, more than seven thousand three hundred feet above the level of the ocean that can be seen as a glittering cord stretched along the horizon fifty miles away ... I have climbed it many a time when pilgrims by thousands wound up its rugged path by torchlight, singing as they went; I have camped with them in its sheltering caves; and with them I have kept vigil the long night through on the cold wind-swept summit, waiting for the rising sun to announce that the time has come to pray; for there is an element of sun-worship in these religions that come to the surface then, and the shouts of the multitude ring out like the cries of Hosannas in the Bible ... where the legends of all religions are interwoven; for the footprint on the rock, that which men go out into the wilderness to see, is sacred to them all. It is only a shallow depression in the rock, some two yards long, but to Buddhists it is the footprint of their founder, and they call the mountain simply Sri-Pada the sacred footprint, Hindus name it Siva's. Mahomedans of both sects call the mountain Father Adam's Hill; and though the modern name follows this in calling it Adam's Peak, Eastern Christians believe the mark to have been imprinted by the foot of St Thomas, who is peculiarly the apostle of India. Another common name is 'Samanala-kanda', the hill of the god Saman has given to butterflies their euphonious Sinhalese title, samanalaya. For at certain times of the year when countless millions of butterflies stream out on migration they are supposed to be going on pilgrimage to end their short lives on the sacred mountain.

Elizabeth Bisland, when visiting the island, was told a charming legend about the banishment of Adam from Eden:

Adam was first banished to this place that he might not feel too sharply in the beginning his loss and the contrast.

Upon Adam's Peak – a soaring pinnacle seven thousand feet high, of which we caught a glimpse of while still at sea – stood the father of men and wept for his lost Eden, for which even Ceylon might not console him; the bitter rain of his immeasurable grief trickling down the mountain-side into the rocks, the rivers, the sea and the sands, where it is found today as clear shining gems and pearls like tears. It was upon this peak that, having clothed himself in skins of beasts, he shed abroad to the winds the first green garments that hid his primal nakedness, and these, scattered far and wide by the breeze, sprang up in spice plants – so ambrosial a potency had even the leaves of the trees in Paradise.

The other mountain, Petrogalle, or Pidurutagala, at 2524 metres, is the highest mountain on the island. Bertie was able to climb to its summit, but today this is a high security zone and access by the public is denied, as the government has its central communication and radar system there.

Monday Dec 28th

Up at 6.   Herbert does not have his bath in the morning, but before dinner (a warm one).   Went for a walk with Herbert & Amy & caught a few butterflies. Herbert tells me that a Tamil woman often has 2 or 3 husbands. This is in order that the estate belonging to 2 or 3 brothers shall not be divided. The garden at Nillo Mally reminds me somehow of "Fairlawn" but when you begin to look at the shrubs & flowers the similarity soon vanishes. Bamboo, large Hibiscus, Datura, (trumpet flower) Pawpaws, oranges, Blue gums, Sacred tree, fine Colias, Japanese lilac, & many others. The pretty little sun birds come to the window after flies. Leeches that look like stick caterpillars have been busy at my ankles. Caught a few butterflies.

'Fairlawn' was one of the large houses in Camberwell. It was bombed in World War II, and now is a primary school.

Nillumally bungalow in 2017 when visited by Berties grandchildren

29 December

I have had the most enjoyable day in the jungle after butterflies & have been most successful. Caught 16 different species & amongst them a fine black one with a yellow patch. Herbert sent my lunch up by a coolie & I had it on the bridge on the Bray road near the place where they are digging holes for 'Cardemons' (an orchid). Saw a jungle fowl. Back at Nillo Mally at 3pm with a grand thirst. I have bought some putties & also ordered some 'karki' Knickers. The Ceylon Magpie Robin is plentiful, it has a note something like our bird.

Sri Lankan Birdwing butterfly, Troides darsius [curtesy of the WA Museum]

'Putties' or puttees were made by winding a long strip of cloth around the lower part of the legs, from ankle to knee. The name comes from a Hindi word 'patti' meaning bandage. They were first worn by hill tribes in the Himalayas and introduced into the Indian army in the second half of the nineteenth century. Later they were used in other armed forces until the Second World War. 'Karki' or Khaki Knickers also originated in the Indian army. The Knickers were short baggy trousers reaching just below the knees which could be tucked into the puttees. The colour of Khaki was first introduced into the Indian Army in 1846 by Sir Harry Lumsden, an officer in the Corps of Guides. He realised that traditional British military red coats were too hot and conspicuous for warfare in India. He ordered cotton pyjamas to be dyed brown using mud and vegetable dyes. The word Khaki originates from a Hindi word meaning soil-coloured. Possibly, Bertie decided to wear his puttees and knickers as protection from the leeches he mentioned that were previously attracted to his ankles.

Bertie was finding the clothing he had bought in England was not suitable for forays into tropical jungle. F.W.Burbridge in his book, *Gardens of the Sun*, suggested that for the good of their health, gentlemen travelling in the tropics should wear belts of soft flannel round the stomach and that clothing should consist of flannel shirts, tweed trousers, woollen socks, a light pith helmet and robust English walking boots. It was his opinion that it did not harm you if you got wet in the tropics, so long as you changed into dry clothes in the evening to avoid becoming chilled in the cool night air. He also recommended flannel pyjamas for sleeping in.

The fine black butterfly with a yellow patch mentioned,is the Sri Lankan Birdwing butterfly *Troides darsius*. This is one of the largest found on the island, with up to 15 cms wing-span, so Bertie was delighted to catch one. It is now Sri Lanka's national butterfly and strictly protected. He did not mention any butterfly books, but several had been written in the nineteenth century, including Frederic Moore's well known book, *Lepidoptera of Ceylon (1887)* which he may have consulted.

Cardemons, [cardamoms] are a member of the ginger *Zingberaceae* family. They are one of many spices grown for medicinal and culinary purposes in Sri Lanka. The plant originated in India and Ceylon; there are two main varieties, Black Cardamom and Green Cardamom. The pods, when harvested are an important component in traditional Ayurveda and Chinese medicine, as a cure for many different afflictions. These include problems of the mouth, throat or digestive system and even tuberculosis. Nowadays cardamom tea or coffee is popular in Asia as a refreshing drink as well as for its therapeutic properties. It is frequently used in Indian and Middle Eastern cooking, and also some Scandinavian baking recipes.

The Sri Lankan Jungle fowl, *Gallus lafayetii,* is found widely throughout the island. The hens are speckled brown, but the cock birds are spectacularly gaudy and may be heard crowing in the jungle. They are one of four *Gallus* species found on the Indian subcontinent which are closely related to the domestic chicken. They now have been named as Sri Lanka's national bird.

The Sri Lankan Magpie Robin, Copsychus saularis is a sub species of an attractive little bird found widely throughout tropical Asia. It is a member of the fly catcher family. As its name suggests, it is black and white and has been popular as a cage bird because of its pretty song. It is still frequently to be seen flitting around among the bushes on the island.

Bertie's account continues:

30 December
Went amongst the tea after butterflies, caught a few but missed a fine 'Kallima'. Fox came over to breakfast. In the afternoon Herbert and I went over to Wattakelly (Mr. Gordon's) & stayed the night.

31 December
Got up at 5.30 & went up Watakelli [Watekelli] peak with Herbert & four coolies. It was a hard climb, especially the first half to the 'bald rock' where we had a rest & a grand view of the valley below. We were on the edge of a precipice. After this the climb was through very stunted growth of trees. Plenty of rhododendrons, but few of them in

flower. There was a kind of bilberry, also some pretty blue flowers & orchids (terrestrial). We came across the footprints of Elephants, also plenty of their dung. Part of the path was along tracks made entirely by game. At the top we got into a thick mist so got no view. We had some beer which we had brought - it was very acceptable. Got back to Mr Gordon's bungalow at 10.30. We went straight on to Nillo Mally as we were very wet about the knees. Watakelli is 3600 feet above sea level.

01 January 1897   Nillo Mally
Wet in the morning. In the afternoon I went out for a short walk.

02 January
Went into the tea gardens after butterflies. Caught a few, but could not secure a single 'Ornithoptera' although I saw about eighteen. They seem to fly slowly, but in reality go very fast & also fly high. Douglas has a dinner party - Xmas pudding & turkey.

Sunday 03 January '97   Nillo Mally
Early tea before 6. After pig with Douglas. No sport.

The next day Bertie set off to explore other parts of Ceylon. His journal continues:

Kandy, showing the roof of the Temple of the Tooth in the foreground and across the park, the Queen's Hotel where Bertie stayed. [from Bertie's album]

Monday 04 January '97 Kandy
Left Nillo Mally 10.30. Arrived at Kandy in time for tiffin at the Queens
Hotel. A guide told me that I could see the sacred tooth. Got into the
temple by a side entrance. Like a fool I gave one of the rascally priests a
rupee. Having received this he told me I must wait till the Governor had
seen it. The fight to get into the temple after the Governor had seen it,
I enjoyed watching rather than participating in.

The Temple of the Tooth 1897 ... and in 2016

When Sir William Gregory was appointed as Governor of Ceylon and one of his first duties was to travel to Kandy with his wife, Lady Gregory, to be formally introduced to the still powerful Kandyan chiefs. In their honour, on the first night, there was a grand procession, or perahera, which he recorded in his memoirs:

Each chief or head man of the temple marched up the avenue at the head of his band, playing the most awful instruments. Behind the chiefs, painted and bedizened with brass ornaments rattling and ringing, and throwing themselves into every kind of contortion, followed the devil-dancers; and then slowly emerged from profound darkness of the background, dimly shown by torches, the enormous, stately elephants. It was indeed a weird sight ... The next morning I was brought out at early dawn for a constitutional round the hill, at the foot of which stands the Pavilion; and still higher rose my admiration of the natural beauties of Ceylon. Never had I taken such a walk. The morning mists were rolling up from the valleys at the other side of the hill, the mountain peaks had emerged, and gradually a vast extent of the country came in view. Below us roared the Mahswelliganga [Mahaweli], the largest river of the island, as it dashed along its rock-encumbered channel, and the sides of the hill down to it were clothed with trees all new to me in foliage. As we turned the hill homewards we came in view of other mountain peaks, and below us was the Temple of the Sacred Tooth of Buddha, his most venerated relic, which we were to visit in the evening ... In the evening we were conducted with much gravity to the Temple of the Tooth, to see the relic of Gautama Buddha ... It is brought out and shown to the multitude once or twice a year, but on other occasions no one, unless of princely station, or a representative of royalty, such as governors or ambassadors, are permitted to behold it. We were led upstairs to a very small room on the upper floor, full of yellow-robed priests. The heat was terrible, and the odour of coconut oil and many perspiring human beings was detestable. In a portion of the room inside a glass case was a profusion of jewels, chiefly rubies ... A huge silver-gilt dagoba contained minor dagobas, it is said of pure gold, and within the last was the relic which appeared to me like a crocodile's tooth. It was on a stand, supported by a narrow gold band, so the whole of it was to be seen.

Bertie was more interested in botany than temple relics and hurried off to visit the famous Peradeniya gardens. The satinwood bridge he mentions was a remarkable single span over the river constructed in 1833 entirely of beautiful yellow satinwood with no nails or bolts. It is no longer there, having been replaced by an iron bridge in 1905.

05 January '97   Kandy
Went to Peradeniya Gardens by 10.40 train. Saw Indiarubber tree, avenue, & Cabbage Palms. The flowering tree I admired most was a kind of Acacia (Amherstia) with a cluster of beautiful red flowers (hanging). I saw two fine blue kingfishers & lots of parrots. Went on the satinwood bridge. 2.28 back to Kandy. In the afternoon I listened to the native band, watched the people & the sunset. The colours in the sky & on the lake were beautiful. Bill at Queens 24.52 Rps.

Kandy had been the centre of a powerful Monarchy founded around the fourteenth century. The Kingdom managed to retain its independence until the mid-nineteenth century, in spite of intense pressure from the colonial powers, which had conquered the rest of Ceylon. It was, and is still considered to be, the spiritual heart of Sri Lanka because it is in the Temple of the Tooth that the most revered Buddhist relic has been housed. This is a tooth which is believed to have come from the Lord Buddha. Reputedly it was stolen from Buddha's funeral pyre and smuggled into Ceylon during the fourth century.

Queens Hotel at Kandy is one of the oldest hotels in Sri Lanka. It was first built as a residence for the Governor of Ceylon in the nineteenth century and was also used as a barracks for the Ceylon Rifle Regiment. It was later turned into an elegant hotel, which has long been a favourite place for visiting dignitaries to stay. These included Rudyard Kipling, Lord Louis Mountbatten, while he was Supreme Allied Commander of South East Asia during the Second World War, and in 1954, Queen Elizabeth II and Prince Philip, Duke of Edinburgh. It is still a busy hotel with a distinctly colonial flavour. It is a favourite venue for wedding parties and large groups of chattering multi-national tourists. Guests can enjoy a cool drink or a refreshing cup of tea in the Lord Mountbatten Lounge, or by the pool at the back of the building.

The beautiful Royal Botanical Gardens at Peradeniya were originally the site of a Royal palace and temple first created by King Wickramabahu in 1371. The present gardens were laid out in 1821 and were formally established as botanical gardens in 1843, when plants were introduced from Kew Gardens and other places around the world. It has always been famous for its grand avenues of trees and beautiful flowers. For many years the director was Dr G. H. K. Thwaites, a distinguished botanist who preferred the gardens to look natural and wild, which did not fit in with the usual Victorian conventions. He became a close friend of Sir William Gregory while he was Governor of Ceylon and also of Marianne North, the famous Victorian botanical artist, who visited the gardens in 1877. She painted many pictures there and these can be seen to this day, with hundreds more from all over the world, in the Marianne North Pavilion at Royal Kew Gardens in London. An account of her impressions of the places she visited during her travels is in the book, *A Vision of Eden: The Life and World of Marianne North*:

I found the dear old gentleman delighted to see me; and in spite of the drizzling rain, we had a charming walk round the garden for two hours. He planted half the trees himself, and had seldom been out of it for forty years, steadily refusing to cut vistas, or make riband-borders and other inventions of the modern gardener. The trees were massed together most picturesquely, with creepers growing over them in a natural and enchanting tangle. The bamboos were the finest I ever saw, particularly those of Abyssinia, a tall green variety 60 to 100 feet high. The river wound all around the garden making it one of the choicest spots on earth.

'India Rubber Trees', photograph from Bertie's album ... and painting by Marianne North

Sir William Gregory was also a visitor to the Royal Botanical Gardens at Peradeniya and he wrote:

It is about three miles from Kandy, a very pretty drive, and you enter it by a row of Indiarubber trees of great height and size. Their huge roots spread widely above the ground looking like the intertwined limbs of prehistoric monsters, or uncanny tentacles of gigantic cuttlefish. We drove down an avenue fringed on each side with palms and diverse tropical trees ... We came to the residence of Dr Thwaites, a small, slight elderly man, who had tea and excellent bread and butter for us ... He took us over the garden and showed us his magnificent clusters of gigantic bamboos, growing by the river side, and the Amherstia nobilis, a tree from Burmah, with the most beautiful blossoms I have ever seen, and all kinds of other trees and plants.

The tree that both Bertie and Sir William Gregory admired, *Amherstia nobilis*, is also known as Pride of Burma, or Orchid tree. It is a spectacular tree originating in Burma (Myanmar), with hanging clusters of vivid red flowers. It is now grown widely in tropical gardens. It is named in honour of the wife of Lord Amherst who had been Governor General of India early in the nineteenth century. Lady Amherst also had a beautiful pheasant named after her. Many splendid specimens of this colourful tree are still displayed at Peradeniya, including one planted by Lord Louis Mountbatten in 1947. They are in full flower during January.

The Palm avenues and huge stands of bamboo are still there today. They are larger than they were in 1897, but sadly the Indian Rubber Tree (*Ficus elastica*) avenue that Marianne North painted and of which Bertie had a photo, is gone and only a few remnants of the trees remain.

Cabbage Palm Avenue in Peradeniya Gardens in 1897 - photo from Bertie's album ... and in 2016

The following morning Bertie set off for Nuwara Eliya and Nanoya (Nanu Oya). These towns are situated in the hills where the climate is pleasantly cool. The area was valued by the early Sinhalese as a place where rubies and other precious stones were found, but was considered even more vital as a source of water for the cities and agriculture on the plains. It was first discovered by Europeans in 1818 when a hunting party led by Dr John Davy came across a beautiful valley high in the hills and informed Governor Barnes about it. A small settlement was established and used as a sanatorium where people could go to recover from fevers such as malaria contracted in the low country. One such person was Samuel White Baker who had travelled to Ceylon in 1845 because he had heard it was a paradise for big game hunters. After twelve months in the jungles, he nearly died of 'jungle fever' (a severe form of malaria) and was told he must go to the highlands to recover. After only two weeks he had regained his strength and fallen in love with the area. He resolved to settle there and found an agricultural and residential community. This he did, starting in 1848. In his book *Eight Years Wanderings in Ceylon*, he writes of how they set up their little community, but the foundation seems to have consisted of one disaster after another:

Old postcard of Newara Eliya in the highlands

I purchased an extensive tract of land from the government, at twenty shillings per acre. I engaged an excellent bailiff, who with his wife and daughter, with nine other emigrants, including a blacksmith, were to sail for my intended settlement in Ceylon.
I purchased farming implements of the most improved descriptions, seeds of all kinds, saw-mills etc., and the following stock: A half-bred bull (Durham and Hereford), a well-bred Durham cow, three rams (a Southdown, Leicester and Cotswold), and a thorough-bred entire horse by Charles Xll; also a small pack of hounds and a favourite greyhound (Bran).

My brother had determined to accompany me; and with the emigrants, stock, machinery, hounds, and our respective families, the good ship Earl of Hardwick ... sailed from London in September 1848 ...

The Earl of Hardwick arrived after a prosperous journey, with passengers and stock all in sound health ... In a few days all started from Colombo for Newera Elia (known now as Nuwara Eliya). The only trouble was, how to get the cow up? She was a beautiful beast, a thorough-bred shorthorn, and she weighed about thirteen hundredweight. She was so fat that a march of one hundred and fifteen miles in a tropical climate was impossible. Accordingly a van was arranged for her, which the maker assured me would carry an elephant. But no sooner had the cow entered it than the whole thing came down with a crash, and the cow made her exit through the bottom. She was therefore obliged to start on foot in company with the bull, sheep, horse and hounds.

The emigrants started per coach, while our party drove in a new Clarence carriage [four-wheel enclosed carriage] which I had brought from England … Four government elephant-carts started with machinery, farming implements, etc., etc., while a troop of bullock-bandies [carts] carried the lighter goods. I had a tame elephant waiting at the foot of the Newera Elia Pass to assist in carrying up the baggage and maidservants.

All went well and all the emigrants arrived safely except the Clarence carriage, which was so heavy the horses were unable to haul it up over the pass. Therefore a groom, two more horses and an elephant were sent back a few days later to collect the carriage and luggage. Baker's narrative continues:

Now this groom, Henry Perkes, was one of the emigrants, and he was not exactly the steadiest of the party; I therefore cautioned him to be very careful in driving up the pass, especially in crossing the narrow bridges and turning the corners. He started on his mission. The next day a dirty-looking letter was put in my hand by a native, which being addressed to me, ran something in this style:

Honord Zur I'm sorry to hinform you the carriage and osses has met with a haccidint and is tumbled down a preccipice and it's a mussy as I didn't go too. The preccippice isn't very deep bein not above heighty feet or thereabouts – the hosses is got up but is very bad – the carriage lies on its back and we can't stir it nohow … Plese Zur come and see whats to be done.
Your Humbel Servt, H. PERKES

Upon investigation of the accident, it was discovered that the horses were so badly injured, they did not survive their fall and the carriage was lying upside down in the ravine. Also, to add to the woes, a message was received saying the precious pure-bred shorthorn cow had died on her journey from Colombo. Worse was still to come:

I sent the blacksmith with a gang of men, and Perkes was ordered to accompany the party. I also sent an elephant to assist in battling the carriage up the precipice. Perkes, having been much more accustomed to riding than walking during his career as a groom, was determined to ride the elephant down the pass; and he accordingly mounted, insisting at the same time that the mahout should put the animal into a trot. In vain the man remonstrated and explained that such a pace would injure the animal on a journey: threats prevailed and the beast was soon swinging along at full trot, with the delighted Perkes striding across its neck, riding an imaginary race.

This was to have disastrous consequences as the poor elephant literally died of exhaustion and as Samuel Baker remarked in his book, *'Mr Perkes was becoming an expensive man; a most sagacious and tractable elephant was now added to his list of victims.'* After these early set-backs, work on clearing the jungle and preparing the land commenced on an area of about 200 acres which they called 'Moon Plains'. The cultivation began with three teams, as the account continues:

Lord Dulcie's patent cultivator drawn by an elephant; a skim, drawn by another elephant, and a long wood plough, drawn by eight bullocks … It was an interesting sight to see the rough plain yielding to the power of agricultural implements, especially as some of these implements were drawn by animals not generally seen in plough harness at home.

The crops were successfully planted, however more tribulations were to come:

Many were the difficulties to contend against when the first attempts were made in agriculture at Newera Elia. No sooner were the oats a few inches above the ground than they were subjected to the nocturnal visits of elk and hogs in such numbers that they were almost wholly destroyed.

A crop of potatoes of about three acres on the newly-cleared forest land was totally devoured by grubs. The bull and stock were nearly starved on the miserable pasturage of the country, and no sooner had the clover sprung up in the new clearings than the Southdown ram got hoven [bloat] on it and died. The two remaining rams, not having been accustomed to so much high living since their arrival at Newera Ellia, got pugnacious upon the clover, and in a pitched battle the Leicester ram killed the Cotswold, and remained solus. An epidemic appeared among the cattle, and twenty-six fine bullocks died within a few days; five Australian horses died during the first year, and everything seemed to be going into the next world as fast as is possible.

In spite of early failures the new settlement was successful. They discovered that vegetables grew well including potatoes, peas, turnips, cabbages, beans, carrots and many others. They also found they could make excellent beer, so they established a brewery. Also:

The solitary Leicester ram had propagated a numerous family, and a flock of fat ewes with their lambs throve to perfection. Many handsome young heifers looked very much like the emigrant bull in the face, and claimed their parentage. The fields are green: the axe no longer sounded in the forests; a good house stood in the centre of cultivation; a road of two miles in length cut through the estate, and the whole place looks like an adopted 'home'. All the trials and disappointments of the beginning have passed away, and the reality was a picture I had ideally contemplated years before. The task was finished.

It was largely thanks to Samuel Baker's vision, that Nuwara Eliya became the thriving centre of the hill country that Bertie so enjoyed visiting. To this day, it is surrounded by successful vegetable market gardens which supply the whole of Sri Lanka with fresh produce. There is also a wide selection of hotels and guest houses. Nuwara Eliya became a favourite destination for people wishing to escape from the heat. It was regarded as a sanatorium where people were sent to recover from bouts of 'jungle fever', as malaria was called. It was also sometimes called 'Little England', where recreational activities such as tennis, fox hunting, polo, cricket, trout fishing and golf could be enjoyed.

In 1872, Sir William and Lady Gregory travelled to Nuwara Eliya from Kandy. This was before the railway had been built between the two towns. Though it was not an easy drive, they still enjoyed the experience.

Every new excursion that we made enchanted us more and more with the varied beauty of Ceylon scenery. The drive, from Kandy to Nuwara Eliya, of thirty-six miles was no exception. The scenery was very beautiful among the peaks starting up boldly, some close, some at distance. The road was trying enough, from its narrowness and the tremendous declivities along which it ran ... The roads themselves were admirable, but, for reasons of economy, far too narrow, and one of my first resolves was to obtain a vote of money to widen them, and erect protective embankments in all the dangerous places throughout the island ... We halted at Ramboda, at the foot of the famous pass, by which we ascended something over 3500 feet in five miles, to reach the highest range of tableland above it. It was a spot of extraordinary beauty; from the veranda of the rest-house we saw eleven cascades tumbling from the mountain in every direction. Right above us a stream plunged from a rocky height, and became as it were a ribbon of mist as it fell ... The ascent was one series of zigzags, and through primeval forest of a totally different character from the tropical vegetation from the lower country ... At last we reached the top, and looked down on the plain of Nuwara Eliya. It was then far from prepossessing, being a long extended dismal swamp ... Now, few come up the road we climbed, for the iron horse has reached Nuwara Eliya by another route. The first sight that now catches the eye is a deep blue lake, called after me ... It was one of my early undertakings, and this wonderful improvement was carried out at a cost hardly exceeding 1,200 pounds ...

We all enjoyed the climate of Nuwara Eliya ... We rode and drove, and had long walks through jungle, by the side of tumbling streams, where we were liable to meet a leopard or an elephant at any minute, and we gave breakfast-parties on the top of Pedrotallagalla, the highest mountain of Ceylon ... the crest of which we reached by an easy riding path ... It was a very pleasant time, interspersed with little adventures. One morning a leopard was espied in the fork of a tree within the precincts of our bungalow ... On another occasion we were visited by an elephant, who after eating whatever vegetables he found in the garden, poked his nose, or trunk through the back window, in order, I presume, to see what was doing inside.

By 1897 the 'iron horse' made travel to Nuwara Eliya much easier and quicker for Bertie and while there, he enjoyed an active and sociable few days.

6th January '97 Newara Eliya
Started at 10.40 from Kandy for 'Nanoya', the station four miles from Newara Eliya. The scenery on the railway is grand but one gets rather tired of the tea plantations. Newara Eliya is 6000 feet & Kandy only 1800 feet above sea, consequently one feels the air rather fresh at first. Newara Eliya reminds me of parts of the New Forest but there are mountains all round. Furze, lilies, rhododendrons, scabious.
There is plenty going on here - bicycling, golf, cricket, boating, fishing, tennis. There are a fine lot of 'Wattle' trees growing here with their pretty little bell shaped flowers.

7th January Newara Eliya
Short walk before breakfast. After, I went for another walk along the

View of the tea plantations from the train

valley to the east, where you get a lovely view of the distant mountains.
Tiffin at 2pm.
Drove to Hakgale [Hakgala] gardens, saw a large monkey, also some
fine flowers of St Johns Wort. In the gardens I saw for the first
time a beautiful creeping begonia. They grow pear and oak trees, also
strawberries, but these don't do well. The red flowers of the Chinese
plantain, also Balsam were pretty.

Hakgala Gardens were first established in 1861 as a place to grow Cinchona trees. This is a plant that originated in Peru, where it was recognised by the native Peruvians to have powerful properties as a cure for malarial fever. The Jesuit missionaries carried some back to Europe in the seventeenth century, where malaria was widespread at the time. King Charles II of England was cured of his malaria by a decoction of Cinchona bark and so was the son of the French King Louis Xl. Quinine is extracted from the bark of Cinchona. The Peruvian government attempted to retain their monopoly on this powerful drug by banning the export of seeds or plants, but some were smuggled out and plantations established elsewhere. This included Ceylon, where, by 1883, there were 64,000 acres under cultivation and it became a very lucrative crop earning £16 million in 1886.

The Hakgala Gardens were also where some of the first tea was grown in Ceylon as a trial, to ascertain whether it could be established commercially on the island. Modern visitors to these beautiful gardens are shown some of those original tea plants which now have grown into substantial trees and also a specimen of Cinchona tree. Hakgala had developed into the beautiful botanical gardens that Bertram visited and today is still enjoyed by many people of all ages and nationalities. There are even charming little electric buggies driven by knowledgeable garden staff, some of whom are fourth generation employees at Hakgala. They delight in telling visitors about the flora of the park and seeing how fast they can whip round the hair-pin bends when coming down the hill.

Like Sir Gregory, Bertie ascended Pedrotagalla mountain, but he climbed it on foot, not horseback.

8th January Newara Eliya
Went up Pedrotagalle [Pedrotallagalla] (8000). There is a splendid path all the way & I went up without a stop. The rhododendron trees are very large. I hear they are in full flower about May. At the very top I caught after a good chase a specimen of Lathona (in my hand). Good view from the top. Back to breakfast at 10 am. Went for a walk round the lake with a young chap staying at the Hotel. The previous night when playing billiards with me he lost his temper, cursed & called the poor marker names, but said nothing to me.

9th January Newara Eliya
After butterflies, but caught none. Tried to paint in the afternoon. A Mr. Bond is staying here with his wife, they come from Wargrave. He knows the Clemandsons. Major Charlie is staying here & seems a good chap.

10th January   Newara Eliya
Went for a sail in the morning with Major Charlie. The Keena is one of the finest trees in the jungle. The tints are lovely.
Bill 65 rupees.

The Keena tree, [Callophylum walkeri] is a handsome tree which occurs naturally in the mountains of Sri Lanka. It has sweet-smelling pale pink flowers in January. Early photos of Newera Eliya, often featured Keena trees in the foreground.

After his visit to Newera Eliya, Bertie boarded the train to Kandy and then on to Nillo Mally and more social activities.

11th January '97   Kandy, left Newara Eliya.
Arrived safely at Kandy & like the place more than ever. Saw a large tree in the Lake View Road covered with Bougainvillea. Sunset lovely. There is a

fine creeper near the lake rather like convolvulus (3 stamens & 1 stigma). Outside my window grows a Hibiscus like the one I have seen in Percy Smit's buttonhole in the city. I also saw it at Wattegamma station & at many other places.

12th January '97   Kandy
Fine. Went after butterflies in the morning. B. Bressey came with me for a short time & then a beastly Sinhalese tacked on to me. I caught a few which are new to me, but should have done better by myself.
Played football at 5pm with the Northern Provinces & the North Lancashire regiment. Very warm work & I got rather short of wind, all the others seemed in the same condition.

13th January '97   Nillo Mally
Left Kandy 11.20 for Wattegamma. Major Charlie was in the train going to Martele [Matale], just for the railway journey, & then going back to Colombo in the same train. One of the Miss Woods came to dinner & I don't think much of her. Major Charlie tells me that the railway to Wargeling has more curves than the one to Newara Eliya — in fact you can almost shake hands with the engine driver in places.

14th January '97   Nillo Mally
Went with Herbert and Amy (in a chair) to breakfast with Mr and Mrs Wright (about 6 miles) at 'Monsagalle'. Met Mrs Powell there who came out in the same boat as the Governor when she was Miss Wright. Wright had a stuffed Cheetar, also the tusks & foot of a large elephant shot by him in the low country. Met a 'creeper' there who had worn out 5 pairs of boots in two months.

It was the custom for ladies to be transported in chairs when the paths were too rough or steep for carriages. Mary Steuart in her book *Every Day Life on a Ceylon Cocoa Estate* (1905) wrote:

I had the great delight of an utterly new experience, namely being carried four miles almost straight up hill in a chair, the poles thereof resting on the shoulders of four coolies. It was an experience. To begin with, I am by no means a light weight, and one of the coolies was such a short, slight, weak-looking little man, that I felt very much as if I ought to carry him, and not him me … The chair was of light cane, with a head well thatched with palm leaves. It was much after the pattern of the old sedan chair, excepting that it was open instead of being closed in. The road by which we went was simply a mountain path, leading first through groves of palms … then we went through paddy fields, forded an unbridged river where I expected momentarily to be deposited in the water, and then up the side of a mountain gorge, where huge boulders encroached on the already narrow pathway, on the lower side of which, without the slightest parapet, was a precipice of several hundred feet. One false step and, for me there would have been an end of all things, but the false step never comes.

15th January '97   Nillo Mally
A fine day. Went up to the jungle after butterflies, saw very few, too cold. Lunch was brought to me at the bridge on the Bray road. Saw a jungle fowl.

16th January '97   Nillo Mally
Fine. Shot a sunbird in the morning & skinned it. In the afternoon caught a few butterflies.

Bertram was a keen lepidopterist who would hunt for butterflies or moths whenever the opportunity occurred. He obviously came well prepared with all the paraphernalia required. We know he had several butterfly nets, since later in his journey he was able to give one of his spares away to a small boy he befriended.

He would also have needed killing jars. These are glass jars with screw tops which contain some plaster of Paris which has been impregnated with a toxic substance. In the nineteenth century this may have been a cyanide compound, but chloroform or ether were sometimes used. All these substances are hazardous, so modern-day insect collectors prefer to use ethyl acetate. (nail-polish remover)

When butterflies die, their wings naturally fold together and as they dry out, become very brittle. To mount the butterflies, the wings can be pinned out into position when freshly killed while their joints are still soft and pliable. This is done on a special mounting board made of soft wood, or cork which has a groove along the middle to hold the body of the butterfly while the wings are arranged to each side and pinned down with paper strips. A special thin type of pin is used to hold insects which are pushed through their thorax. At all times, the handling of butterfly specimens must be done with care to avoid damaging the delicate coloured scales on their wings.

An alternative method, which Bertram may have chosen, was to allow the butterflies to dry out with their wings folded, stored in envelopes, which he would have kept in air-tight boxes. At a later date, he would have placed them in a container with some moistened absorbent material for a day or more until the wings become relaxed. He could then have manipulated the butterfly and mounted it in position until it dried out again. To transport large numbers of butterflies in envelopes would have taken up less space than if pinned and mounted.

It is not known what happened to the bird specimens he collected. He records that he skinned them and perhaps he intended to have them mounted for display purposes later. Cabinets of colourful stuffed and artistically mounted birds were popular in Victorian households. None of Bertram's descendants can remember such displays, so they may have been donated to a museum.

17th January '97   Nillo Mally
Went to breakfast with B. Bressey at the White's bungalow. Shot at swinging bottles. In the afternoon Herbert & Amy went to the Foxes. Wood came to tea & a conjurer came & performed, a very poor one I thought.

18th January Nillo Mally
Fine. After butterflies in the morning - Poor sport. Douglas & I left at 3pm to catch the train for Martele on our way to Anuradhapura. Stayed the night at the rest house there.

Anuradhapura was an ancient city which was believed to be the capital of Ceylon from the fourth century BC until the eleventh century AD. It was also the centre of Theravada Buddhism for many thousands of years and there is a wealth of ruined temples and other magnificent buildings. There were a series of large lakes, (or 'tanks' as they were known), constructed to provide an elaborate irrigation system. This has long been recognised as one of the most significant archaeological sites in the world and is now designated as a UNESCO World Heritage site.

Over time the magnificent buildings fell into ruins and were covered by the jungle, although the area continued to be revered by the local Buddhists as a holy place. One of the early Europeans to explored the ancient city was Thomas Skinner, who as a very young army officer was responsible for building many of the roads throughout the island. He wrote:

In 1832 I was ordered to open a road from Aripo, on the western coast, where the pearl fishers were situated, to Anarjapora [Anuradhapura], the capital of the district of Nuwara Kalawa, about which less appeared to be known than about the most recently discovered lake in Central Africa. In the latest maps of the island then published, this district was described as a mountainous unknown country, so that to ascertain its position I had to survey into it in the first place. This was a very slow operation … Moreover, it seemed to be the policy of the Kandyans in those days to keep this sacred retreat as inaccessible as possible to Europeans; the low, over-growing jungle paths, which alone led to it, were so extremely tortuous, that it was difficult at times to pass along them.

My astonishment, therefore, was the greater when I reached the place, to find extensive ruins, large dagobas, [stupa] magnificent tanks of colossal dimensions, and instead of the 'mountainous country' represented in the so-called maps, I found a thickly-populated district, with evidence of it having been, at some remote date, the granary of the country.

Nearly fifty years later Sir William Gregory visited Anuradhapura in 1880, by which time some roads had been built, but it still took several days to reach the site. He wrote:

In September I made my first excursion to Anuradhapura, the once famous capital of Ceylon. This city was a considerable place when Wijayo, in the fifth century before Christ, the William the Conqueror of Ceylon, came over from India with his Aryan hordes and conquered the country. It became the capital about a century afterwards.

We had a drive of extraordinary beauty from Kandy to Dambulla, breakfasting at the very pretty town of Matale on the way, and visiting the remarkable rock temple of Alu Vihara, a short distance from the road. In the afternoon we reached Dambulla, which lies at the foot of an enormous round mass of gneiss, said to be five hundred feet high. About half way up is an immense cavern, lined with statues of Buddha, most solemn and striking, partly natural and partly artificial excavation. The walls and ceiling are painted with scenes from the life of Buddha … Up to this, about forty-seven miles from Kandy, the road was very fairly good, but henceforward we were warned we must not trust to wheels, as the Great Northern Road, extending to Jaffna, was a mere track running through jungle and paddy fields, and without a single bridge over the many, and at times dangerous, rivers which intersected it. We accordingly mounted our horses and rode the rest of the way …

Our journey was auspicious enough. We safely forded the rivers, and if rough enough, the track was dry. On the second day after leaving Dambulla we reached Anuradhapura. I was immediately struck with its picturesque appearance. The huge Dagoba rose above the forest, and as we advanced the remains of its former magnificence was apparent. The ground was strewn with broken pillars; in some places the columns stood erect, with richly carved capitals. The so-called Brazen Palace of the great and chivalrous King Datugammenu [Dutugemunu], who reigned about 160 BC, was, according to Mahawanso, supported by sixteen hundred columns of rock, and they still stand, though shorn in number. Everywhere were seen the entrances to private dwellings, decorated either by dancing dwarfs graven on stone or by vases of flowers … The jungle, wherever one penetrates, is full of these remains, and in the thick of it, where a clearance is made, appear here and there all alone sitting statues of Buddha. We were brought to see the bathing place of the King and another of the Queen, lined with stone, and gigantic stone troughs in which the royal elephants are said to have been given their rice, and a stone couch in which the dying King Datugammenu lay watching for the completion of the great Ruanwelle [Ruwanweli] Dagoba, which, if finished, would render his end a happy one.
The great sight at Anuradhapura was, of course the celebrated Bo tree, said to be an offshoot of Ficus religiosa under which Gautama Buddha reclined just before his death.

Someone else who came to know the ruined cities of Ceylon well, was John Still who wrote in his book, *Jungle Tide* how, when he worked in the archaeology department as a young man in the early part of the twentieth century, he was asked to guide a Governor to a temple which was deep in the jungle:

I once lost the reigning Governor of Ceylon. This disaster was not gazetted, for I found him again, but for most of the day his wife was very anxious, and her agitation was conveyed to various minor officials … It happened this way. The Governor wished to visit a certain ruined temple where some remarkable frescoes still retained their colours after six centuries of neglect, and he asked me to take him to see them … I mistook one cattle track for another, where all looked much alike … On we went, and when we had been a couple of hours afoot I knew we had missed the frescoes, lost our way, and were heading for very wild uninhabited country. There were plenty of game paths, and they bore fresh imprints of buffaloes, that might or might not be wild, and of elephant, leopard, bear, and several kinds of deer. Also were damp hollows where wild pigs had dug, and in the trees above us endless tribes of monkeys moved. So the Governor had many interests added to what must normally prove a tedious career. But it was hot, and he was more than sixty years old, and he became very tired and thirsty …

That Governor was a great gentleman. When at last I found the way out, and we stumbled wearily along to the door of the circuit bungalow he occupied, I began to voice my apology; but he cut me short with, "I have enjoyed my walk, and you must come to dinner."

I do not know how many miles we walked, but I do know we never passed outside the limits of the buried city. The places where the animals' footprints were held in record by the mud had once been public baths, reservoirs for washerwomen to beat clothes in, ornamental ponds, or pools where lotus blooms were grown for temples. The mound where grew the trees I chose to climb were compact of tile and brick, and their earth had once been beams and rafters; where streamlets had run after heavy rain the dry sand was full of broken pottery, and the game paths we walked cut through ridges whose soil was red with bricks that one were walls.'

By 1897, it was easier to get to Anuradhapura. Bertie went by train to Martale, then by coach and bullock cart; a journey that took only two days, with one night spent at the Martale rest house. The ancient ruins were still being excavated, but many of the sites had been cleared of jungle.

19th January 1897   Anuradhapura
Fine. Up at five ready for the coach, but it did not start till 6.30. Three Frenchmen are also going. Two in the coach the other on a bicycle. They stayed at Dambulla. The scenery was grand. At first mostly palms but later forest trees. There was a broad clearing on either side of the road where there were plenty of butterflies. Lunched at Dambulla 11am, nothing after this but bananas & milky coconuts till we arrived at Anuradhapura 7 pm.

Anuradhapura city ruins, photo from Bertie's album and photo taken in 2017 by the author

20th January 1897 Anuradhapura

Did the ruins. The tomb of King Elala [Elara] is being excavated now under the supervision of Mr Bell who has 200 coolies working under him in different places. The rock temple, where there is an image of Buddha cut out of the rock & painted yellow, this is supposed to be the first made in Ceylon. From the top you get a good view & can see Mihintale in the distance (8 miles). There is near this temple one of the large 'tanks' so plentiful in Ceylon. This one is 3 miles round, there are large crocodiles in it but they are not often seen. The water is let out daily by a sluice into the paddy fields. They catch a fish called a 'hula', which is fairly good eating. The natives catch the fish in a most ingenious way. They have long strips of bamboo tied together with a hook & line at the end. This they can guide out to any distance they like, the bamboo floating on the water. There is a large jail here, convicts being sent from Kandy & other places. The prison walls are most curious; about 14 feet high, the four feet at the top being of loose brick stacked loosely. If the convicts tried to climb over this of course they would fall, make a noise & attract the warders. I saw this sort of wall round the prison in Colombo. Also a large Dagoba near the prison is being repaired, the funds coming from the King of Siam who is one of the chief supporters of Buddhism. There is a fine tree grown here with red flowers called Spathodia. A Mr Parker was staying at the rest house, he knows a lot about birds of Ceylon. I saw the Paradise Flycatcher, also green & black Bulbuls (2). The green one is a match for 12 of the others & is also a splendid mimic.

Isurumuniya Rock Temple, Anuradhapura, photo take in 2017 by author and photo form Bertie's album 1897

H. C. P. Bell was the first Archaeological Commissioner in Ceylon, who worked tirelessly from 1890 until 1912, excavating the ancient treasures all over the island until his retirement. The work was always difficult, and sometimes dangerous. Many of the sites were covered in thick jungle which had to be cleared and some involved hazardous rock climbing, and there was always the threat of malaria and other tropical diseases. Some of the coolies Bertie saw assisting with the dig may have been inmates from the prison. It was the policy at that time to use prisoners for labouring jobs such as road building and other public works.

H. C. P. Bell was born in India where his father was a Major General. He was sent to England to be educated, but returned to Ceylon to join the Civil Service. He had been in the legal department, but had a keen interest in archaeology, so went to work in the field without any formal training. After he retired, he pursued his passion for archaeology in the Maldives and was able to prove that the people of the islands had practised Buddhism before they converted to Islam.

The *Spathodia*, or *Spathodea campanulata*, the African Tulip tree, originates from West Africa. It has been introduced to many other parts of the world where it is a popular tree in gardens and parks and is prized for its showy red flowers. It grows well in tropical and sub-tropical climates, and in some places has become an invasive weed species.

21st January 1897 Anuradhapura
We got up early & went after snipe. I did not care much about the experiment. We had to wade nearly up to our knees in mud & water & saw very little snipe. I shot 3. There were lots of waders of all sorts about, also some large hawks which were very tame.

22nd January 1897 Mihintale
We left Anuradhapura in a bullock wagon for Mihintale. My foot is bad. I have a boil & also my old complaint. Douglas shot a mongoose, also some bee-eaters of which species we saw plenty. We brought beer, bread, sugar, sardines, jam and ham with us. There is a beautiful climbing begonia growing over the portico, like the one I saw at Hakgale gardens. The sunbird I had previously seen at Nillo Mally comes to it, & also another species - black with a metallic head. We went to bed at 9pm after dinner of sardines on toast, fowls & green plantains. When I had been asleep some time the rest housekeeper woke me up & told me that there were some deer outside - I thought at first he had said bear - Douglas went out, as I did not feel inclined to turn out with my bad foot. He brought his ox out, & behind it he and Douglas stalked and shot a large stone.

Sunday 23rd January 1897   Mihintale

A lovely morning & plenty of all sorts of jolly birds about, but worse luck my foot is very bad. Douglas shot some pretty ones, some of which I skinned. In the afternoon I went to a tank nearby with Douglas. There was plenty of bird life everywhere. I saw a crocodile which I socked with the rifle at about 35 yards, he wriggled into the water & we did not see him again. There were lots of large water tortoises. A Mr Fox came on his bicycle & drank 3 bottles of our beer without thanking us much for it. Douglas went out at night after pig, saw a large one, but missed it. I have a 'comboy' on my bed instead of a sheet & first night a filthy pillow that belonged to the rest house keeper. The table cloth is also filthy & covered with egg-stains although there have been no Europeans for 4 months. There is also lots of Nux Vomica (strychnine) growing here. The fruit looks very pretty, rich orange, round and hard.

A 'comboy' is a sarong, known in Sri Lanka as a kambaya.

Sunday 24th January 1897   Mihintale

Tried to go round the tank, but failed. We have had nothing decent to eat all day. The rest house keeper has turned out to be a dirty, slovenly, lazy rascal. He spends all his time quarrelling in his cottage (night & day) & tells some story about his mother-in-law wanting to take his little girl to Anuradhapura, I don't believe a word of it. For breakfast we had ham and eggs which had been cooked in a 'chetty' in which coconut oil had been boiled (probably for his dirty head). We could not eat the mess, also a fowl done in the same pot. This meal was an hour late. For dinner (also an hour late), we had a piece of beef gristle (smoked) which I told him to give to his mother-in-law, & some rice full of grit, we finished our beer. At 9pm he had not made our beds nor emptied the water away we washed in in the morning.

Mihintale 25/I/97

Foot better. Shot two golden oriels, one of which I skinned. Went into the jungle & saw lots of skulls & human bones. We have discovered something. The rest house keeper has always kept Douglas's room rather dark & this is the reason. The dirty table cloth that I mentioned before has served also for a sheet for his bed. He had complained that it felt rather gritty — Of course it was the crumbs left at dinner. I have given him a bit of my mind. We ordered tea only for breakfast, (at 11am) as we wanted to start for Aradhapura at 12 O'clock. Nevertheless he was ¾ hour late & we did not start till 1.30. He also cheated us

81

over the bullock wagon. I had my revenge, reporting him at head-quarters at Aradhapura when I got there. He will be sacked at the end of the month & have his wages stopped for January. There are some birds that go about in small flocks, something like thrushes with thick plumage & a white eye. They are a sort of ground thrush & are called the Seven Sisters - They make enough row for a dozen. We slept the night at Aradhapura.

When Bertie mentioned his infected foot, it was the only occasion, apart from motion sickness, he suffered from ill-health on his journey. This is quite remarkable considering that he travelled to unhealthy areas where tropical diseases were common and he also ate some strange and unfamiliar foods. He was lucky to recover from his infection so quickly. Nineteenth century travellers did not have the benefit of modern medicines, but there were remedies available which he may have used. F.W. Burbidge's book, The *Gardens of the Sun* suggested that people travelling to remote areas take with them a supply of Cockle's pills, Collis Brown's chlorodyne, and Howard's sulphate of quinine, also, a bottle of brandy, a roll of sticking-plaster, needles, silk thread and bandages. Cold compresses could be made from towels and poultices made from mustard. It suggested taking a bottle of carbolic acid to mix with oil for treating insect bites, scratches, or flesh-wounds and gave useful instructions on how to set a broken bone.

Cockle's Anti-bilious pills were an invention of Dr James Cockle. They were widely advertised as a sovereign remedy for troubles with bile, liver, headaches, heartburn and constipation. Their main component was aloe, which is a laxative with several other ingredients, some of which were trade secrets.

Collis Brown chlorodyne was promoted by Dr John Collis-Brown and became popular at home and an essential item in the luggage of nineteenth century explorers of the world. It was marketed as a remedy for cholera, diarrhoea, insomnia, neuralgia, migraine, coughs and colds and asthma. It was considered an effective panacea and had the added bonus of making patients feel up-lifted. This is hardly surprising, since its main constituents were morphine dissolved in alcohol, cannabis and other substances to make it palatable. It could also be highly addictive and dangerous if over-used, so it was eventually withdrawn from the market.

Howard's sulphate of quinine was a medication used for the prevention and treatment of malaria and other fevers. John Howard was a pharmacist who was largely responsible for the introduction of Cinchona plantations throughout the British Empire. He was a pioneer in the development of medications derived from quinine which was extracted from the bark of these trees. These previously only grew in South America. Sulphate of Quinine was effective in the fight against malaria, but prolonged use of the drug could cause unpleasant side effects.

All did not go well for Bertie on their return journey.

Aradhapura/ Martele 26/1/97
Caught the coach at 6.30am for Martele, but did not arrive until 1.30am.
We were on the box seat & there were six inside who had to turn out in
places & push the coach up the hills. Nothing to eat from 12 till we got
to Martele except a few bananas. The last six hours it pelted. Dambulla
was closed as the governor was there. When we got to Martele there
were 3 English chaps who had been fighting with the Malays. One of
them had been locked up & then bailed out by the others (100 rupees.)
When let out, he knocked the chief officer down & there was another
row.

Nillo Mally 27/1/97
Caught the 12.50 train from Martele to Wattagamma. Had some difficulty
getting a trap. Amy is away staying at the Foxes.
Nillo Mally 28/1/97

Went up to the jungle & shot one jungle fowl. Dinner with Douglas. He
has a good cook. He dined in pyjamas.

Nillo Mally 29/1/97
Early tea by myself. Wrote letters in the morning. Caught some
butterflies on the gymkana grounds & shot a fine parrot (blossom
headed.) It was feeding on the seeds of the gravilia. Mr Parker gave
me an example of the honesty of Singalese. He engaged a Singalese boy
& another came & told him that he was dishonest." How do you know
that?" asked Mr. P " He robbed me," said the man. " Why did you not
prosecute him?" asked M. P. " Because I had two enemies in the town
& prosecuted them," said the man.

While on his travels, Bertie sent several letters home to his family which were preserved
by his son. This one was written to his sister, Kathleen.

NilloMally
Jan 27th

Dear Kathleen,
Douglas and I have returned from our trip to Anadhrapura. We enjoyed
ourselves very much, had some funny experiences, but no sport. We
started from Martele by coach at 7 (very late) on 19th. There were 3
Frenchmen also going as far as Dambulla. They could not speak a word
of English so I was obliged to air my French which is very rusty. One
of them was riding a bicycle. The road was in very good order, but we did

not get to A. until 1pm. We did the ruins the next day & they are certainly very interesting. The Boo tree is not much to look at. We were very much amused at the prison at A. (modern) The walls are about 14 feet high, the four feet at the top being of loose bricks put on the top of one another in this way. If a convict tries to climb over this of course they all fall down making a great noise & attracting the warders. I believe this dodge is common in Ceylon.

There are some lovely trees growing near the Rest house with large clusters of red flowers. Spathodia it is called.
 There are two Englishmen & a lady staying at the rest house, who are Buddhists. They have got a fat priest who goes about with them & looks as if he did himself jolly well. They are the cause of great excitement & there is always a crowd of natives hanging around their door who fight to look in directly it is opened. I should like to catch the dirty fellows hanging around mine, I would give them something to talk about.

21st.   We got up early & went after snipe in the paddy fields. I don't think that either of us will try the game again in a hurry. There were very few snipe. (We got 3) after wading sometimes up to our knees in thick mud & water for three hours in the hot sun.

We had to leave A on 22nd as the Governor had taken the whole of the rest house for the 23rd, 24th & 25th so we went on to Mihintale which is about 8 miles off in a bullock wagon. There is a rest house, but we were obliged to take provisions with us, as they keep nothing there. We had a ham, bread, two tins of sardines, two of biscuits & 14 small bottles of beer. It was a nice rest house in a lovely situation with the most lovely creeping begonia growing over the porch, to the flowers of which the little sunbirds used to come every day – They are just like hummingbirds. I am sorry to say that I was laid up here with a small boil on my ankle. Also with the old swelling of the ankle brought on, I think by wading about in that mouldy paddy field. We had a decent dinner the first night but that was the only respectable one we had. The rest house keeper woke us up in the night to say there were three deer just outside. My foot was too bad, so Douglas went out in his pyjamas. They got the bull belonging to the rest house keeper & stalked along the side of it till they thought they were near enough, when Douglas fired. They then both rushed on the quarry in great excitement as it had not moved, & discovered that they had stalked & shot a large stone.
A Mr. Fox turned up the next day & drank 3 of our precious bottles of

beer, hardly saying thank you for it, a most cool proceeding.

I amused myself skinning birds as Douglas shot them. There are a great number about. I managed to get to a large tank close by in the afternoon & put a bullet into a large crocodile, but could not get him, in fact I think he liked it. There are some birds that go about in small flocks in Ceylon. They are rather like thrushes with very thick plumage. I am told they are called the 7 sisters. They certainly chatter enough for a dozen. On 26th we caught the coach (on our way back to Martele) at 6.30 in the morning, as it is only 60 miles, but we did not reach our destination till 1.30am the following day (18 ½ hours.) Douglas and I sat on the box seat. Inside there were two half-casts who spoke English & 4 coolies. We had two eggs each when we started & 3 more at 12 at Kekirawa, after that we had nothing till we got to Martele at one at night. The Dambulla resthouse was closed as the Governor was there. For the last 6 hours it rained & we got very wet. The horses could not pull the coach up the hills & the beggers inside would not get out, so Douglas & I, who wanted to get to Martele at some time or other, walked round to the back of the coach & turned them out. They tumbled out pretty quick when they saw we meant business. Douglas was very anxious to kick one of the half-casts in a tender place, but I would not allow it. They gave us no more trouble, bolting out in future directly we got off our seats. We had to push the coach up all the hills as the coolies could not move it. We were jolly hungry & thirsty when we got to Martele as there are no pubs on the road where you can get a snack of bread and cheese & a pint.

27. We are safe back at Nillo Malley & seem little the worse for our privations. Amy is away staying with the Foxes & Herbert is going there to dinner tomorrow, so I shall dine with Douglas. I have decided to leave Ceylon on 7th Feb for Singapore. I shall be sorry to leave the island as I have had a jolly time here, but want to see some more places.
Does Claude's clockwork mouse run fast?

With best love to all & hoping that you are all well.
Your affec. Brother, Bertie Bristowe

ಬಿಡಿ

30th January 1897 Nillo Mally
Got two parrots near the factory with walking stick gun. Skinned them after lunch.

It was normal for well-dressed gentlemen in the Victorian era to carry a walking stick, cane or umbrella in public. These were not so much for support, but more as a fashion statement, just as he would wear a smart hat and gloves. The walking stick guns were developed as gun technology improved in the nineteenth century to allow a small bore shotgun, usually .410, to be built and concealed in a walking stick. It was not illegal to carry a concealed weapon, as it is now. Most of these guns were sold to gentlemen who had no intention of using them for harming anyone, but to have with them, just in case they saw some small game they might want to shoot, such as a rabbit.

31st January 1897 Nillo Mally
Went after pig, but no sport. The Woods came to breakfast.

1st February 1897 Nillo Mally
Went to the jungle with net & walking stick gun. Saw pig amongst the tea. Collected a few orchids. Shot a small flycatcher which I skinned.

2nd February 1897 Nillo Mally
Went up into the jungle again, but did not see the pig. Shot a small bird after the style of a yellow hammer, but knocked it about too much for a specimen. Herbert met me & took me for a long walk round by Blair's factory. Mr Campbell (the superintendent) is here. Gordon came over to tea. Shot another parrot. Douglas calls his three puppies Ling, Longer & Loo.

After his enjoyable time in Ceylon with his family, it was time for Bertie to continue on his journey.

3rd February 1897 Nillo Mally Last Day
Was busy all the morning packing. In the afternoon I took it easy as I have a boil under my arm. Douglas came to dinner & we had champagne. I am really very sorry to leave as I have had a jolly time with Herbert & Amy.

4th February 1897 Colombo
Amy & I left Nillo Mally 6.30. We broke the journey at Kandy & had tiffin, also a rickshaw ride round the lake. We met Mr. Chamberlain at the "Queens" with his sister & a Miss Brodie. They are also sailing in the Kaiser-i-Hind.

5th February 1897 Colombo
Grand Oriental Hotel. Early tea 6.45. Breakfast 9am. Bought a tin box, two white suits, chair and photos. Sent off my butterflies & birds (vp.

90 cents the two.) Bought a small Frena (75) Went to the museum after tiffin, but being Friday it was closed. Went with Amy for a drive & saw polo & football.

The 'Frena' is the name sometime used for a woollen knitted hat, also known as a 'beanie' and Bertie purchased a deck chair to be used on board ship. It was the custom for passengers to supply their own chairs on sea voyages if they wished to sit on deck.

Saturday 6th February 1897 Colombo
Went to the museum 10 - 11am
11.50 train to Mount Lavinia, one certainly gets more air there than at Colombo. I saw plenty of fish of many sorts & sizes from the header board, also a shark. We had a very nice lunch.

Mt Lavinia lies aapproximately six miles south of Colombo and the Grand Hotel Mt Lavinia that Bertie visited had been there since 1877. Before this time, the beautiful mansion built by the sea, had a varied and romantic history. It was originally constructed as an elegant country residence for the second British Governor of Ceylon, Sir Thomas Maitland, in 1806.

Sir Thomas Maitland arrived in Ceylon in 1805 at the age of 46 and the romantic legend is that soon after his arrival, he fell passionately in love with a beautiful dancer named Lovina Aponsuwa. She was a member of a local dancing group which had entertained the new Governor. He named his new house Mt. Lavinia in her honour. She was part Portuguese and part Sinhalese, and society in those days would not tolerate an open relationship between them. Their liaison, which lasted six years until he left Ceylon in 1811, was always kept a secret. It is claimed Sir Thomas had a tunnel constructed between his cellar and her garden which was in the village close by, so they could enjoy clandestine meetings. When he left Ceylon to go to his new appointment in Malta, Sir Thomas provided Lovina with a pension and some land as a gesture of his esteem.

After his departure, subsequent Governors used the house as their country retreat, but it gradually fell into disrepair and in 1842 was sold for £124. For some years it became a hospital until 1877, when the railway line was constructed between Mt Lavinia and Colombo. It was then bought by some local businessmen and converted into a hotel. This became a popular place for people to escape the city and enjoy the cool sea breezes.

Sunday 7th February 1897 Colombo.
The Kaiser has not arrived. The Arcadia arrived on Saturday night & the hotel is full. The Kaiser arrived at 7 & we sail tomorrow at 10 am. I shall have to get a pass to go on board on account of the plague at Bombay where she comes from.

Bertie's second ship, the *Kaiser-i-Hind* belonged to the Peninsular and Orient Steam Navigation Company (P&O). This great shipping company started with the partnership of two men early in the nineteenth century. They were Brodie McGhie Willcox, who was a London ship broker and Arthur Anderson, a Scotsman from the Shetland Islands. Wilcox had been in the Navy, but when paid off and nearly starving, obtained a job as a clerk with Anderson. They became partners in the newly-formed company of Willcox and Anderson. When the business started, they only had one small ship which they bought as a repaired salvage-wreck. With this sole vessel, then other ships they later acquired, they operated a fairly precarious trade between England and Portugal. In 1837 they obtained mail contracts to Portugal and Spain and changed the name of their company to the Peninsular Steam Navigation Company. This was later renamed the Peninsular and Orient Steam Navigation Company when they were awarded a mail contract to Alexandria. From Alexandria, mail, or passengers to India and other Asian destinations, were transported overland to the Red Sea to connect with a ship there. After 1869, when the Suez Canal was built, P&O ships could eventually travel more easily to the Orient and the company prospered.

S.S. "*Kaisar-i-Hind*" passing Cape St. Vincent.

Kaiser-I-Hind from P&O Pocket Book 1887

Kaiser-i-Hind was named in honour of Queen Victoria, whom was created Empress of India in 1877. The ship was launched at the shipyards of Caird and Co at Greenock, in

1878, and mostly travelled between England and India. She was to become a popular ship, nicknamed *The Bridge to India*.

She was the first P&O ship to have refrigerated holds used for transporting meat and fruit from Australia to Britain. She also carried mail and had accommodation for 176 first class passengers and 64 second class. Her length was 400 feet, and was of 4,023 gross registered tonnage.

P&O was justly proud of the excellent service extended to its passengers, with accommodation and food of a high quality. When she was first launched, it was reported in the *Maitland Mercury* on 30 July 1880, that she had been described in the *British Mercantile Gazette* as:

Certainly the finest vessel that has ever been launched ... ''a floating palace'' are the words that best convey any idea of the luxurious appointments and convenient arrangements of this steamer ... Every improvement has been added that science and art have invented.

By the time Bertie was a passenger on *Kaiser-i-Hind*, she was an ageing ship. In October 1897, a few months after he sailed on her, she was extensively damaged by a typhoon while cruising between Singapore and Hong Kong. This was to be her death knell. She was sold and broken up in January 1898.

Bertie was not impressed by the *luxurious appointments of the Kaiser-i-Hind*, but perhaps his opinion of the vessel might have been coloured by the fact that, once again, he was overtaken by the misery of sea sickness.

Chapter Six

Penang, Singapore, Java, Hong Kong

Colombo - photo from Bertie's album

Colombo 8/2/97
Breakfast 8.45. On board the Kaiser-i-Hind 9.30 Weighed anchor at 1pm.
The ship is 18 years old & this is my first experience of a P&O. Does not
impress me favourably. Lascar sailors & many Lascar waiters at table,
some of whom can't understand English. The grub is inferior to that
which we got on the Orient, & is badly served up. There are about 50
1st Class passengers, most of them off the Arcadia. My cabin is large,
but the vibration of the screw is awful.

After a passage of five days, the next port of call was to be Penang. Once the vessel
cleared the outer breakwater from Colombo, she headed south, down the west coast
of Ceylon. After passing Point de Galle Light and rounding Dondra Head, an easterly
course was steered across the Southern Bay of Bengal. Three days later Bertie noticed
several islands, including Pulau Bras Island. This lay off the north coast of Sumatra.
Then, the Penang Light vessel would be visible before arriving at Georgetown harbour.

Kaiser-i-Hind   9/2/97
I was ill directly after my bath & could eat no breakfast, & very little lunch or dinner.   On this ship 1st class deck is aft. There are no 3rd class passengers on P & O boats.

Kaiser-i-Hind   10/2/97
Seedy, calmer.

Kaiser-i-Hind   11/2/97
Dull. Feel alright today & have done myself well at meals. Played cricket in the afternoon.   The captain is a jolly chap & the officers seem nice.

It was unfortunate that Bertie had such a noisy cabin and was once again struck down by seasickness which may have coloured his view of the Kaiser i Hind. Many of her regular passengers became extremely fond of the old ship. If he had been feeling better, he might have appreciated the food more. Once he was recovered, he would have discovered there were plenty of activities for him to partake in. There is an account in an article, (*P&O Passage to India)* as written by a fictional Rupert Scott- Padgett which gives an idea of what it was like to sail with P & O.

At the time of Bertie's journey, there was intense rivalry between the shipping lines to provide the most comfort and top quality food to the passengers. This was generally equal to what they would have expected from a first class hotel. Passengers were summoned to their meals by a fanfare from a bugle. Dinner was a formal occasion, where passengers dressed up, except traditionally the first night after embarkation and while in the Suez Canal. It was served at long tables with sparkling silver cutlery and white linen, which might be dampened to prevent the plates sliding around. In rough weather fiddles (long boards) were attached to the tables to stop the food from sliding off into peoples' laps. Originally there were cloth fans overhead which circulated the air operated by a crew member, later electric fans were installed. Dinner consisted of several courses. The first course was a choice of soups, one nearly always being mutton broth. This was followed by up to seventeen main courses to choose from. These usually included various roast meats, duck and peas, roast goose, sea pie, (a rich beef pie with a suet pastry crust) and always curry. These dishes were all placed on the table at the same time for passengers to make their choice. When the main course dishes was finished and cleared away by the stewards, they were replaced by up to twelve desserts. There was also a wide variety of alcoholic and non-alcoholic beverages to accompany the meal which were served without charge.

In addition to dinner, passengers could expect a substantial breakfast, luncheon, afternoon tea, (tiffin) and a late night light supper. Second class passengers had a less extensive menu, but were nevertheless well fed. P&O ships did not have a third class.

P & O stewards were mostly recruited from Portuguese Goa. They served at the table were also expected to look after the cabins too, so they had to work long hours. The deck crew were Indians known as Lascars which was originally a Portuguese term. The officers were all British, who in the tropics wore immaculate white uniforms.

Between meals, many passengers socialised on deck walking up and down or sitting on their deck chairs. Alternatively there was a smoking room, writing room, music room and general sitting saloons with room for dancing and concerts in the evenings. There was a barber shop which also functioned as a shop stocked with useful items passengers might require.

All entertainments, whether of a sporting or cultural nature, were organised by the passengers. At the beginning of each voyage it was one of the First Officer's duties to encourage some of the passengers to form sports and entertainments committees. These would organise the various games which were played with enthusiasm and much jollity during the day, while in the evenings there might be impromptu concerts and dances, including the obligatory fancy dress ball. Passengers showed much ingenuity in creating outfits from any material they could lay their hands on. Ship-board romances frequently occurred under the tropical skies.

Every Sunday, the Commander (Captain) would make a formal inspection of the ship and its crew and he also conducted a Sunday service which all passengers would be expected to attend, unless the weather was too bad.

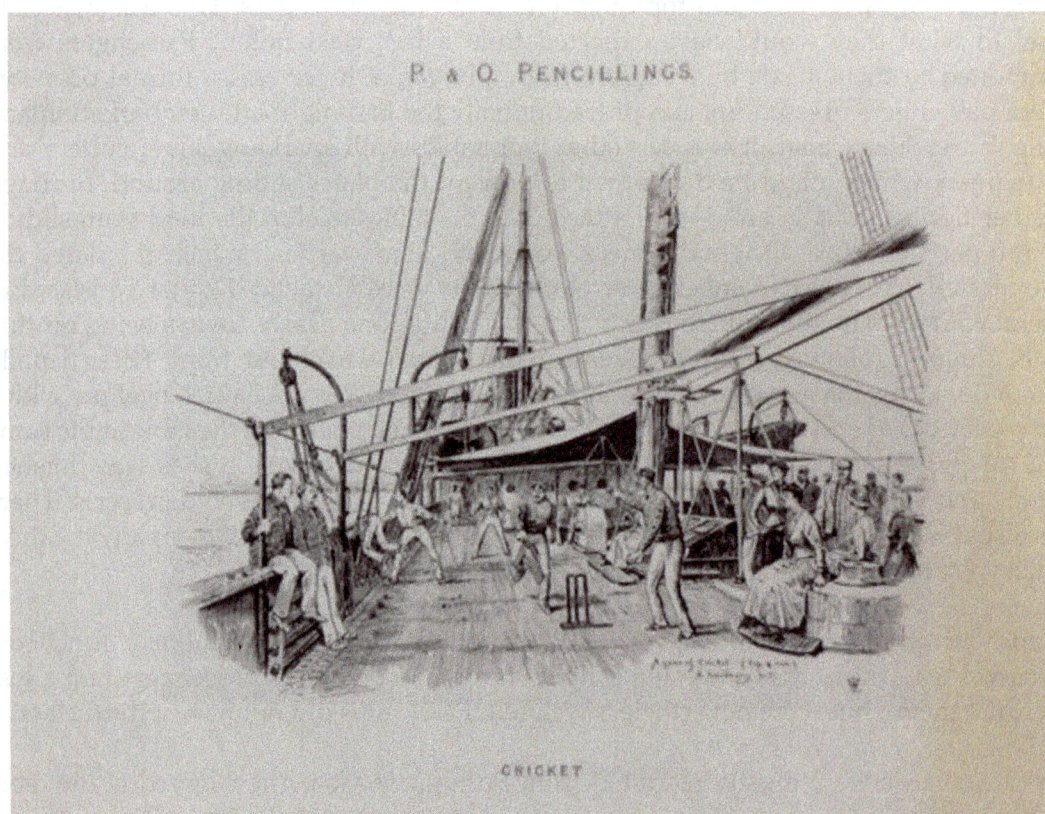

Deck Cricket P&O Pencillings, WW Lloyd (P&O Heritage)

In 1889, the American journalist, Nellie Bly travelled some of the way on her round the world trip on a P&O Ship, *SS Victoria* and wrote of some of the activities on board. Like Bertie, she was not impressed by the Lascar sailors:

'In the daytime the men played cricket and quoits. Sometimes in the evenings, we had singing, and other times we went to the second-class deck and listened to better music given by second class passengers. When there were no chairs we would all sit down on the deck, and I remember nothing more enjoyable than these little visits.... Better than all to me. It was to sit in a dark corner on deck, above where the sailors had their food, and listen to the sounds of a tom-tom and weird musical chanting that always accompanied their evening meal. The sailors were Lascars.... They were the most untidy looking lot of sailors I ever saw. Over a pair of white muslin drawers they wore a long muslin slip very like in shape to the old-time night shirt. This was tied about the waist with a coloured handkerchief, and on their heads they wore gaily coloured turbans, which are really nothing but a crown of straw with a scarf-shaped piece of bright cloth, often six feet in length, wound about the head. Their brown feet are always bare. They chant, as sailors do, when hoisting sails, but otherwise are a grim, surly looking set.'

Kaiser-i-Hind   12/2/97
A lovely morning. We passed some islands (Pulo Brass). They seem to be covered with vegetation to the water's edge. We pass later along the north coast of Sumatra. 89 in the shade.

While Bertie had not enjoyed some of this section of his journey, F. W. Burbidge, who was travelling to Asia to collect plants suitable for Victorian gardens, obviously experienced a better passage. He waxed lyrical about the joys of sea travel in these waters. As he wrote in his book, *Gardens of the Sun*:

'A long sea voyage has its pleasures as well as its drawbacks; and in travelling eastward, more especially, it is quite possible, after crossing "the Bay" to get a smooth voyage all the way. There are times when the Mediterranean, the Indian Ocean, and the China Sea lie sleeping in the sunshine, and a steamer runs as smoothly as a canal boat.... It is most pleasant to passengers on board steamships who can lie and read under the cool shade of the awning, drinking in the fresh ionized sea air, untroubled for the nonce [present] by the cares of business or the whirl and bustle of the town.

A curious feeling comes over one on viewing the boundless ocean for the first time on a calm, cloudless day. It makes one feel extremely small to gaze on what appears to be the eternity of sea around, with not a speck or a sail to break the view on all sides. Then when a breeze springs up a sense of freedom animates the breast as the vessel rushes through the water and shakes the milk white foam from her bows, as though also glad to be free.... The exhilarating motion of the ship stirs one's blood and sends it coursing through one's veins, as she "walks the waters like a thing of life," and the strong pure breeze fans our cheeks and the cool spray comes in our faces like a shower of dew.'

Bertie enjoyed his short visit to Penang and commented on the colourful Chinese lanterns.

Penang
Dull but no rain. We arrived at Penang 5.30. I went ashore with Chamberlain,
Maynard & a chap from Bombay. A very pretty place but we only had ½ an
hour of day light. Saw lots of Chinese, one on a bicycle. They seemed
very sturdy after the Singalese & Tamils & the rickshaw men have legs
wonderfully developed. Had dinner at the Eastern & Oriental after a drive
round. The Chinese lanterns are finer than any I have seen in England.
(dinner 1 Mex. dollar.)

Red Lanterns in Penang in 2017

Below: Eastern and Oriental Hotel,
Penang. Old postcard

VICTORY ANNEXE, EASTERN AND ORIENTAL HOTEL, PENANG.

Elizabeth Bisland, who travelled around the world in 1889, but in the opposite direction to Bertie, wrote about her impressions of Penang:

' . . . Penang. – Its peaks shoot sharply up into the blue air 2000 feet, wrapped in a tangle of prodigious verdure to their very tops, enormous palm forests fringing all the shore. The ship anchors some distance from the docks, and will remain but a few hours. We are ferried to land in crazy sampans, the only alternative from out-rigger canoes – a narrow trough set on a round log and kept upright by a smaller floating log connected to the boat by bent poles. Only a native, a tight-rope walker, or a bicyclist would trust himself to these.

A gharry and a pitiful little horse take us towards the gardens and the famous waterfall. The road skirts the town and intersects lagoons, where Malay houses of cocoanut thatch stand upon piles like ancient lake dwellings. They live over this stagnant water by preference, and apparently suffer no harm. Further on, where the ground rises, there are huge stone bungalows of English officials and rich Chinese merchants, the entrance to the grounds of the latter adorned with ornate doors and guarded by carved monsters, curiously coloured.'

By the end of the nineteenth century, Penang was a thriving port. It had benefited greatly from the construction of the Suez Canal which had increased the number of ships coming to trade in the East. The Industrial Revolution had created a great demand in Europe for commodities such as tin, rubber, coconut and cotton, as well as pepper and other spices. The island became a cosmopolitan society as people flocked there, attracted by its business opportunities.

Originally, Penang, or Ping-lang-yu as it was once known, was a small settlement, and the first Europeans to use its sheltered harbour were the Portuguese traders from Goa in the sixteenth century. One of the first British ships to arrive, was the merchant ship *Edward Bonaventure* in 1592 under the command of Captain Sir James Lancaster. This gallant gentleman had previously served under Sir Francis Drake in the defeat of the Spanish Armada. He spent some profitable months cruising around Penang Island, during which time he attacked and pillaged any ships he encountered.

In 1786 Penang was ceded to Britain when Captain Francis Light made an agreement with the Sultan of Kedah, that the British should have the use of the island and harbour to trade in the area, in exchange for a yearly honorarium of 6,000 Spanish dollars. Included in the deal was a promise to protect the Sultanate from Thai and Burmese raiders. This made Penang the first British possession in South East Asia. The promise to protect the Sultan was not honoured, but the honorarium was increased over time, and Captain Light declared it a Free Port to encourage traders. He named it Prince of Wales Island, with the port being Georgetown in honour of King George III. Fort Cornwallis was built to protect the settlement and in 1800, a keen young army officer, Lt Colonel Arthur Wellesley was appointed to superintend the defences. In time, he was destined to achieve greater things and became the Duke of Wellington, the hero of Waterloo. Another bright and extremely able young man working as a junior officer in the administration, was Thomas Stamford Raffles. He became fluent in the Malay language and was extremely interested in the culture and natural history of the region. He, too, was to make his mark in the world.
In 1867, Penang was declared a crown colony as part of the Straits Settlement which included Malacca, Penang and Singapore. Thirty years later, when Bertie arrived in

Penang and also during his time in Singapore, it was the time of Chinese New Year, which would account for the explosions of crackers and the colourful lights everywhere that he reported.

After leaving Georgetown, Kaiser-i-Hind would have taken a southerly course into the Straits of Malacca. The sea is usually calm there as it is sheltered by the Island of Sumatra and the Malaysian coast. Bertie mentions the heat. Being just north of the Equator this area is generally hot and humid with frequent rain showers and thunderstorms. Altering course around the Pulau Pisang Lighthouse, the vessel then entered the Singapore Strait and sailed past the Brothers and Raffles lighthouses, through the islands to Singapore.

The letter from Bertie to his mother was written over several days as he travelled from Penang to Singapore. This first section was written as he left Penang on the Kaiser-i-Hind:

Kaiser I Hind off Penang
Feb 13th

Dear Mater,

We got to Penang at 6 o'clock tonight & I have been on shore with some friends I have made on the ship. It is a most picturesque place & I should have liked to have seen more of it by day light. We had a drive round & then went to dinner at the Eastern & Oriental Hotel. They gave us a very good one for a dollar. (Mexican dollar about 2s/1). There seems to be a large colony of Chinese here & they are fine chaps after the Singalese. The rickshaws are all drawn by them & we also had them to wait on us at dinner. I saw one riding a bicycle, & he looked very funny with his pigtail hanging down behind. The town looked very nice lighted up at night. In front of lots of the houses there were fine Chinese lanterns, better than I have ever seen in England. We landed and returned to the ship in very curious boats. They did not look very safe but were managed by the men in fine style.

I left Colombo at 1 o'clock on the 8th. As the Kaiser came from Bombay nobody could land. (She was in quarantine) & I had to get a pass to go on board. I was not favourably impressed with the P&O up till now. This is a very poor boat in which you feel the vibrations dreadfully. The first class promenade is aft & the quarter deck is given up to the second class passengers. They let you find out everything for yourself. The food is very poor indeed & served up by Laskars, some of whom can't speak English. Most of the sailors too are Laskars. They look very picturesque but I think they should have Englishmen. Perhaps I should not have found so much fault if I had not been sea sick again. It has not been really rough &

there were only three ladies ill to keep me company. It was 89 in the shade yesterday, & today it is 87. We have passed some very pretty islands & apart from the sea sickness and bad ship I am enjoying myself.

The Eastern and Oriental Hotel in Georgetown, Penang, where Bertie and his friends dined, was founded by the Sarkies brothers, Tegan and Martin, who were Armenians born in Isfahan. Originally they set up a hotel in Penang which they called the Eastern Hotel, then another called the Oriental. These were later combined into the Eastern and Oriental, (or E&O) in 1889. Other famous hotels founded by the Sarkies family include the Raffles Hotel in Singapore and the Strand in Rangoon. The E&O still stands in Penang: it is now a luxurious five star hotel and is proud of its heritage.

Kaiser-i-Hind   Sunday 14/2/97
Too wet in the morning for divine service, fine but dull later. I am glad to say this is the last day on board this ship. I have slept very badly on account of the vibration & heat. I hear the coast along the straights swarms with crocodiles.

This was to be the last day sailing on the *Kaiser-i-Hind* before arriving at Singapore. Other travellers recorded their impressions of the journey between Penang and Singapore.

In 1830 Major Thomas Skinner sailed from Ceylon to the 'Eastern Archipelago' to visit Penang, Malacca and Singapore in an attempt to recruit men to join the ranks of the Ceylon Rifles. He was commanding the Government barque *Anne*, a small sailing ship which was heavily armed, in case they encountered pirates. After visiting Penang and Malacca they sailed south and he wrote in his memoirs:

'We sailed from Malacca on Monday 11th October, but the winds being light and contrary we were four days working down to Singapore, the usual run occupying from thirty-six to forty-eight hours. The scenery was very beautiful. We were continually sailing between wooded islands and narrow channels, and the number of vessels which met and passed us enlivened the otherwise monotonous voyage. The passage into Singapore, leading through groups of islands, was very fine, the town and harbour opening abruptly immediately on rounding St. John's Island, which forms the western boundary of the harbour.

There were ships of all classes in the harbour: European square-Rigged; Chinese junks of enormous size; buggis prows from the Celebese, Borneo, and all the islands of the Malayan Archipelago; no less than 349 sail at anchor....

Singapore is a wonderful instance of the advantage of the unrestricted enterprise of free trade; so late as the year 1822 there was scarcely a native hut, certainly not one European habitation on the island; in eight years it had not only grown into the most important settlement in the whole of the Malay Archipelago, but was the emporium of more trade than the whole of the other ports put together. The trade us almost exclusively one of barter, The English merchants procuring profitable exports in exchange for English goods. The annual value of importations in 1830 was five millions sterling.'

Whereas Major Skinner was travelling in a sail boat, F.W. Burbidge arrived at Singapore some forty years later, by which time steam ships were widely used. (This was about twenty years prior to Bertie's visit). He too, was impressed by the vitality of the port and the town and wrote:

'This port, which is also the seat of the government of the Straits Settlement, has not inaptly been called the "Liverpool of the East," and the applicability of that title soon becomes evident to the stranger from "home," who finds himself on the landing stage at Tanjong Paggar for the first time. Here is a range of warehouses or "godowns" for the storage of goods, and coaling sheds for the supply of mail and other steamers moored alongside. One is soon glad to get away from the heat, the noise of the steam winch, and the coal-dust; and a gharry or cab having been procured, the dusky Jehu springs to his seat on the shaft from which "coign of vantage" he uses both whip and voice in urging on at a gallop a plucky little pony, scarcely larger than a donkey, most probably bred either in Sumatra or Pegu. You meet other little ponies in other little gharries coming full tilt down the road to the wharf, a string of buffalo-carts, or occasionally a neat little private carriage, and you soon become aware that Singapura, as it is still called, of the Malays is both hot and dusty....Of course you have kept your eyes open as you came along past the rough hedges on the right clothed with red lantanas, the neat police-station on the bank to the left, with those beautiful crimson and buff coloured hibiscus bushes before the door. Then the rows of Chinese homes and shops, an elaborate Hindoo temple or two of white stone, and then street after street of whitewashed red tile roofed shops, until you reach the square where you meet your agent, or to the hotels, nearly all of which are clustered around the tall spire of the cathedral, which you will have seen as the ship steamed slowly into the harbour.'

On her race around the world in 1889, Nelly Bly only had one day at Singapore. She went ashore with friends and hired a carriage drawn by a *'pretty spotted Malay pony whose speed is marvellous compared with its diminutive size.'*...

'There are no sidewalks in Singapore, and blue and white largely predominate over other colors. Families seem to occupy the second story, the lower being generally devoted to business purposes. Through lattice windows we got occasional glimpses of peeping Chinese women in gay gowns, Chinese babies bundled in shapeless wadded garments, while down below through widely opened fronts we could see people pursuing their trade. Barbering is the principle trade. A chair, a comb, a basin and a knife are all the tools a man needs to open shop. ...Chinamen have their heads shaven back almost to the crown, when a spot about the size of a tiny saucer is left to bear the crop of hair which forms the pig-tail. When braided and finished with a silk tassel the Chinaman's hair is "done" for the next fortnight.

The people here, as at other ports where I stopped, constantly chew betel nut, and when they laugh on would suppose they had been drinking blood. The betel stains their teeth and moths blood-red. Many of the natives also fancy tinting their finger-nails with it.

Nothing is patronized more than 'rickshas in Singapore, and while they may be had for ten cents an hour it is no unusual sight to see four persons piled in on jinricksha and drawn by one man. We visited a most interesting museum, and saw along suburban roads the beautiful bungalows of the European citizens. People in dog-carts and wheelmen on bicycles crowded the splendid drives'.

While in Singapore, Bly could not resist purchasing a small monkey which was later to cause her some problems. Firstly it bit her cabin stewardess and then, when the ship ran into rough weather crossing the Pacific ocean, the superstitious sailors wanted to throw it overboard, since they believed it might be the 'Jonah' causing the storm. She was only able to save her little friend by pointing out that there were two priests on board the ship. As it was also a superstition that priests were considered unlucky to have as passengers, Miss Bly said she would be willing to sacrifice her monkey, if they were thrown overboard with him.

Bly's rival in the race around the world, Elizabeth Bisland, also observed the hustle and bustle of the port, but expressed her concern about the modes of transport in the East. She wrote:

'Queer little square carriages, made for the most part of Venetian blinds, wait for us, drawn by disconsolate ponies the size of sheep. Conveyance in the East is a constant source of unhappiness to me. I was deprecatory with Jinrickasha men in Japan, I humbled myself before the chair-bearers of Hong Kong, and now I go and make an elaborate apology to this wretched little beast before I can reconcile it to my conscience to climb into a gharry, or let him drag me about at a gallop.'

Miss Bisland did board the Gharry and was shown the sights of the port, before arriving at her hotel. She did not name it, but obviously spent a disturbed night.

'Mine is a huge dim apartment with a stone floor opening directly upon a lawn and into the dining room, and has only slight jalousies for doors; but no one peers or intrudes. The bed is an iron frame; the single hard mattress is spread with a sheet, and there are no covers at all. Even the pillow is of straw. My bath-room, a lofty flagged chamber, opens into this one, and contains a big earthenware jar which the coolies fill for me three times a day, and into which I plunge to rid me of the burning heat.

. . .That night I have the most terrible adventure. Immediately I get into bed and blow out the candle, I hear what sounds like some great animal stalking about. I am cold enough now – icy in fact.

. . .What can it be? . . They tell me tigers come over from the mainland and carry off one person on an average per day.

. . . This is probably a tiger. He could easily push open those blind doors and walk in!

. . . He is coming towards the bed with heavy stealthy rustlings. There is not even a sheet to draw

up over me. The room is hot, utterly black and still, save the sound of those feet and the loud banging of my heart against my ribs.

. . . The hotel seems dead, so horribly silent it is. Has the tiger eaten everyone else?

. . . The darkness is of no use; he can see all the better for that; so I will strike a match and at least perish in the light.

As the blue flame on the wick broadens I meet the gaze of a frightfully large, calm grey rat who is examining my shoes and stockings with care. He regards me with only very faint interest, and goes on with his explorations through my possessions. He climbs the dressing-table and smells critically at my hat and gloves.

. . . This is almost as bad as the tiger, but I have no intention of attacking this terrible beast and my notice seems to bore him. I blow out the candle and go to sleep, leaving him to continue those heavy rustlings which so alarmed me.'

Bertie was met by friends on his arrival at Singapore who were there to greet and entertain him while he was in port.

15th February 1897 Singapore
10.15 Graham Paterson met me. The entrance to the harbour is simply lovely; the sea a lovely colour & the islands covered with vegetation. Went to lunch at the Club of which I am a member pro tem. Played billiards with an officer of the rifle brigade & was in good form. Went for a drive with Graham to the botanical gardens. Went to dine with the Simons.

Singapore Harbour in 1897, from Bertie's album .... and in 2019

100

Bertie's friends Graham Paterson and Henry Simons were prominent Singapore business men. According to an article written by Arnold Wright in 1908, Patterson was Vice Chairman of the Singapore Chamber of Commerce, a Justice of the Peace and a committee member of the Singapore Sporting Club and owner of several race horses. He was a partner in the firm Paterson and Simons Co. It was also reported in the Singapore Free Press and Mercantile Advertiser on 25 June 1897 that Patterson was one of the distinguished guests attending the State Diamond Jubilee Ball at Government House, hosted by the Governor Sir Charles Mitchell and Lady Mitchell. Paterson may have been a friend of Bertie's before he arrived in Singapore in 1891, as he was born in London and received his commercial training there.

Bertie's letter to his mother continues once he arrives in Singapore:

> Raffles Hotel
> Singapore Feb 16
>
> There was a party of four on board with which I became very friendly. Mr and Mrs Chamberlain from Brighton, Mr and Mrs Brodie from Edinburgh, they are travelling round the world & I shall very likely come across them again in Japan. We arrived at Singapore at 10.30 yesterday & I was glad to get off the Kaiser I Hind on which I have been able to get little sleep owing to the vibration – I think some of the machinery was right under my cabin. I thought Colombo was grand when we steamed into the harbour, but Singapore beats it for beauty into a cocked hat. You enter by a narrow channel amongst the most lovely islands & then steam right up to the landing stage. G.Paterson met me. The Simons would have put me up but their bungalow is full, so I am sleeping at Raffles Hotel in a splendid bedroom with a large open room in front where I have early tea with letters and smoke. A bathroom at the back – You don't get into the bath here, but chuck the water over you with a small pail. Like the one Kathleen uses on the sands at Bournmouth. I have breakfast there, lunch at the Club – (of which I am a member for the time) & the Simons want me to dine with them always. Graham is living with them just now. Tomorrow I am going to the island of Johore with a party. I shall probably leave for Java on the 18 where I shall stay some time. I shall most likely leave Singapore for good about the middle of March en route for China and Japan. Write to the Post Office, Yokohama. I played billiards (never in better form) at the club yesterday with an officer in the Rifle Brigade (quartered here) & gave him a rare doing (300 up). I went for a drive yesterday evening with Graham round the botanical gardens, very beautiful! I am getting quite used to Chinamen now: they swarm here. One of the officers on board the Kaiser goes

101

in for butterflies and birds. Funnily enough he has stayed in the house next door to Mr Fraser at Greenhithe but never knew him. One of our party to Johore tomorrow is a chap who used to be on the S.E (Stock Exchange). I knew him well by sight. He is now managing some company out here. I don't remember how many photos of Ceylon the Governor bought? I purchased 2 doz. Today is cracker day at Singapore amongst the Chinese. They are very busy letting them off. (It is supposed to keep the devils away.) Tonight, I hear that the noise will be dreadful.

Hoping that you are all well & best love to all. Your affect son,
Bertie Bristowe

Singapore Island is situated at the tip of the Malay Archipelago, and at the beginning of the nineteenth century was inhabited by approximately 1,000 Malay fishermen and their families. At that time, commerce in the area was dominated and controlled by the Portuguese and Dutch, making it hard for the British merchants to trade. In 1819 Sir Thomas Stamford Raffles managed to negotiate an agreement with local leaders to allow the British to establish a port. When Singapore was made a free port, it became hugely successful, and by 1897 the population had swelled to about 200,000 residents, coming to Singapore from China, India and other countries. It had also changed from being an unruly Straits settlement into a better-governed Crown Colony.

A few years after the foundation of Singapore port, Sir Stamford Raffles wrote:

'Here all is life and activity; it would be difficult to name a place on the face of the globe with brighter prospects or more pleasant satisfaction. In a little more than three years it has risen from an insignificant fishing village to a large and prosperous town, containing at least ten thousand inhabitants of all nations actively engaged in commercial pursuits which afford to each and all a handsome livelihood and abundant profit. There are no complaints here of want of employment, no deficiency of rents, or dissatisfaction at taxes. Land is rapidly rising in value and in respect of the present number of inhabitants we have reason to expect that we shall have at least ten times as many before many years have passed. This may be considered as the simple but almost magical result of that perfect freedom of Trade which has been my good fortune to establish....

I am at present engaged in establishing a constitution for Singapore, the principles of which will I hope ensure its prosperity,'

As time went by, the jungle which had previously covered the entire island was gradually being cleared, because as the population grew, the need for more farm land increased. When Burbidge visited the island in 1874, he was told that tigers were seldom seen and attacks had become rare, but Alfred Russel Wallace, who visited the island in 1854 wrote:

'There are always a few tigers roaming about Singapore, and they kill on average a Chinaman every day, principally those who work in the gambir plantations, which are always made in newly-

cleared jungle. We heard a tiger roar once or twice in the evening, and it was rather nervous work hunting for insects among the fallen trunks and old sawpits, when one of these savage animals might be lurking close by waiting an opportunity to spring on us.'

Gambir bushes, Unicaria gambir, were grown for their astringent sap, which was extracted from the leaves. This was used in the brewing, tanning and dying industries and became an important export from Singapore.

Things had become more civilized by 1897 and Bertie makes no mention of rats or lurking tigers, however, the last tiger killed in Singapore was in 1902. This poor bewildered creature somehow wandered into the billiards room at the Raffles Hotel, where it was cornered and shot, but there was a suspicion that it may have been an escapee from a visiting circus and was not really a wild tiger.

While in Singapore, Bertie stayed at the Raffles, which was considered the best hotel in town. Originally the building was a private seaside house in the 1830s. This was converted into a hotel and boarding house and in 1887, was bought by the Sarkies brothers, who named it Raffles Hotel after Singapore's founder. They converted it into a smart ten-room establishment, which became popular with visitors to Singapore. Over the years many famous people stayed there, including royalty. The hotel was enlarged and renovated, but it has always been the epitome of luxury and impeccable service. It survived the 1930 Great Depression, which bankrupted the Sarkies brothers. It also survived Japanese army occupation during the Second World War, when it was named, Syonan Ryokan. There have been several changes of ownership since then. Due to extensive land reclamation, it is no longer right beside the beach, but is still, as always, a magnificent hotel.

During his time here, Bertie seems to have enjoyed an active social life amongst the British residents, who were extremely hospitable and showed him around the city and beyond. They even arranged for him to join one of the many clubs that catered for gentlemen in town.

There were several clubs in Singapore where Bertie might have become a 'pro tem' member. The Singapore Sporting Club was founded in 1842, the Singapore Cricket Club in 1852, the Singapore Golf Club in 1891, and the Tanglin Club, with started with a membership of '40 good men,' in 1865. These clubs originally were only open to white gentlemen. Since his friend Graham Paterson was on the committee of the Singapore Sporting Club, it is likely this is the one he patronised.

The Singapore Botanical Gardens visited by Bertie, were founded in 1859 and developed by Lawrence Niven. Sir Stamford Raffles, who was a keen botanist, had previously established a 'Botanical and Experimental Garden' in 1822, but this venture closed in 1829. One aim of the botanical gardens was to establish suitable crops to be grown in tropical conditions. In 1877 rubber tree seedlings were introduced, having been smuggled out of South America. These grew so well that they were propagated widely throughout Malaya and rubber became a major export. Singapore Botanic Gardens also became famous for their colourful orchid displays, which present day visitors can enjoy.

Tuesday 16th February 1897   Singapore
In the morning I looked round the town & took a ticket to Batavia, by the
Holt Line (Mansfield & Co).   She will probably start on 18th (day light.)
Lunched at the Club & dined with the Simons. It was a "cracker night"
with the Chinese & I had difficulty in getting a "gharry". A very wet night.

A gharry is a horse drawn cab, or carriage for hire. The word originates in India where the driver is known as a 'gharry wallah'. The fact that it was Chinese New Year would have accounted for the colourful display of lamps, the crackers and the difficulty in obtaining transport.

The Cavenagh Bridge over the Singapore River, 1897, from Bertie's album - and in 2019

Wednesday 17th February 1897
Singapore

Breakfast 7.45.   A soaker.
Went with Graham, Holland
& Bowden in the "Bankok" to
Johor & then round the island,
did not get back till seven & it rained the whole time.   Good lunch at
Johor, went to a gambling place & played "Po" I won 12 dollars, Bowden
lost 40, Holland, 14 & Graham came out even. 7½ inches of rain at Johor.
The floods have not been so bad since '93.

104

18th February 1897   Singapore
Walked down Beach Road & watched the Chinese at work.   Lunched at the club & played billiards with Lloyd Thomas. In the evening went with Pickenpack (a German) to Malay St. & then to a Chinese theatre. I was foolish enough to go only in a vest & white coat on.

19th February 1897   Singapore
The "Telamon" will not sail now before Sunday morning. They drink a good many "Stingers" in Singapore. This is Malay for a half & means a small whisky & soda.

Stengahs were a favourite drink in Singapore, especially when consumed at the famous Long Bar at the Raffles. They consisted of half measures of whisky and soda poured over ice. If Bertie had been in Singapore a few years later, he might have been offered the sensational Singapore Sling cocktail. This potent Gin-based pink cocktail was invented at the Raffles Hotel in 1915 and has become an iconic drink to have while in Singapore. Nowadays they even serve them on Singapore Airlines flights.

20th February 1897   Singapore
Went to see the Telamon & took my luggage on board. A Spanish band played at Raffles in the evening & a few people danced. I went on board the Telamon at 10.30. Left my porthole open & was badly bitten by mosquitoes. Over 70 bites, 29 on one foot.

21st February 1897   On board Telamon
1500 tuns.   Holt Line (Mansfield & Co.) flying the Dutch flag (Capt. Purdu.) Three passengers. A German, a long chap (in the wine trade) & myself. Good food, but can't do justice to it. I think I caught a cold when I went out with Pickenpack.

Went through the Banka Straits today. There are large tin mines on this island. Fine in the morning, a storm after lunch.

Eliza Ruhamah Scidmore, in her book *Java the Garden of the East* wrote of sailing from Singapore to Java in 1896. She commented on the expense of the fare. It was fifty Mexican dollars or ninety Dutch guilders, which she considered, *'an excessive and unusual charge for a voyage of such length'*. She did, however enjoy the two days of the journey.

'Breakfasting by candle-light and leaving the hotel in darkness, there was all the beauty of the grey-and–rose dawn and the pale yellow rays of the early sun to be seen from the wet deck when our ship let go from the wharf and sailed out over a sea of gold. For the two days and two nights of the voyage, with but six passengers on the large blue- funnel steamer, we had the deck and

105

the cabins, and indeed the equator and the Java Sea to ourselves. The deck was furnished with the long chairs and hammocks of tropical life, but more tropical yet were the bunches of bananas hanging from the awning rail, that all might pick and eat at will... The ship slipped out from the harbour through the glassy river of the Straits of Malacca, and on past points and shores that to me had never been anything but geographic names.... There was a magic stillness of air and sea; the calm was as of enchantment, and one felt as if in some hypnotic trance, with all nature chained in the same spell. The pale pearly sky was reflected in smooth stretches of liquid, pearly sea, with vaporous hills, soft green visions of land beyond....We were threading a way through the thousand islands, the archipelago lying below the point of Malay Peninsula, a region of unnamed, uncounted "summer isles of Eden," chiefly known to history as the home of pirates.'

Another person who made the passage between Singapore and Java, was His Highness Jagatjit Singh Raja-I-Rajgan of Kapurthala who was travelling in great style with his entourage around various Asian countries in 1902. He was much displeased with the conditions he found on the ship.

'The steamer on which I embarked for Java on December 5 was a wretched little tub of seven hundred tons, which, unluckily for me, carried a cargo of dried fish; consequently she was filled with vile smells. One other person comprised the passenger list, if I omit the large crowd of Chinese and Malays who swarmed all over the boat, and who slept, and bathed on deck, to our great discomfort.'

Like Eliza Scidmore, Bertie also sailed on a blue-funnel ship. The Telamon was launched in 1885, built by Scotts of Greenock, for brothers Alfred and Philip Holt for their shipping line, known as the Holt Line, or 'Blue Funnel Line', because the funnels of their vessels were painted a cerulean blue. They sailed between England and Asia, with ships carrying cargoes of mainly cotton and woollen goods to the Far East and returning with commodities such as tea, tobacco and tin. There was competition between shipping lines at this time, so shippers had to be flexible as to where their vessels went and what cargoes they carried. To improve trading possibilities with the Dutch colonies, Telamon was registered under a Dutch Flag in partnership with the Nederlandsche Stoomvaart Maatschappij Oceaan Compagnie. Since this name is not one that trips easily across the tongue, (unless you speak Dutch), it was generally known as NSMO. This ship was to continue trading until she was scrapped in 1902.

23rd February 1897   Batavia Java
Hotel Nederlanden. Arrived here this morning. 20 minutes by train from Tanjong Priog to Wetlervraden (Batavia). Country very flat. The place is beautifully green & there are some lovely orchids in the garden of the hotel.. At tiffin they give you a soup plate in which you put rice & all you wish to eat with it & mix it all up. ½ Guilden for a small soda. (10d.) Went for a drive in the afternoon with Shulter.

Hotel der Nederlanden was originally built, towards the end of the eighteenth century, as a private residence occupied by Dutch colonial administrators. In 1840 it was converted into a hotel and named Hotel Palais Royale. The name was changed to Hotel der Nederlanden in 1846 and it continued to operate under that name until 1958. With Indonesia's independence, came more name changes and the original building was demolished. Now on the site, stands the Bina Graha buildings (Presidential Office).

Scidmore also stayed at Hotel der Nederlanden on her arrival in Batavia in 1897. Her first impression was of amazement at the standard of dress among the Dutch residents. She wrote:

'...driven into the long garden court of the hotel Nederlanden, and there beholds a spectacle of social life and customs that nothing in all travel can equal for distinct shock and sensation. ... There in the hotel was an undress parade that beggars description, and was astounding on the last as on the first day in the country. Woman's vanity and man's conventional ideas evidently wilt at the line, and no formalities pass the equator, when distinguished citizens and officials can roam and lounge about the hotel courts in pyjamas and bath slippers, and bare-ankled women, clad only in the native sarong, or skirt, and a white dressing jacket go unconcernedly about their business in the street and public places until the afternoon. It is a deshabille beyond all burlesque pantomime, and only shipwreck on a desert island would seem sufficient excuse for women being seen in such ungraceful , unbecoming attire....The hotel is a series of one story buildings surrounding the four sides of the garden court, the projecting eaves giving a continuous covered gallery that is the general corridor. The bedrooms open directly upon this broad gallery. And the space in front of each room, furnished with lounging- chairs, table and reading lamp, is the sitting room of each occupant by day....The whole hotel register is in evidence, sitting or spread in reclining chairs. Men in pyjamas thrust their bare feet out bravely, puffing clouds of rank Sumatra tobacco smoke as they stared at the new arrivals; women rocked and stared at the new arrivals as if we were the unusual spectacle, and not they; and the children sprawled on the cement flooring, in only the most intimate undergarments of civilised children.... We were sure we had gone to the wrong hotel; but the Nederlanden was vouched for as the best, and when the bell sounded, over one hundred guests came into the vaulted dining-room and were seated at the one long table.... Rice is the staple of the midday meal, and one is expected to fill the soup plate with boiled rice and on that heap as much as one selects from eight or ten dishes, a tray of curry condiments being also passed with this first great course. Bits of fish, duck, chicken, beef, bird, omelette and onions rose upon my neighbours' plates and spoonfuls of thin curry mixtures were poured over the rice, before the conventional chutneys, spices, cocoanut, peppers, and almond went to the conglomerate mountain resting upon the "rice table" below. Beefsteak, a salad, and then fruit and coffee brought the midday meal to a close....After the riz tavel everyone slumbers, as one naturally must after such a very "square" meal - until four o'clock.'

The city of Jakarta was named Batavia by the Dutch when they were in power. The Dutch East Indies Company was known as Vereenigde Oost-Indische Compagnie, shortened to VOC. The traders were in search of the much-valued spices when they took over the island of Java in 1602. This powerful institution ruled the country with a rod of iron until 1800 when the company ran into financial troubles and the Dutch government took control.

In 1811, at the time of the Napoleonic war, France annexed Holland, so Java became a French possession. Since Britain was at war with France, the decision was made to invade Java and remove the French influence. Between 1811 and 1815 Raffles was appointed as Lieutenant-Governor of British Java. During his tenure he relaxed some of the more draconian conditions imposed on the native Javanese population by the previous Dutch rulers. Raffles also commissioned engineers and archaeologists appointed by the British administration to begin the excavations of the amazing ancient temples on the island. These had been buried by volcanic ash and forgotten for thousands of years. Another of Raffles' interests was botany, so he undertook landscaping projects in the botanical gardens at Buitenzorg (Bogor). Sadly, while he was there his wife Olivia, died and he constructed a memorial shrine to her in the gardens. He remained as Governor until Java was returned to the Dutch government at the end of the war. Raffles was a busy man and able administrator. He later was responsible for the founding of Singapore. He also wrote a book; *The History of Java*, which was published in 1817.

By 1897 the city of Batavia had a population of about 115,500, of mixed ethnicity, but since it was a very unhealthy place to live, rife with malaria and other tropical diseases, most of the Europeans chose to live outside the old city and had their houses up in the hills. Improvements had occurred in infrastructure: schools, hospitals, factories and the development of the port etc. An extensive network of rail lines were constructed starting in 1864.

While staying at the Nederlanden Hotel, Bertie sent a letter to his sister, Kathleen, in which he wrote of the journey to Java, his activities in Singapore and first impression of Batavia:

Hotel der Nederlanden
Batavia,
Java Feb 23

Dear Kathleen,

I arrived here today in a steamer flying the Dutch flag (1500 tons.) The Captain was English & also the 1st officer & 1st engineer. 'Telamon' was the name of the boat & there were two passengers besides myself, a German & a chap who calls himself English. I did not get away from Singapore when I expected to (18th) but had to wait there until the 21st, the weather being so bad they were unable to get the cargo on the boat. I went on board on the night of the 20th as they were starting at day light on the 21st. Slept with my porthole open & woke up in the morning with 70 mosquito bites, 29 on one foot. They seem to go principally for the wrists & ankles.

While at Singapore I went to dine twice with the Simons. I went on the 17th in a private steam boat to the island of Johor with Graham Paterson & two officers in the Rifle Brigade. We started at 9 in the morning, got to Johor a little before 2pm, had lunch & then went to a gambling house kept by a Chinaman where we played a game called "Po" for 20 minutes. I think it was lucky we had not time to stay longer as the others might have lost more. As it was one lost 30 dollars. I played very small only putting in a dollar or two at a time & coming away a winner of 12.

A regular tropical downpour had been coming down all morning & it continued to do so all the afternoon. After leaving Johor we went all round the island of Singapore getting home again at 7pm. There is not much going on at Singapore except boozing. I amused myself walking about the Chinese quarter looking into the shops which I found very interesting. I met a very nice German chap at the Raffles Hotel who has gone up to Bangkok in Siam. I hope to meet him in Hong Kong & we shall in that case travel through Japan together. He is also travelling round the world.

I went to a Chinese theatre one night. They keep up a continual noise (music) while the performance is going on. The dresses were very pretty & the show was certainly worth seeing. We only stayed about 30 minutes. I have not had time to see much of Java yet, but Batavia lies very low & I should I think must be very unhealthy. I am only going to stay here two days & then am going up into the hills to see volcanoes & ruins. There are very few English on the island & the Dutch (they tell me) will help one little, although a lot of them can speak English. There are no English papers so I shan't know what's going on till I get back to Singapore. There are not many Chinamen in Batavia, nearly all Malays.

I have sent my 12 bore gun home as I was told I should have great difficulty in bringing it into Java. I know I would get no shooting in Japan & shall not have time in America. I am very disappointed as I wanted to shoot some birds here. Batavia is a large but very quiet place. Everything is beautifully green & there are some lovely orchids growing in the trees in the garden of this hotel. I am going to start taking photos soon & hope I shall manage it properly.

I may stay a fortnight or three weeks on the island & then go back to Singapore from which place I shall catch a P & O on 28th or 29th March to Hong Kong, stay a week & see Canton, & then go on to Japan as I want to be there in time for the cherry blossom. I think you had better write to the post office Yokohama as I shall go there for letters soon after getting to Japan. Kobe will be my landing place & I shall stop *at the Oriental Hotel there, but might miss your letters. I expect to be in Japan about the 2nd week in April & shall leave about the first week in July.*

Hoping that you are all well at home & with best love to all.

Your affect. Brother, Bertie
It is what you would call rather warm here.

Both Bertie and Scidmore commented on the exceptionally high population of the island of Java, which they were informed was 24 million in 1897. They would have been shocked to hear that one hundred and twenty years later, (2016) the population had risen to over 141 million, which is claimed to be the most densely populated island in the world. Bertie's description of Batavia (Jakarta) as being large but quiet and green certainly is not so today. Its population has risen to over 10 million with many high-rise buildings, not too many trees remaining and a huge traffic congestion problem.

24th February 1897   Batavia
Went for a walk before breakfast. After I went to the Hong Kong Bank & Police Station for a passport (1 guilder 80.) They asked me my age, where I came from, what my business was, what boat I came on & the name of the Captain. Tasted "Durian" & smelt it. I tried to engage a boy, but he wanted 2/2 Guilder a day. The pedlars try hard to make you buy their rubbish.

Scidmore also discovered there were limitations to being a tourist in Java. She wrote:

'The Dutch do not welcome tourists, nor encourage them to visit their paradise of the Indies. Too many travellers have come, seen, and gone away to tell disagreeable truths about Dutch methods and rule….Although the tyrannic rule and the "culture system" of forced labor is a thing of the past, the Dutch brain is slow and suspicious, and the idea being fixed fast that no stranger comes to Java on kindly or hospitable errands, the colonial authorities must know within twenty-four hours why one visits the Indies. They demand one's name, age, religion, nationality, plus nativity, and occupation, the name of the ship that brought the suspect to Java, and the name of its captain – a dim threat lurking in this latter query of holding the unlucky mariner responsible should his importation prove an expense or embarrassment to the island….The tourist pure and simple, the sight-seer and pleasure traveller, is not yet quite comprehended, and his passport usually accredit him as travelling in the interior for "scientific purposes." Guides or efficient couriers in the real sense do not exist yet. The English-speaking servant is rare and delusive, yet a necessity unless one speaks Dutch or Low Malay.'

Bertie never developed a taste for eating Durian, but Scidmore considered it *'agreeable to the palate, but offends the nose.'* Burbidge, on the other hand, became quite an addict of this foul smelling, but deliciously flavoured fruit. He wrote:

'The regal durian (Durio zibethinus), like the finest of nectarines or melting pears, must be eaten fresh and just at on particular point of ripeness, and then is, as many think, a fruit fit for a king.... It is the universal favourite, both with Malays and Chinese, but the opinions of Europeans vary as to the merits of this "delectable epitome of all that is perfect in fruit food." It is a paradox. "The best of fruits with the worst of character," as the Malays say... Its odour – one scarcely feels justified in using the word "perfume" - is so potent, so vague, but withal so insinuating, that it can scarcely be tolerated inside the house....an odour like that of a putrid sewer when half supressed by holding a perfumed handkerchief to the nose – a blending of a good deal that is nasty with a touch of something rather sweet.... The flavour of the durian is perfectly unique... The unceasing popularity it enjoys is like the music of a well-played violin on the ear, rich soothing and sweet, piquant. it is satisfying, but never cloys; the richness seems counteracted by a delicate acidity, the want of grape –like juiciness is supplied by the moist creamy softness of the pulp as it melts away ice-like on your tongue....Whoever is lucky enough to taste a good fruit to begin with, soon develops into a surreptitious durian eater; just as a jungle tiger becomes a man-eater after its first taste of human blood. There is scarcely any limit to durian eating if you once begin it; it grows on one like opium smoking, or other acquired tastes; but on the other hand, the very suggestion of eating such an "unchaste fruit" is to many, intolerable.'

Like Bertie, most travellers to Java did not choose to linger too long in the hot and steamy lowlands, and would head for the cooler climate of the hills. His Highness Raja Rajgan wrote of his departure from Batavia by train to Buitenzorg, where he was to make an official visit the Governor General:

'Heavy rain was falling when we left on January 5 for Buitenzorg. I had reserved a carriage, which was fairly comfortable. Most of the carriages have leather-covered or ordinary cane bottomed seats... Buitenzorg was reached after about two and a half hours journey. The rain continued the whole way, but did not suffice to obliterate the beauty of the scenery en route. On both sides of the line, as far as the eye could reach, there was a dense mass of the most profuse tropical vegetation one could imagine.

Buitenzorg has an altitude of about two thousand feet above sea level.... After reaching our destination, we drove to the Hotel Bellevue, which, by the way, seems to be very appropriately named, inasmuch as the outlook from the hotel verandah was a particularly fine one, extended over beautifully wooded and extremely fertile valleys.

The salubriousness of Buitenzorg attracts many people of Batavia to live there, as by so doing they avoid the heat and other disadvantages of life in the latter place. For the same reason the Governor General has his principle residence at Buitenzorg.'

Bertie also enjoyed the train ride to Buitenzorg and commented on the beautiful prospect from the Hotel Bellevue.

25th February 1897   Buitenzorg (Bogor)
Arrived here 10.30 after 2 hours in the railway through lovely country. At all the stations fruit was brought for sale - Rambutans & Mangosteen.

The Belle Vue Hotel is beautifully situated, the view from my balcony is grand. I think the botanical gardens are finer than those at Peradineyar. A fine avenue of high trees with beautiful creepers, ferns & orchids on them. Double cocoa nut, lotus (Nelumbium speciosum,) a talipot in full flower.

Buitenzorg, meaning 'without care' in Dutch, was the name given to the city of Bogor by the Dutch colonialists. In the eighteenth century, a palace was built there as a summer residence for the Governor, and many of the Dutch residents chose to live there. In 1814, the famous botanical gardens were first established and the city became the centre for scientific study.

The double coconut referred to, was the Coco de Mer palm, *Lodoicea malvica*. For many years it was a mystery and the stuff of legends. The large double palm nuts sometimes washed up on beaches around the Indian Ocean. People believed they had magical properties and that they had grown under the sea, hence the name 'Coco de Mer'. In 1768, the secret of their origins was revealed when Jean Duchemin in his ship *L'Heureuse Marie* discovered groves of them growing on the uninhabited Seychelles Islands. These nuts are the largest seed in the world and since their double form closely resemble a certain part of ladies' anatomy, their earlier Latin name was *Lodoicea callipyge* derived from the Greek word for 'beautiful buttocks'.

Talipot palm trees, *Corypha umbraculifera*, are native to Southern India. They only flowers once when they reaches maturity, which can take up to 80 years. They then put on a spectacular display of creamy- white flowers, and soon after, die.

The lotus, *Nelumbo nucefera*, has been considered sacred in many religions, ranging from ancient Egypt to Buddhism and Hinduism. It is a beautiful form of water lily like plant with pink and white flowers that open on tall stalks above the flat leaves.

Scidmore fell in love with Buitenzorg which she described as: *'one of the enchanted spots where days can slip by in dateless delight.'* She also visited the botanical gardens and observed the same abundance as Bertie recorded in his journal:

'The famous Botanical Gardens at Buitenzorg is the great show-place, the paradise and pride of the island. The Dutch are acknowledgedly the best horticulturists of Europe, and with the heat of a tropical sun, a daily shower, and nearly a century's well-directed efforts, they have made Buitenzorg's garden first of its kind in the world, despite the rival efforts of the French at Saigon, and the British at Singapore, Ceylon, Calcutta, and Jamaica....Graceful kanari trees arching one hundred feet overhead in a great green cathedral aisle, have tall straight trunks covered with stag-horn ferns, bird's-nest ferns, ratans, creeping palms, blooming orchids, and every kind of parasite

112

and air-plant the climate allows; and there is a fairy lake of lotus and Victoria regia beside it with pandanus and red-stemmed Banka palms crowded in a great sheaf or bouquet on a tiny islet. When one rides through this green avenue in the dewy freshness if the early morning, it seems as though nature and the tropics could do no more, until one has penetrated the tunnels of warigentrees, the open avenues of royal palms, the great plantations of a thousand palms, the grove of tree ferns, the frangipani thicket, and have reached the knoll commanding a view of the double summit of Gedeh and Pangerango, vaporous blue volcanic heights, from one peak of which a faint streamer of smoke perpetually floats.'

Bertie enjoyed the botanic gardens so much, he made a second visit.

26th February 1897   Buitenzorg
Went to the botanical gardens again & through the village. The hats worn by the natives are all sorts and sizes. I hear that tea grows well here & that they get a crop averaging 600 pounds (dry) to the acre, sometimes as much as 1100 lbs.

Marianne North found the botanical gardens at Buitenzorg to be a botanical artist's paradise. She spent more than a month painting the abundant flowers growing there. She wrote:

'The Botanic Garden was a world of wonders. Such variety of the different species was there. The plants had been there so long that they grew as if in their native woods – every kind of rattan, palm, pine, or arum. The latter are most curious in their habits and singular power of emitting heat. All the gorgeous water lilies of the world were collected in the lake in front of the palace. The Director was most kind in letting me have specimens of all the grand things I wanted to paint. The palms alone, in flower and fruit, would have easily employed a lifetime. The blue thumbergia and other creepers ran to the tops of the highest trees, sending down sheets of greenery and lovely flowers.'

From Buitenzorg, Bertie travelled to Garoet [Garut], which Scidmore described as: 'a favourite hill and pleasure resort of the island.'   This town is set in a valley surrounded by active volcanoes some of which are liable to erupt at any time, but are popular excursions for intrepid visitors. Both Bertie and Scidmore chose the same hotel while in Garoet. Bertie wrote:

27th February 1897   Garoet
Hotel van Horck
2.30 They speak little English here & I converse with the proprietor in French. Dinner at 8pm. There are lots of Pomeloes growing here in the garden, but not ripe. I saw some fine pigeons in a cage.

While Scidmore stayed at Hotel van Hork and she described it as:

'The Garoet hotel is one of the institutions of Java, and the Vrouw van Hork and her excellent Dutch housekeeping are famed from Anjer Head to Banjoewangi. All the colonial types are represented at the long table d'hote, and every language of Europe was heard. There were always nice neighbors at table, able and anxious to talk English, and the cheery Dutch ladies were kindness and friendliness personified. At no other resort on the island did we receive such a pleasant impression of the simplicity, refinement, and charm of social life in the colony. But, although two thousand feet above sea-level, in a climate of mildly tempered eternal spring, the ladies all wore the sarong and lose dressing –sacque in the morning, as in scorching Batavia or lowland Solo. Even on damp and chilly mornings, when a light wrap was a comfortable addition to our conventional muslin gowns, the Garoet ladies were bare-ankled and as scantily clad as the Batavians; and there were shock and real embarrassment to me in seeing in sarong and sacque the dignified elderly matron who had been my charming dinner neighbor the night before.'

Bertie wasted no time in setting off to explore the volcanoes in the area.

28th February 1897   Garoet
Up at 4.30. Went to Papanjan (Papandayang) Mountain to see sulphur springs. The natives seem very polite. Went to bed after lunch for 2 hours. Dinner 8pm

Scidmore also ascended the mountain and saw the spectacular five acre pit of boiling sulphur, but unlike Bertie who rode up, she was carried in a sedan chair.

'At the foot of the mountain, we changed to clumsy djoelies, or sedan chairs, each borne by four coolies, whose go-as-you-please gait, not one of them keeping step with any other, was especially trying. Despite their churning motion, the way was enjoyable; and beginning with a blighted coffee plantation at the base of the mountain, we passed through changing belts of vegetation, as by successive altitudes we passed botanically from the tropic to the temperate zone....We met strings of coolies descending with baskets of sulphur on their backs, the path was yellow with the broken fragments of years' droppings, and infragrant, murky sulphurstreams crossed and ran beside the path, in promise of the stifling caldrons we were fast approaching. We had a magnificent view back over the Garoet plain, with its checker-board of green and glinting fields, marked with the network of white post roads and dotted with clumps of palms that bespoke the hidden villages, and then we passed through a natural gateway or cutting in the solid mountain-side made by the eruption. The broad passage or defile led to the kawa, or crater, a bowl or depression deep sunk in rocky walls, with pools of liquid sulphur bubbling all over the five acre floor and sending off clouds of nauseous steam. These pools, vats of purest molten gold, boiled violently all the time, scattering golden drops far and wide from their fretted honey-combed edges. There was always suggestion of the possibility of their suddenly shooting into the air like geysers, and deluging us with the column of molten gold.'

Papadayan had erupted in 1772, which blew the top off the mountain and the resulting avalanches destroyed forty villages and killed about three thousand people. In 1897, it was considered safe to venture close to the crater, but another major eruption occurred in 2002 and the whole area is now much less stable. There have been frequent earthquakes and the emission of noxious gases makes the whole crater area hazardous.

1st March 1897   Garoet

Got up at 4.30 again & went to Kewar Manoek at the top of which there is lots of mud & water boiling & bubbling up from holes. The ride through the jungle was very enjoyable.   It started to rain when I was on the top, so I walked down to the rest house where a carriage with three ponies was waiting for me. The Dutch do not allow the natives to wear shoes & the women must not wear white jackets. Heard a good story about a Dutch lady finding a newspaper left by an Englishman & catching a cold. (Wren)

In modern times, this area has been converted to a geo-thermal power plant, but tourists can still visit the bubbling, steaming vents.

2nd March 1897   Garoet

Up at 6 & went to see the Milk Lake in the mountains. I am getting rather tired of these long rides up mountains & besides am rather sore in places. It rained when I was half way down & I got wet again.

Talaga Bodas (White Lake) is the crater of a semi quiescent volcano which has filled with sulphurous water to form a beautiful milky-white lake. The temperature of the lake is around 95 degrees Centigrade, so swimming is not recommended, but nowadays there are thermal baths and a proper road to the attraction.

Bertie's letter to his sister, Ethel seems to indicate he was just as interested in the people as he was in the natural phenomena he visited. He mentioned that the trains were slow and never ran at night. All the passengers were accommodated overnight at Moas, the next place he was to stay. It was the Dutch Government's policy not to allow trains to run at night for security reasons.

Garoet, Java , March 2nd

Dear Ethel,

The first two days here at Garoet the only conversation I could have was with the proprietor of the Hotel Van Vlorck (where I am staying) in French! Now there are some Dutch who speak English & an American & Englishman having turned up tonight. Buitenzorg where I stayed before coming here is a lovely spot.   From the balcony of my bedroom I had a grand view. A valley full of tropical vegetation, with a river running through it & mountains on the far side. I enjoyed the Botanical gardens there which I hear are the finest in the world.   Everything is very dear in Java. Half a gulden (10d) for a bottle of soda (made on the island) or lemonade. They charge for all extras at the hotel & finish up by charging for the receipt stamp they put on your bill. The stamp on your letter is it. The natives wear all sorts of funny sun hats, some as big as a brolly. They are very polite, taking them off long before you get to them & not putting them on again till you have passed. I hear this politeness is enforced by the Dutch. They are not allowed to wear shoes & the women must not have white coats. The Dutch ladies appear at tiffin in native costume. Slippers, no stockings, a tight fitting " sarong" which passes for a skirt and shows off their fine figures. (They are nearly all fat) a little white jacket, very open at the neck & a little shirting underneath. Their hair a foot long, and they go to bed for a couple of hours - 2 til 4. All the Dutch turn in at this time. I don't like their style of eating. You mix all the food in a soup plate, then shovel it down with a spoon.

Yesterday I got up at 4.20 & went first in a small carriage drawn by three ponies for a long distance, I then rode on a pony up a mountain through lovely jungle to the top where there is steam squirting out in large quantities & lots of sulphur. Today I got up at the same time. I went the same way up another mountain where there is boiling water and mud spouting out from lots of holes in what looks like an old crater. Tomorrow I go to see the Milk Sea! Whatever that may be! After that I am going to the middle of the island to see some wonderful ruins.

It is very slow travelling here by the train. They stop at nearly all the stations & no train run at night. I had no idea that Java was so large & that there are 24 million people living in it. This is the rainy season I am sorry to say. Yesterday it was fine in the morning, but today I got a good soaking. Umbrellas are no use for a tropical shower. We don't have dinner until 8pm here & the custom is to bow to everybody near you when you take your seat, or leave the table.

The native cottages are very picturesque built almost entirely of bamboo. They are making preparations here (Garoet) for a grand fete. I should have liked to have been here for it They have fights between leopards & wild pigs, also between other wild animals in a large square surrounded by bamboo platforms for the people to sit on. This takes place in the open & I wonder the leopard does not go for the people.

I expect to find letters when I get back to Singapore sent on by Amy. I have had none since I left Ceylon.   Hoping that you are all well at Durlsone
With best love to all - Your Affec. brother, Bertie

10 pence may not seem much for a drink, but in England, at that time, a pint of beer could be bought for one penny and 10d in today's money is equivalent to about four pounds, fifty pence.

3rd March 1897   Moas

Gillespie & I with his "boy" arrived here about 7pm and had to wait till 8.30 for dinner. Along the line today I saw lots of flying foxes, also creeping palms, splendid forests of bamboo. The first half of our journey was through a thickly populated country, well cultivated; the latter half through swampy jungle.

4th March 1897   Boro Budhar

We arrived at Djojakarta today from Moas & started off after lunch for the ruins of BoroBudhar (a four hour drive). They are building a railway between these places. We passed plenty of sugar cane, also the ruins of Mendout. One gets a splendid panoramic view from the top of the ruins of BB. We saw men climbing coconut palms after sugar. We tasted some & found it rather like toffee.

Marianne North also visited the 'Boro-Bodo' ruins as part of her exploration of Borneo and Java in 1876. Conditions then were a challenge for a lady travelling alone, but she managed to produce a quantity of beautiful paintings of the tropical flowers and the scenery. She too was impressed by the view from the top of the ruins. She wrote:

'We came to the great pyramid or monastery of Boro-Bodo, or Buddoer, … a perfect museum, containing the whole history of Buddha in a series of basso-relievos, lining seven terraces round stone-covered hills, which, if stretched out consecutively, would cover three miles. From the top terraces was the finest view I ever saw: a vast plain, covered with the richest cultivation – rice, indigo, corn, mandioca, tea, and tobacco, with one giant cotton-tree rising above everything else, and groves of cocoa-nuts dotted all over it, under which the great population hid their neat little villages of small thatched baskets. Three magnificent volcanoes arose out of it, with grand sweeping curves and angles, besides many other ragged-edged mountains. Every turn gave one fresh pictures; and if Boro-Bodor were not there I should still think it one of the finest landscapes I ever saw.'

Eliza Scidmore spent some time exploring Chandi Mendoet and wrote:

'Chandi Mendoet, two miles the other side of Boro Bodor, is an exquisite pyramidal temple in a green quadrangle of the forest, with a walled foss and bridges. Long lost and hidden in the jungle, it was accidentally discovered by the Dutch resident Hartmann in 1835, and the space cleared about it. The natives had never known of or suspected its existence, but the investigators determined that this gem of Hindu art was erected between 750 and 800 AD. The workmanship proves a continued progress in the arts employed at Boro Boedor…. The body of the temple is forty-

five feet square as it stands on its walled platform, and rises to a height of seventy feet. A terrace or raised processional path, around the temple is faced with bas-reliefs and ornamental stones, and great bas-reliefs decorate the upper walls. The square interior chapel is entered through a stepped arch or door, and the finest of the Menoet bass-reiefs, commonly spoken of as the "Tree of Knowledge," is in this entrance way. There the Buddha sits beneath the bo-tree, the trunk of which supports a pajong, or state umbrella, teaching those who approach him and kneel with offerings and incense. These figures, as well as the angels overhead, the birds in the trees and the lambs on their rocky shelf, are listening to the great teacher.'

Bertie did not seem to be particularly interested in the spiritual or artistic aspects of the monument.

5th March 1897   Djoejakartar
We spent a jolly morning among the ruins. It was the 5th March (Malay New Year) & they swarmed about the ruins letting off crackers & enjoying themselves. We went into a tent and saw some acting. We tasted Durian, Guava & bamboo curry. I saw Durians growing here. The natives all seem rather frightened of us.

Borobudur has been designated a world heritage site by UNESCO and has around 2.5 million visitors a year, making it one of the most revered and visited sites in Indonesia. It is now surrounded by extensive car parks and stalls selling souvenirs.

THE LATTICED DAGOBAS ON THE CIRCULAR TERRACES.

The summit of Borobudur in 1899 (Java, The Garden of the East: E.R.Scidmore)
The same scene in 2017, when visited by the author

118

It was originally built around the 8th and 9th centuries AD at the time of the powerful Sailendera Dynasty and consists of nine stacked platforms each of which has marvellous carved panels depicting the tenets of Buddhist beliefs and the life of Lord Buddha. The top three levels are circular with carved Stupas and statues of Buddha.

As beliefs changed, the temple was gradually abandoned. It became covered in volcanic ash and jungle and was more or less forgotten until the early part of the nineteenth century when it was uncovered and excavated. Unfortunately the exposed temple became vulnerable to damage from the weather and humans in the form of 'souvenir hunters' and wear and tear from many feet climbing it. In recent times there has been the added threat of sabotage from religious extremists, so security had been increased. However, it is still an intensely spiritual and beautiful place to visit.

Borobudur in 1897 (ER Scidmore, Java the Garden of the East   -   and in 2017)

6th March 1897   Moas
Left Djoejakarta for Moas 2.30. There were two Chinamen in the carriage with us who smelt rather.

7th March 1897   Buitenzorg
Left Moas 5.28. Lunch in the train. Gillespie & I both have rooms looking over the valley.   We had a swim in the bath before dinner.

8th March 1897   Buitenzorg
Went to the gardens with Gillespie.   Took some seeds of " Caesalpina pulcherima," a pretty sort of acacia with red and yellow flowers. I also saw Victoria Regia in full flower.

Caesalpinia pulcherrima is a spectacular flowering bush, or tree, which originated from the tropical region of the Americas. It is widely cultivated in tropical gardens because of its beautiful bright red and/or yellow flowers. It is a member of the pea family and its seeds are housed in large pods. It is sometimes known as the dwarf Poinciana or 'Pride of Barbados'.

Victoria regia is the name originally given to the huge Brazilian water lily in honour of Queen Victoria. It is now *Victoria amazonica*. Its exquisite flowers are pure white when they open at night, but become rosy pink as they mature. Seeds were taken to England in 1836 and there was intense rivalry between Victorian gardeners to produce the first flowers. The two main contenders were the Duke of Devonshire and the Duke of Northumberland, both of whom had large heated glass houses. The winner was the Duke of Devonshire, (or his head gardener, Joseph Paxton), at his stately mansion, Chatsworth. The event was reported in the *Illustrated London News* on 17th November 1849 when one of the first flowers was presented to Queen Victoria. To accompany the article, there was an illustration of the lilies in flower, with a small girl standing on one large leaf and the caption:

> '*On unbent leaf in fairy guise, reflected in the water.*
> *Beloved, admired by hearts and eyes, stands Annie, Paxtons's daughter.*'

Joseph Paxton was not only a gifted horticulturist, he could create glass houses, and it was his design that was accepted and used to build the vast 'Crystal Palace' that housed the Great Exhibition in 1851.

Bertie's next letter was to his mother, in which he describes the places he has been to and the strange fruits he has sampled.

Hotel Belle Vue
Buitenzorg, Java
March 8th

Dear Mater,
I am glad I did not miss Java as it is a most lovely island imaginable. Everything seems to grow here to perfection. The rice is twice as fine as in Ceylon & you see it in all stages of growth: when young it is the most beautiful green & when ripe it looks just like a field of barley. Tea & coffee grow splendidly & the sugar cane I have seen for the first time. When I was in Batavia I tried to get a Malay boy who could speak English. There was only one & he wanted 2 ½ guilders a day (4/1d.). They can live well on 5d a day, so of course I refused. Two days after I got to Garoet, an American arrived & funnily enough he had engaged this boy. We got on very well together & he decided to go on the ruins with me. I therefore got the services of the interpreter very cheap. I expect we will travel together until we shall get to Singapore. It took us 2 days

to get to these ruins from Garoet & at the end we had to drive for 4 hours from a place called Djojakarta. They were rather disappointing & much smaller than I expected. But they improved on closer inspection being a mass of beautiful carving. Boro-Budha is the name of the temple. We stayed the night at a rest house close to the ruins & the following day saw them under the most favourable conditions. The 5th March – the new year of the Malays & a great holiday for them. They swarmed all round & on the temple, (it is built on terraces), making the place look quite gay with their various gaily coloured dresses. We bought and tasted various fruit; Durian I tried again holding my nose meanwhile. But this is the last time). I also had bamboo salad (the root) & sugar from coconut palm which tasted like toffee.

Mangosteen is the best fruit I have come across yet. We went to see some Malay dancing & acrobatic feats in a tent, a very poor show, but interesting. In the afternoon we drove back to Djojakarta which is a beautiful town. It looks very pretty at night as all the natives are compelled by Dutch law to carry lanterns after 8pm. I fancy this must be to prevent the Javanese from holding revolutionary meetings. One day I saw hundreds and hundreds of flying foxes, (very large bats) hanging from lofty trees. I hear they do great damage among the fruit. I also saw lots of nests of the weaver birds hanging from the branches high up. We are now back at Buitzorg where we have stopped to have another look at the gardens. Tomorrow we go to Batavia & then as soon as we can, get a boat to Singapore. I am very anxious to see some English papers, having had no news since I have been on this island. I also expect letters sent on by Amy. I don't like the Dutch much, they are too sleepy and greedy.

With best love to all & hoping that you are all well at home.
Your loving son,
Bertie

Bertie mentions how rich the soil is and how well the crops grow on the island. This is due, in part, to the high rain fall and the tropical climate, but also because of the wonderful volcanic soil. It was only fourteen years since the huge volcanic eruption of Krakatoa which convulsed the whole island and covered it in ash.

Scidmore was told by fellow hotel guests of their terrifying experiences during the summer of 1883:

'They told one thrilling stories of that summer of Krakatau's prolonged activity; of Batavian folk running frequent excursion-steamers to the Strait of Sunda to witness the spectacle of a volcano *in eruption; and of that August Sunday of horror when the very end of the world seemed to have come to all that part of Java. A dense pall of smoke covered all of Buitenzorg's sky that day; Salak was lost in the darkness, and it was thought that it or Gedeh was in eruption when crashes and roars beyond those of the most terrific thunder-storms, the bang and boom of the heaviest artillery's bombardment, and the sound of frightful explosions filled the air, shook and rocked the ground, and rattled houses until conversation was impossible. Compass needles spun around and around, barometers rose and fell, clouds of sulphurous vapors half strangled the people in the gloom of that awful Sabbath night, and no one slept with this dread cannonading and the end of the world seemingly close at hand. The next day-light brought the climax, a series of prolonged and awful roars, and then the very crack and crash of doom, when half of Krakatau's island was torn away with the final explosion…. Those whose plantations were near the Sunda Strait had yet more gruesome times during the days of darkness and of greenish, horrid twilight, when the heavens seemed to be falling about them in the rain of ashes and hot stones.*

Batavian folk had as terrifying experiences, and each entering ship brought more awful tales of being caught by the waves or the eddies of that sickening sea, with hot stones setting decks and rigging afire, and the weight of hot ash threatening to sink the vessel in a sea of pumice before they could be shovelled away…. Pumice drifted into Batavia harbor in a surface-layer so deep that planks were laid on it and men walked even a mile to shore.'

It was estimated that well over 36,000 people died following the Krakatau eruption. Some were killed by the noxious gas, the ash or super-heated rocks that fell to earth, but also many thousands were drowned in the series of huge Tsunamis that swept through the region. Over 165 villages and towns were destroyed completely and large areas of crops and trees died. The blast was heard as far away as Australia, India and Ceylon, up to 5,000 kilometres away. The ash was blown high into the stratosphere where it circulated around the world and affected the weather patterns for several years causing a world-wide drop in temperature of several degrees and spectacular sunsets, sunrises and other strange atmospheric phenomenon.

9th March 1897   Batavia
We left Buitenzorg 10.30. Bought our tickets for a boat to Singapore. 85 guilders (7 pounds.) They also made us pay 10 cents for the stamp. This for 48 hours at sea.

It is noticeable that when Bertie mentions the price of things, it is because he considers he is being charged too much. The amount does not seem too expensive to us, but we have to consider that seven pounds sterling in 1897 would be about 693 pounds sterling in 2016.

Wednesday 10th March 1897   Batavia
We went to the museum in the morning & saw some fine things. Among others, a gold chain that belonged to the King of Borneo.   In the afternoon we went to a Chinese shop & bought some pretty ornaments.

11th March 1897   Batavia
I went in the morning after butterflies with Nicholson, (a chap from Queensland bound for Celebes.)

12th March 1897   On board Van Dieman
I sit next to the Captain, a Dutchman & two Dutch ladies sit opposite who can't speak English.   The food is good & I think it ought to be for the money.

No blue funnels on this journey. *Van Diemen* was built in 1890 by the Nederlandsche Stoomboot Mij. at Rotterdam. She was a Dutch cargo boat owned by the Koninklijke Paketvaart Mij. of Amsterdam. She must have been extremely well constructed because she survived as a hard-working cargo ship, plying various ports in the Far East until 1945, by which time she was 55 years old. During her career she was owned by six different companies, had six names and finally ended her days as the *SS Mikazuki Maru* when she had been seized by the Japanese government in 1941. She was operated by Japanese navy throughout the Second World War, until in 1945, when she was blown up and sunk by a US navy mine in the Grand Canal of the Yangtze, below Woosung in China.

13th March 1897   Van Dieman
Fine and smooth

15th March 1897   Singapore
Went for a drive with Gillespie in pelting rain to the botanical gardens.

16the March 1897   Singapore
Packed in the morning & went to say goodbye to Graham. Went on board the Thames after tiffin. She was to have sailed at 5pm, but will not start till tomorrow, daylight. I bought some pretty shells.

As Bertie prepared for his next sea journey, he had had time to write a letter from the Raffles Hotel. It is noticeable that letters he wrote to his father contained more about financial matters, including information which could be relevent to his Stock Exchange activities.

Raffles Hotel
Singapore

March 16t

Dear Governor,
I got back here on 14th & leave here this afternoon for Hong Kong in the P&O boat "Thames". I found a letter from Kathleen here (sent on by

Amy) & one from Mr. Fraser.   I had to wait 3 days in Batavia for a boat & then came in the Dutch mail boat "Van Dieman" for which they charged me the modest sum of 85 gulden (7 pounds) single passage; you are only 48 hours at sea.   It is quite a treat to get back to an English colony again, where you can get decent food & the people are a little more lively. I don't think the Dutch are keen on having English people travelling in Java & I expect that is why they are loth to give you information, or help you in any way.

You would laugh if you saw some of the Javanese costumes:-   They are compelled by the Dutch to wear turbans & sometimes you see a coachman with his turban & a topper stuck on the top; the porters also wear their official caps on their turbans.   At all the principal hotels in Java, Gin & bitters is put in the veranda before dinner, & you can help yourself gratis: You should see how the greedy Dutchmen go for it I bought a few curious silver ornaments at Batavia as worn by the native women. I also bought a sarong for a "gulden" for which they asked 13 at first. I did not want it but having offered one gulden, did not cry off when they came down to my price. I did not have any time to catch butterflies in Java as I was continually on the move. I met a man from northern Queensland at Batavia who told me that there is a rush now to British New Guinea, where alluvial gold has been discovered. He says that as many as 500 left on one steamer for that place. The "Thames" I hear is very full. I hope that I will find it a better boat than the Kaiser I Hind. I have not decided yet which way I shall cross to America. If I can get a boat that touches at Honolulu on the way to San Francisco I shall very likely go that way.   I am going to stay a week at Hong Kong & go up to see Canton & perhaps shall go to Shanghai.

Hoping that you are all well at Durlstone & with best love to all.
Your affect. Son
Bertie

I shall look out at Yokohama for letters at the Post Office up till the beginning of June.

෩෨

On the "Thames" 17/3/97
Singapore to Hong Kong.
This is a much better boat than the Kaiser I Hind & the food is good
enough. I played cricket in the afternoon. The weather is all that I
could wish.

The Thames, from Ian Farquhar collection

Bertie seems happier on the *Thames* than on the old *Kaiser I Hind*. Since he was travelling first class, he had a cabin to himself. This had electric lighting and an electric bell to be used if he wished to summon the cabin steward. The standard cabins were quite compact, usually holding bunk beds with metal railings to stop passengers rolling out of them in rough weather. The furnishings included some chairs and a wash-stand with a patent fold -away basin and a cold water tap. This was combined as a dressing table, with a mirror, and had a chest of drawers and shelving for toiletries and clothing. A stand up wash could be accomplished in the cabin, but passengers had to walk to the communal bathrooms if they wished to take a bath, or use the toilets.   There was no air-conditioning, so the port hole could be opened to allow fresh air into the cabin. In hot weather, battens were fitted , so the breeze could be directed into the cabin. In the extreme heat of the Red Sea, many passengers, especially the men, chose to sleep on deck.

Each morning at 7am, the steward would bring tea and biscuits to the cabin and at eight-thirty the bugle sounded to summon passengers to a hearty breakfast with plenty of choices in the dining saloon.

Bisland also sailed on the *Thames* for part of her journey. She arrived on board in a state of exhaustion after a busy visit to Hong Kong and was enchanted by the ship, and the feeling of relaxation it engendered:

'*It is a beautiful ship; like a fine yacht in its spacious commodiousness. Here and there hang canary cages thrilling with song. Narcissus bulbs in bowls are ablow with fluttering white flowers, and everywhere are deep-colored jars full of palms and ferns. The space assigned to me is a large, pleasant white room, from which a great square lifts up outwards on the water-side, leaving me on intimate terms with the milky, jade-tinted sea. Beneath this window is a broad divan, and here laved in tepid sea winds and soothed by rippling whispers against the ship's side, I sleep – the languorous, voluptuous sleep of the tropics; . . . sink softly into that dim warm flood where one lies drenched, submerged I unconsciousness; a flood that ebbs slowly, slowly – bearing with all fatigue and satiety – and leaves me on the shores of life again in a pale lilac dusk glimmering with great stars. . . .'*

Thames was a P&O ship. She was built by J. & G. Thompson at Clydebank in 1881 and started service in 1882 with a journey from London to Calcutta. She later made voyages from London to Australia via Colombo. She could accommodate up to 138 first class passengers and 60 second class passengers, and also space enough for 3,012 cubic metres of cargo, some of which would be mail. In 1885 Thames took part in the rescue of another P&O ship, *Chusan* which had run aground near Perim Lighthouse in Yemen. Then in 1886, she herself had to be rescued, when she ran aground near Hong Kong in a sudden fog. On this occasion, the mail she was carrying was taken on by *Tehran*. When Bertie travelled on Thames she had been contracted to the Italian Government to provide a Venice to Bombay service. In 1898 she was withdrawn from service, sold in 1901 and decommissioned for scrap metal at Marseilles.

On leaving Singapore, *Thames* set sail for Hong Kong heading eastward along the Strait to Horsburgh Light and then into the South China Sea. In March, although outside the typhoon season, the weather can be changeable and is often foggy, with poor visibility. After passing Charlotte Bank, Julia Shoal and Bombay Reef, the ship's course was set direct for the entrance to the narrow Lei Yue Mun Passage between Hong Kong Island and Kowloon and on into Hong Kong Harbour.

18th March 1897   On the Thames
Fine and calm.Cricket in the afternoon.

19th March 1897   Thames
89 in the shade at 9.45

20th March 1897   Thames
Tug of war in the afternoon. The wind is getting up.

21st March 1897   Thames
Rough. Went to breakfast, but after putting milk on my porridge, made a bolt for my cabin. I was not very bad and went for a walk in the afternoon.

Nelly Bly on the *Victoria*, also had rough seas on her passage to Hong Kong, but her spirits remained high. She recorded in her diary:

'One night during the monsoon the sea washed over the ship in a frightful manner. I found my cabin filled with water, which however did not touch my berth. Escape to the lower deck was impossible, as I could not tell the deck from the angry, pitching sea. As I crawled back into my bunk a feeling of awe crept over me and with it a conscious feeling of satisfaction. I thought it very possible that I had spoken my last word to any mortal, that the ship would doubtless sink. …If the ship does go down, I thought, there is time enough to worry when it's going. All the worry in the world cannot change it one way or the other, and if the ship does not go down, I only waste so much time. So I went to sleep and slumbered soundly until the breakfast hour.'

She was happy, next day to reach Hong Kong and dry land. Her first impression was of the beauty of the port, but when she went ashore, reality struck.

'We first saw the city of Hong Kong in the early morning. Gleaming white were the castle-like homes in the tall mountainside. We fired a cannon as we entered the bay, the captain saying that it was the custom of mail ships. A beautiful bay was this magnificent basin, walled on every side by high mountains. …Mirror-like was the bay in the bright sun, dotted with strange craft from many countries. Heavy Iron-clads, torpedo boats, mail steamers, Portuguese lorchas, Chinese junks and sampans. …Hong Kong is strangely picturesque. It is a terraced city, the terraces being formed by castle-like, arcaded buildings perched tier after tier up the mountain's verdant side….*

Hong Kong Harbour from the sea. Photo from Bertie's album,

The doctor, another gentleman and I left the boat, and walking to the pier's end selected sedan chairs, in which we were carried to the town. The carriers were as urgent as our hackmen around railway stations in America. There is a knack of getting into a chair properly. It is placed upon the ground, the carrier tilts the shafts down, and the patron steps inside, back towards the chair, and goes into it backwards. Once seated, the carriers hoist the chair onto their shoulders and start off with a monotonous trot, which gives the chair a motion not unlike that of a pacing saddle horse.

We followed the road along the shore, passing warehouses of many kinds and tall balconied buildings filled with hundreds of Chinese families, on the flat house plan. The balconies would have lent a pleasing appearance to the houses had the inhabitants not seemed to be enjoying a washing jubilee, using the balconies for clotheslines. Garments were stretched on poles, after the manner of hanging coats so they will not wrinkle, and those poles were fastened to the balconies until it looked as if every family in the street had placed their old clothes on exhibition.

The town seemed in a state of untidiness, and the road was dirty, the mobs of natives we met were filthy, the houses were dirty, the numberless boats lying along the wharf, which were invariably crowded with dirty people, were dirty, our carriers were dirty fellows, there untidy pigtails twisted around half-shaven heads.

On arrival, Bly's first priority was to visit the offices of the Occidental and Oriental Steamship Company to find out when the next ship would be leaving for San Francisco. It was here that she was informed for the first time of the existence of Elizabeth Bisland, who was attempting to beat her in her race around the world. Consequently she was disappointed to hear she would have to wait five days before the *Orient* would embark. However this delay did give her time to explore Hong Kong and Canton. She seemed to have a very enjoyable time, being entertained royally by the many charming young men there.

'There are bachelors enough and to spare! And a most happy time do those bachelors have in the East. They are handsome, jolly and good-natured. They have their own fine homes with no one but the servants to look after them. Think of it, and let me whisper, "Girls, go East!"

Bisland experienced a trouble-free visit to Hong Kong. She faced no shipping delays and found waiting at the quay, servants in smart uniforms who had been sent to convey her in a sedan chair to the luxurious house of a friend up on the Peak.

'There are four Chinamen for each chair, dressed in my friend's livery – loose trousers and tunic of white cotton bordered with rose color. Their feet are bare and their queues are gathered in Psyche knots on the back of their heads.

They lift the poles on their shoulders and start off in a swift swinging trop. We pass across the narrow strip of level land that lies on the water's edge – the business quarter of the city built handsomely and solidly of native stone – and begin to mount the broad steep ways that lead to the residence quarter. These are cool and shadowy with great trees, with the clattering feathered spears of tall bamboos, with gigantic ferns, and the prodigious satiny leaves of tropical lilies. The streets are paved with asphalt and have no sidewalks; here and there they resolve themselves into broad flights of shallow steps up which the bearers carry us with perfect ease. . . The verdure is magnificent; the town is submerged in it, and flowers are everywhere. On every wall stand rows of earthen jars full of greenery and blossom – rows on rows of them in the courtyards – more rows on both ends of every flight of steps, and on all balcony railings. Every nook and corner that will hold a jar is filled with bloom, and the rarest orchids are strewn carelessly about, industriously producing flowers, in delicious provincial ignorance of their own value.'

During the three days she spent in Hong Kong, Bisland was shown around the city, including the shops, which she found irresistible. She was introduced to Sir Catchick Paul Chater, a gentleman of Armenian extraction, born in Calcutta, who came to Hong Kong as a young man. He was reputed to be probably the richest and most successful businessman in the colony. Among his many business interests, he was largely responsible for the development of Kowloon. He was happy to show her some of his ventures.

Bisland rode on the tram that ran from Murray Barracks up to Victoria Gap. Some of the more affluent residents of Hong Kong had built fine residences high on the Peak, as it was cooler there than at sea level, but the only transport up had been by foot, or sedan chair. Alexander Finlay Smith, who had previously worked on the Scottish Highland railways, conceived the idea of building a funicular tram line. He studied similar railways in places such as San Francisco and in Europe and the Peak tram was completed in May 1888.

Bertie only had time for a quick look around the city of Hong Kong, before boarding a ferry to Canton.

22nd March 1897   Hong Kong
We arrived here at 6am. Rather misty, but no rain. At the Hong Kong Hotel we had to wait a long time for our luggage. Went round Happy Valley in a rickshaw with Dr. Otto Seitz. We went on board the "Fatshan", (named after a town on the river above Canton.) Good dinner. There were loaded rifles in the first saloon.

On board the "Fatshan" (280 feet long) Twin screw, 2260 tuns gross, 1425reg.   Fare 5 pounds (max) single.   Meals on board for 1.50 each, this includes wine, Sherry, claret, Porter, Ale, Brandy, Whisky & aerated waters.

When Bertie arrived in 1897, Hong Kong Island had been under British rule for 57 years. It had a population of approximately 265,000 and was a thriving port. Originally it had been a remote and insignificant place in the far south of the Chinese Empire. It consisted of a few villages of Cantonese-speaking people who made a living from fishing, salt production and pearling. It was also an area plagued by pirates. It was named Heung Gawng (Fragrant Harbour) because of the sandalwood trees which grew there.

Happy Valley, Hong Kong, from Bertie's album

Over the centuries there were incursions by various European traders attracted to China by its silk, tea, pearls, jade, beautiful porcelain and other art works. The Portuguese established a settlement at Macau. The Chinese imperial government was suspicious of these traders and imposed restrictions on them. Also the Chinese were not particularly interested in purchasing the manufactured goods offered by the Europeans, except for limited luxury items like clocks and watches, so the British introduced a terrible commodity which became much sought after by the Chinese. This was opium, which was extensively grown in India. This caused huge social problems for the Chinese, and their government attempted to ban the trade, which annoyed the British traders and resulted in the Opium Wars. The British got the upper hand in 1841 and the Union Jack was first raised on Hong Kong Island. On 26th June 1843 the Island was officially declared a British Territory, and in 1860, Kowloon was added to allow Britain to control the entrance to the Pearl River.

The *Fatshan* which Bertie boarded, was operated by the Canton & Macau Steamboat Co in partnership with China Navigation Co. She had been built by Ramage & Ferguson of Leith in 1887, specifically to be a fast overnight ferry between Hong Kong and Canton. She was considered to be a very modern ship with her powerful triple expansion engines with twin screws. Bertie travelled in comfort, first class, but the *Fatshan* could accommodate 1,000 or more deck passengers. The guns he mentioned being kept in the Saloon, were needed for the very real threat from pirates which were active in the area. In fact, a sister ship, *Hankow*, was attacked, set on fire and entirely destroyed by pirates. *Fatshan* was to carry passengers between Hong Kong and Canton for forty-six years, until 1933, when she was replaced by *Fatshan 2*.

23rd March 1897   Canton

We arrived off Canton 6am. The river boats I shall never forget. I read in the guide book that there is a population of 3000,000 that live entirely on the river. The small boats here they call slipper boats. These take the place of "sampans" which we saw in Singapore & Penang. They swarmed round the ship directly we anchored. An old one eyed woman, (Chinese) called "Susan" came on board, also a guide. We went in a slipper boat & were punted by a coolie & two Chinese girls to the Victoria Hotel on the island of Shameen. (Shamian) The Japanese consul was staying there, also some Germans & the only room we could get to sleep in was the smoking room. A good hotel, good food, a billiard table & two skittle alleys. We had breakfast and started with our guide in sedan chairs at 8am. Crossed the bridge , guarded by Chinese soldiers, into Canton & stayed there till 15.30. Saw 5 storied Pagoda, temple of 500 Buddas, water clock, examination hall, prison & went to many shops at some of which we made small purchases. I bought a few broaches made of silver and birds' feathers, a pipe, chop sticks, a few silk articles & paintings on rice paper. The narrow streets & the coloured dazzling sign boards hanging thickly above you are most curious. Along the streets you are carried through a busy crowd of Chinese, most of whom treat you with indifference, but others make faces, spit & shout at you, no doubt something very insulting, but it was like water on a duck's back, as of course I could not understand.

We had a Chinese lunch, birds' nest soup, Shark fins, mongoose, duck & squirrel. I tried all & it nearly made me sick. I also tried an opium pipe. We saw the execution ground in the afternoon, 12 had been executed the day before. I saw the blood, but could not see the heads. We had tea after & the executioner came in and sat at the next table. He cuts off heads for 25 cents, but there is a reduction for quantity. Saw 22 flower boats in the evening.

Bly was informed that the population of Canton was 'millions of people' in 1889, but a survey was made in that year which estimated approximately 2.5 million. The large numbers of people who lived and carried out their business on river boats, was mainly because land suitable for building was in short supply. The 22 flower boats Bertie noticed were floating brothels. These were often colourful and elaborately decorated.

Canton, or Guangzhou, as it is known now became an important trading post, firstly with the Arabs who travelled overland and by sea to seek the riches of the Orient, then later with the Europeans. The first to arrive were the Portuguese, then traders from other countries. The most sought after exports from China were silk, tea and porcelain.

During the 18th and early 19th centuries, foreign traders were forbidden to operate at other Chinese ports and only allowed access to Canton. Each country had its own compound, or factory as they were known. These were kept separate and well-guarded to protect the traders from the hostile locals who considered them to be 'foreign devils'.

After the treaty of Nanking in 1843 other treaty ports were opened up and the dominance of Canton declined, but during the 19th century it was an important centre for the production of chinaware and porcelain, in particular the beautiful 'famille rose' pattern, which was much valued in Europe.

The Victoria Hotel on Shamian Island was named Shameen Hotel when it opened in 1888, but with a change in ownership in 1895, it was renamed the Victoria Hotel and became popular with well-to-do visitors. In the 1950s, it was taken over by the Chinese government and renamed the Victory Hotel. It is now a modern multi-story establishment with a swimming pool on the roof.

Shamian Island was created by European engineers by enlarging a sand bank in the Pearl River. It housed the British and French foreign concession trading posts and afforded them additional security. Two bridges were constructed between the island and Canton city. These were guarded at all times and closed at night. The island is now gazetted as an historic site and the old European buildings have been restored.

Bly made a short visit to Canton, arriving there on Christmas day. She said of Shamian Island:

'This little island, guarded at every entrance, is Shameen, or Sandy Face, the land set aside for the habitation of Europeans. An unchangeable law prohibits Celestials from crossing into this sacred precinct, because of the hatred they cherish for Europeans. Shameen is green and picturesque, with handsome houses of Oriental design, and grand shade trees, and wide, velvety green roads, broken only by a single path, made by the bare feet of the chair-carriers....
What a different picture Canton presents to Shameen. They say there are millions of people in Canton. The streets, many of which are roughly paved with stone, seem little over a yard in width. The shops, with their gaily colored and handsomely carved signs, are all open, as if the whole end facing the street had been blown out. In the rear of every shop is an altar, gay in color and often expensive in adornment. As we were carried along the roads we could see not only the usually rich and enticing wares, but the sellers and buyers. Every shop has a bookkeeper's desk near the entrance. The bookkeepers all wear tortoise-shell rimmed glasses of an enormous size, which lend them a look of tremendous wisdom.'

Bly's tour of Canton followed much the same lines as Bertie's, including the execution ground. Perhaps, with an object of providing a more dramatic story for her newspaper article, she dwelled at length on the gruesome practises for the punishment and execution of miscreants and she tipped her guide so he would show her one of the decapitated heads which were stored in barrels filled with lime. She also insisted on being shown the leper village and described the misery and degradation of the inmates and was shocked to hear they grew vegetables which were sold in the general markets.

Her tour concluded with lunch:
'As we left the leper city I was conscious of an inward feeling of emptiness. It was Christmas day, and I thought with regret of dinner at home. The guide , Ah Cum said there was a building near-by he wanted to show us and then we could eat our luncheon. Once within the high wall we came upon a pretty scene. There was a mournful sheet of water undisturbed by a breath of wind. In the background the branches of low, overhanging trees kissed the still water just where stood some long legged storks, made so familiar to us by pictures on Chinese fans.

Ah Cum led us to a room which was shut off from the court by a large carved gate. Inside were hard wooden chairs and tables. While eating I heard chanting to the weird, plaintive sound of tom-toms and a shrill pipe. When I had less appetite and more curiosity, I asked Ah Cum where we were, and he replied "in the Temple of the Dead."

And in the Temple of the Dead I was eating my Christmas luncheon. But it did not interfere with the luncheon.'

After her eventful day in Canton, Bly returned to the ferry boat and retired to her cabin suffering from a sick-headache and travelled back to Hong Kong, to continue on her race round the world.

While Bly spent Christmas, 1889 in Canton, her rival, Miss Bisland was at sea travelling westward on the *Thames*. She wrote of the experience:

'It is Christmas Day – Still very hot: and off to our right are to be seen from time to time the bold purple outlines of the coasts of Sumatra. The ship is decorated with much variegated bunting, and the servants assume an air of languid festivity; but most of us suffer from plaintive reminiscences of home and nostalgia. There is a splendid plum-cake for dinner, with a Santa Claus atop, huddled in sugar furs despite the burning heat. We pull Christmas crackers, as in the holidays at home, and from their contents I am loaded with paste jewels and profusely provided with poetry in brief segments and of an enthusiastically amatory nature.'

Bertie decided to visit Macau on the way back to Hong Kong. The ferry boat, *Kiangtung* was operated by the China Merchants Steam Navigation Co (CMSNCo.) This was formed in 1872 to be a Chinese steam shipping company to challenge the foreign monopoly in steam ships in the area). She was built by the Shanghai SN Co in Shanghai in 1871 under the name of *Honan*, then sold and renamed *Kiangtung* by CMSNCo in 1877. She met her end when she was burned out in 1922.

24th March 1897   On board the Kiang Tung
Caught the boat at 8am for Macao. Scenery very fine on the way down the river. Arrived at 4pm & was met by a Portuguese from the " Bon Vista" hotel.   He took us round the place in a rickshaw before dinner. Old

Jesuit church, spinning silk, & boundary between Portuguese and Chinese territory, & the place where the governor was killed. Met Fell again here. In the evening we went to a gambling house where they played "fatsan."

Fantan is a game of chance where the middle of the table is marked into a square with each side numbered one, two, three and four. The dealer [tan kun] places a large handful of beans, counters, or other small objects into the square which are covered by a metal bowl. [tan koi]. The players then bet on one of the numbers. The dealer removes the beans four at a time with a small bamboo rod, until either, one, two, three, or four are left. The winner is the person who has chosen the right number of the last beans remaining. Fantan used to be a popular ancient Chinese gambling game and there were numerous Fantan houses in Macau. It was also exported by the Chinese immigrants to the US where many illegal Fantan houses were established. It gradually became less popular as it was replaced by other casino games.

Gamblers playing fantan - photo from Bertie's album

Macau in 1897 was a Portuguese colony. The first European to arrive there was Jorges Alvares, a Portuguese merchant seaman in 1513 and they set up a trading post. Macau is claimed to be the first port in the Far East to be settled by Europeans. In addition to the merchants, the Jesuit missionaries came to Macau. They built churches, established schools and endeavoured to convert the local Chinese people to Christianity. The Portuguese managed to maintain a thriving trading post, in spite of attempts by the Dutch and other traders, to raid and usurp the Portuguese monopoly of the area. There was also an uneasy relationship between the Portuguese colony and China with revolts by the Chinese inhabitants. This came to a head in 1849 when the Governor was assassinated.

When the British established themselves at Hong Kong in 1841, its thriving port impacted adversely on Macau's trade. In order to increase the revenue coming to Macau, the Portuguese government made it a free port and also, made gambling legal. This move did increase prosperity, but also led to a rise in various illegal activities. Macau became an official Portuguese colony in 1887, but was handed back to the People's Republic of China in 1999.

The Bel Vista Hotel, (or Boa, or Bella Vista) where Bertie stayed, was originally built as a residence in 1870 for a rich trader. It was then purchased by an English sea captain, William Clarke and his wife. They turned it into a hotel in 1890, but later ran into financial difficulties. Over the years it had several different uses, but in 1988 it was again a smart hotel and was used as a location during a TV film version of *Round the World in 80 Days* starring Peter Ustinov and Pierce Brosnan. When Macau was returned to the Chinese government, this historic building became the official residence of the Portuguese Consul General.

Macau - from Bertie's album

135

25th March 1897   Hong Kong
Caught the steamer "Heung Shan" at 8am for Hong Kong (3 ½ hours.)
Tried to go to the station for Victoria Peak, but our rickshaw coolies
misunderstood us & took us round the town.

The *Heung Shan* like the *Fatshan*, was owned by Hong Kong, Canton and Macau Steamship Co. Ltd.   This ship was built by Ramage and Ferguson at Leith in 1889, and during her long career was wrecked twice, once in a typhoon and again when she hit a rock in foggy conditions below Canton. She also had several different owners, operating in various waters. The old ship met her end when she was stranded and sunk in the Yangtze River in 1948.

27th March 1897 On board the Verona

Verona was another P&O ship. She was built by Caird and Co Ltd at Greenock in 1879 and used mostly on the London to Bombay and other Far East ports service. She could accommodate 130 first class and 54 second class passengers. She also had space for 3,754 cubic metres of cargo. The ship was eventually sold to a Dutch firm, which took her to Rotterdam where she was broken up in 1899. Bertie did not have much to say about the journey from Hong Kong to Nagasaki, but at least there is no mention of sea-sickness.

The Verona - (from Ian Farquhar collection)

Hong Kong to Nagasaki
Foggy

Verona 28/3/97
Foggy in the morning

Verona 29/3/97
Foggy in the morning

While Bertie had an uneventful passage through the mists of the East China Sea, Miss Bly, travelling along the same route on SS Oceanic, had a much livelier time. She wrote:

I spent New Year's Eve between Hong Kong and Yokohama.... In the forepart of the evening the passengers sat together in the Social Hall talking, telling stories and laughing at them. The captain owned an organette which he brought intp the hall, and he and the doctor took turns in grinding out the music. Later in the evening we went to the dining-hall where the purser had punch and champagne and oysters for us, a rare treat which he had prepared in America just for this occasion.

When eight bells rang we rose and sang Auld Lang Syne with glasses in hand, and on the last echo of the good old song, toasted the death of the old year and the birth of the new.

Verona was travelling in a northerly direction, and as they approached Japan the temperature would have become noticeably cooler. Early spring time in Japan is cold and wet, so warm clothes, good boots and an umbrella were recommended in Bertie's guide book.

Bertie decided to disembark at Nagasaki, instead of carrying on to Kobe, as originally planned. He spent seven happy weeks exploring the fascinating country of Japan.

Chapter Seven

Japan

Obama - from Bertie's album

During his time in Japan, Bertie used as his guide, a book entitled *A Handbook for Travellers in Japan including the whole Empire from Saghalien to Formosa*, written by Basil H. Chamberlain and W. B. Mason, and published by John Murray.

John Murray Publishing was a remarkable family firm. It was started in 1768 by a Scottish ex-marine, named John MacMurray. He changed his name to John Murray and set up as a book seller and publisher in London. His son John Murray II continued the business and became highly successful. He published books by such authors as Jane Austen, Sir Walter Scott, Charles Darwin and also Lord Byron, whose work, *Childe Harold's Pilgrimage* sold out in five days. Byron also entrusted Murray with the manuscript of his memoirs planning to have them published at a later date, but Murray was so shocked by their scandalous content, that he burned them!

The firm continued for several more generations, until the seventh John Murray sold it to Hodder Headlines in 2002.

Murray's *Handbooks for Travellers* first appeared in 1836. They were published first by John Murray II, and initially, they only covered the British Isles and the European Continent. As Victorian travellers ventured further afield, books were produced to include the

Middle East and Asia. These comprehensive guide books gave information on places of interest, hotels, transportation, costs, the history and culture of the country and many helpful hints. There were also maps and illustrations and suggested itineraries. Murray's Handbooks were really the fore-runners of modern day travel guide books.

Some useful hints in the introduction to *Handbook for Travellers in Japan* were:

'Custom-House – Strict examination of the luggage of passengers is made at the Custom-House, and the best way to avoid trouble and delay is to open up everything freely. Tobacco, liquors, cameras, bicycles, sporting gear, and most other articles, except ordinary personal effects are liable to duty.

Guides – Licensed guides understanding English can be engaged at any of the principle hotels in Tokyo, Yokohama, Kyoto and Kobe. The charge …is 4 yen per day for a party of one or two tourists, and 50 sen more for each additional person. In all cases the guides's travelling and hotel expenses must be paid by his employer. A guide is almost a necessity to persons unacquainted with the language, unless they are expert travellers.

Inns – The hostelries at which travellers in Japan put up are of three kinds – The European hotel, the Eurpeanised or half-European half-Japanese hotel (hoteru), and the purely native inn (yadoya). …. Many inns now provide chairs and tables. Beds are still very rare; but good quilts (futon) are laid down on the mats, wherever may be most convenient; pillows of sorts are now common, or else a small quilt will be rolled up as a pillow…. It is but fair that foreigners should pay more than natives, both for accommodation and for jinrikishas. They usually weigh more and they give infinitely more trouble at an inn with their demands for fresh water in the bath, the occupation of a portion of the kitchen to cook their European food, and a dozen other such requirements, to say nothing of their insisting on having separate rooms, while Japanese guests – even strangers to one another – are habitually required to share a room between them.

Provisions – Except at some of the larger towns, … meat, bread, and other forms of European food are scarce. Even fowls are rarely obtainable; for though plenty may be seen in almost every village, the people object to selling them – partly because they keep them for the sake of their eggs, partly on account of a lingering Buddhist dislike of taking life. Those, therefore, who cannot subsist on the native fare of rice, eggs, and fish, should carry their own supplies with them. … Many who view Japanese food hopefully from a distance, have found their spirits sink and their tempers embittered when brought face to face with its unsatisfying actuality.

Means of Locomotion; Luggage – Take railway or electric tramways wherever available. … Europeans usually avail themselves of the first-class railway cars whenever such are provided, ladies in particular are recommended to do so. … On those plains which no railway yet traverse, take jinrikisha. Avoid the native 'basha' (carriage), if you have either nerves to shatter or bones to shake; and be chary of burdening yourself with a horse and saddle of your own in the interior, as all sorts of troubles are apt to arise with regard to shoeing, run-away grooms (betto), etc…Other possible conveyances are pack- horses (but the Japanese pack-saddle is torture), cows, the 'kago' – a species of small palanquin, uncomfortable at first, but not disliked by many old residents – and lastly chairs borne by four coolies …The pleasantest sort of trip for a healthy man is that in which walking and jinrikisha-riding is combined. In those hilly districts that make japan so picturesque, walking is the only possible, or at least the only pleasant, method of progression. The luggage is then taken on a pack-horse or on a coolie's back. … It is always best to avoid large boxes or portmanteaus, and to divide the luggage into two or three smaller pieces for convenience in piling on the coolie's hod, or for balancing the two sides of a pack horse's load. The Japanese wicker baskets called 'yanagi-gori' are much recommended.

Miscellaneous Hints – Never enter a Japanese house with your boots on. The mats take the place of our chairs and sofas. What would we say to a man who trod on our chairs and sofas in his dirty boots?

If going off the beaten tracks, take plenty of flea-powder or camphor; but those who do not mind the odour of oil-paper (abura-kami), will find sheets of it stretched over the quilts by far the best protection against fleas. Take soap, candles, and some disinfectant to counteract the unpleasant odours that often disturb the comfort of guests in Japanese inns.

Take visiting cards with you. Japanese with whom you become acquainted often desire to exchange cards.

Start early, and do not insist on travelling after dark. You will thus most easily obtain good coolies or horses for the day's journey. By arriving at your destination before sunset, you will be likely to find the bath as yet unused, and will thus avoid the trouble and delay entailed by the necessity of getting other water heated. You will also have a better choice of rooms.

Above all, be consistently polite and conciliatory in your demeanour towards people. Whereas the lower classes at home are apt to resent suave manners, and to imagine that he who addresses them politely wishes to deceive them or get something out of them, every Japanese, however humble, expects courtesy, being himself courteous. … Many travellers irritate the Japanese by talking and acting as if they thought Japan and her customs a sort of peep-show set up for foreigners to gape at. Others run counter to native custom, and nevertheless expect to get things at native prices. …Too many foreigners, we fear, give not only trouble and offence, but just cause for indignation, by their disregard of propriety, especially in their behaviour towards Japanese women, whose engaging manners and naive ways they misinterpret. The subject is too delicate to be treated here. We may, however, be permitted to remark in passing that the waitresses at any respectable Japanese inn deserve the same respectful treatment as is accorded to girls in a similar position at home. Never show any impatience. You will only get stared at or laughed at behind your back, and matters will not move any quicker in this land where an hour more or less is of no account. … Storming will not mend matters….Neither be moved to anger because you are asked personal questions by casual acquaintances. To ask such questions is the Far-Eastern way of showing kindly interest.'

As more shipping lines provided regular services to Japan and more comfortable 'Western' style hotels were developed, the country became the 'in place' to visit for increasing numbers of people. These often travelled in large groups, which scurried around the main tourist attractions. In about 1870, for the first time the term 'Globetrotter' was used in a derogatory way to describe the types of tourists who flocked to Japan and showed an arrogant disrespect for the culture of the people.

Scidmore, the American travel writer, lived for some years in Japan with her brother who was a member of the American consular staff. She wrote in her book, *Jinricksha Days in Japan:*

'In the increasing swarm of tourists some prince, duke, or celebrity is ever arriving, visitors of lesser note are countless, and the European dwellers in all Asiatic ports east of Singapore make Japan their pleasure-ground, summer resort, and sanatorium. That order of tourist known as the "globe-trotter," is not a welcome apparition to the permanent foreign resident. His generous and refined hospitality has been so often abused, and its recipients so often show a half contemptuous condescension to their remote and uncomprehending hosts, that letters of introduction are looked upon with dread.'

Armed with all the useful information in John Murray's *"Handbook for Travellers in Japan"* Bertie was ready for the next section of his journey.

His journal reads:

Nagasaki 30/3/97
" We arrived at 11.30. I decided at the last moment to land here with Dr. Otto Seitz. We slept at the "Belle Vue." We saw some temples in the morning & got a good view of the town from a hill. In the evening we went to see the Geishas. (10 dollars)

Nagasaki had a long history of contact with foreigners because it has a very good harbour and is conveniently situated at the southern end of Japan. The Portuguese traders were the first European arrivals in the sixteenth century who were accompanied by Jesuit missionaries, led by St Francis Xavier. For many years the Japanese government forbade trade with outsiders, but by 1859 this was somewhat relaxed and Nagasaki was declared a free port. In 1889 it was officially proclaimed a city, and by 1897 Nagasaki was one of Japan's major centres of Industry, particularly ship building. Mitsubishi Heavy Industry was based there.

Bertie's guide book, *Murray's Handbook for Travellers in Japan* mentioned three hotels in Nagasaki; the Nagasaki Hotel, Bellevue Hotel and Cliff House. It also stated that:

'Nagasaki is noted for a delicious kind of jelly (kin-gyoku-to) made from seaweed. The fish market has the reputation of being one of three which show the greatest variety of fish in the world. A notable feature of the harbour is the coaling of steamers by gangs of young girls, who pass small baskets from hand to hand with amazing rapidity. One of the "Empress" steamers has had 1,210 tons of coal put on board in this way in 3 ½ hours which as at a rate of 372 tons per hour!'

Scidmore visited Nagasaki several times, but in 1885 when her ship docked in port, there was a cholera epidemic in the town and passengers were confined to the vessel. They had ample time to admire the scenic views and witness the coaling operations alluded to in the guide book. She wrote:

'As travel increases, the harbor of Nagasaki will be everywhere known as one of the most picturesque in the world. Green mountains, terraced and wooded to their very summits, have parted far enough to let an arm of the sea cleave its way inland, and chains of islands with precipitous shores guard the entrance of the tortuous reach. The town seems to have run down from the ravines and spread itself out at the end of the inlet, and the temples, tea-houses, and the villas of foreign residents cling to the hill-side and dot the groves on the heights....

On our way to China we touched at Nagasaki while the epidemic was at its height, so no passenger was allowed to go ashore, and all day we kept to the decks that were saturated with carbolic acid. It took six hours to coal the ship, and from noon to sundown we beheld a water carnival. As the first coal-barge drew near, a man in the airy summer costume of the harbor country – which consisted of a rope round his waist – jumped over the side and swam to the stern of our steamer. He was like a big brown frog kicking about in the water, and when he came dripping up the gang-way the faithful steward gave him a carbolic spraying with his bucket and brush. The barge was hauled up alongside and made fast, and our consignment of coal was passed on board in half-bushel baskets from hand to hand along a line of chanting men and women. Nothing more primitive could be imagined, for, with block, tackle, windlass, steam, and donkey engine on board, it took a hundred pairs of hands to do their work. At the end of each hour there was a breathing spell. Many of the women were young and pretty, and some of them had brought their children, who, throwing back the empty baskets and helping to pass them along the line, thus began their lives of toil and earned a few pennies. The passengers threw to the children all the small Japanese coins they possessed, and when the ship swung loose and started away their cheerful little sayonaras rang after us.'

When Bertie and his friend Dr Otto Seitz arrived at Nagasaki, they spent their first night in Japan at the Bellevue hotel. In 1897, the proprietor was a French lady, Mme Hammand who was the widow of the previous owner. The establishment was first opened in 1863 by Mathew and Mary Green and was considered one of the best in Nagasaki. It had several owners over the years, but the hotel closed down in 1920.

31st March 1897   Onsen (Unzen)
We started at 11 am for Moji where we had lunch. (A lovely spot) We then went on a Japanese steamer to Obama where we saw hot mineral spring baths with plenty of natives in them, male and female together. I counted 8 in one small round bath. From here we walked to Onsen, (7 miles.) We got there at 8pm, had a sulphur bath & dinner at 9pm.

Onsen, [Unze] according to Bertie's guide book:

'Consisted of three hamlets where there are three hotels and several good Japanese inns with

142

private baths and even European furniture. This remarkable spot, 2,550 ft. above the sea, noted for its sulphur springs, its varied and beautiful scenery, and its bracing air, has become a sanatorium, not only for Nagasaki and neighbourhood, but also for the residents of the China treaty ports.'

Onsen - photo from Bertie's album

1st April 1897   Shimbara (Shimabara)
It was raining, but we started to walk to Shimbara from Onsen. (13 miles) & got a good soaking. Got there at 4pm, changed our things, (while the females looked on). Dr Otto putting on a "Kimono" & then we went to the bath where the landlady scrubbed us down.   Somebody snored in the next room. I felt inclined to throw my boot through the partition.

Kumamoto 2/4/97
We left Shimbara at 11 am after a short walk to a well (very clean water & fish in it.) We bought some Japanese pipes (without the help of our guide) & gave too much.

We got on a small steamer which was full of pilgrims. At first it was calm, but before we got over it was rather rough. We had to land in a sampan & the beastly pilgrims swarmed into it. We went broadside to the waves & were almost upset. Rickshaws came into the sea to meet us.

Lunch at the teahouse & then ½ hour train to Kumamoto.

The construction of railways in Japan had been delayed, because the country had been ruled by the Tokugawa Shogunate for 260 years. Their policy was one of strict isolationism and resistance to modern Western technologies. The Meiji government came to power in 1868 and was more willing to consider change.

Prior to the introduction of railways, goods in Japan had been transported around the country mainly by ships around the coasts and on rivers, or on pack-horses, or even on the backs of men. The roads and bridges over rivers were not developed enough for carriages or wagons.

Many people had suggested that Japan would benefit from railways, particularly between the ports and large cities, but the Japanese government was reluctant until 1869. Sir Harry Parkes, the British Ambassador, finally persuaded them to begin the construction of a railway line between Tokyo and Yokohama, a distance of twenty-nine miles. In 1871 a shipment of ten tank locomotives and fifty-eight passenger carriages arrived from Britain. The opening ceremony of the first railway service was attended by the Japanese Emperor and many other dignitaries on 14 October 1872.

After this, many more lines were constructed to other cities, and by the time of Bertie's visit in 1897, there was an extensive network of railway lines connecting the major towns.

Saturday 3rd April 1897   Kumamoto
We went in the morning to see a temple, also a Japanese garden. I saw a very pretty gateway, circular with a square centre. The roads are in a frightful state. In the afternoon we went to a theatre, revolving stage like a turntable on a railway. The Jap play starts between 10 & 12 & lasts till 12 at night. Frequent intervals, & everyone brings refreshments. Kumamoto is a large garrison town.

In 1897 Japan was a rising military power and was developing a strong army and navy. In 1894-1895 they had fought a successful war against China over the control of Korea. This resulted in the ceding of the island of Taiwan to Japan. There was also conflict looming between Japan and imperial Russia which would culminate into the 1904 Russo-Japanese war. Much to everyone's surprise, this resulted in a resounding defeat of Russia. In the 1920's and 1930's the brutal second Sino-Japanese war took place resulting from Japan's desire to expand her empire.

Bertie and his travelling companions were more interested in the culture and beauty of Japan, than its military aspirations.

4th April 1897   Moji
Fine. We started by train at 9.40 for Moji where we intended to get a

Japanese steamer to Hiroshima. Moji is a wretched & most uninteresting place. Birds at present have been very scarce.

5th April 1897   Japanese steamer on the inland sea
In the morning we went to Simonsaki & went on board the steamer at 3pm.

Miyajima & Hiroshima
We arrived at daylight at Miyajima & it is the most lovely place I have seen. The temple is large with some fine paintings by good artists. The maple is just coming out & the vistas about are beautiful. I bought a carved box and a tray & at 10am we left for Hiroshima.   There is not much to see here. The hotel is excellent. The rooms are very prettily decorated.   The little recess with "Kakamonoes," also a bronze with cherry blossom. The short trip from Miyajima here among the islands was excellent. Got rid of Miashta today (swindler) 18 dollars he demands for his return trip to Nagasaki. Bill at Hotel over 10 dollars.

(M 27)   (Three view in Japan) Miyajima Inland Sea Aki.   (内之景三本日) 安藝宮島

Miyajima Great Torii Gate old postcard

Murray's 'Handbook of Japan' says of Miyajima, sacred island:
'Many small, but lovely valleys trend down to the sea; and in these, among groves of maple trees, nestle the inns and tea-houses for pilgrims and the dwellings of the fishermen and image-carvers, who, with the priests and innkeepers make up the population of some thee thousand. Miyajima is a charming summer resort, the temperature being never unbearably high, the sea and fresh water bathing being excellent and the walks numerous…. A number of dear still linger on the island, and feed out of the hands of passer-by…. The temple of Miyajima enjoys great celebrity. The 'torii' in front of it which stands in the sea on piles is a favourite motive of Japanese art; and the temple itself, being partly built over the sea on piles, appears at high tide to float upon the surface of the water…. A characteristic of the temple is its gallery 648 ft. long hung with ex-votos. Many of these are old pictures by famous artists.'

Kakamono, or Kakejiku, are decorative scrolls designed to hang on the wall. They will have a painting or some calligraphy on paper set on a silk backing.   They are often displayed in a tokonoma alcove which may contain a complementary sculpture and flower arrangement to set the spiritual mood.

View overlooking Itsukushima Temple, Miyajima, Japan - from Bertie's album

7th April 1897   Japanese steamer Hiroshima to Kobe
Up at 6am. A ride to the boat in rickshaws. Lovely days but rather cold.
Had three meals on board (good), 3 bottles of beer & 6 of saki for $1.60
– The cheapest bill we have had yet.   Arrived at Kobe at 2am at night,
put our luggage on a barrow & wandered about trying to find the Oriental
hotel.

The Oriental Hotel was opened in 1870 by a Dutch Naval physician and later gained a reputation for superb cuisine when the proprietor was Monsieur Louis Begeux, a French chef. After he returned to France in 1890, the hotel's standards dropped, but M. Begeux's son, also named Louis, was persuaded to return and run the hotel. Judging by Bertie's entry in his journal, things had improved.

8th April 1897   Kobe
Breakfast 9am. This is a beautiful hotel. (French Management.)   Went
to the water fall in the afternoon with "Jasuda," our new guide.   Went
to see public gardens also some private ones.

As Murrays Hand-book says: '

The Nunobiki waterfalls are in two parts. The path first reaches Men-daki, or Female Fall, … then crossing a stone bridge, it climbs to tea houses which command a view of the upper, or Male Fall (On-daki). Ladies are advised only to visit Nunobiki only under the escort of gentlemen, as the tea houses are apt to be noisy'.

9th April 1897   Kobe & Kyoto
It was wet in the morning, but we went nevertheless to Hyogo (rickshaws)
where we saw a fine bronze Buddha. I saw some fine bronze lanterns.
Train in the afternoon to Kyoto. The scenery is not so fine as I expected.
Our little guide is very conceited & in appearance rather like Edgar Tidd.

This comparatively new Buddha is also described Murray's guide:

'The Daibatzu, or great bronze Buddha, at Hyogo is 48 feet high and was erected in 1891, owing to the zeal of a paper manufacturer named Nanjo Shobei. The visitor is taken into interior of the Buddha where there is an altar … and other Buddhist ornaments.'

10th April 1897   Kyoto

Scidmore wrote of Kyoto (Kioto) :
The sacred city, the capital and heart of old Japan, incomparable Kioto. We saw it in the sunset light, the western hills throwing purple shadows on their own slopes, and the long stretch of wheat-fields at their base turned into a lake of pure gold. The white walls of the Shogun's castle,

147

the broad roof of the old palace, and the ridges of temples rose above the low grey plain house roofs and held the sun's last level beams.

View of Kyoto, Japan - photo from Bertie's album

After the imitations and tawdriness of modern Tokio, the unchanged aspect of the old capital is full of dignity. After many long stays in spring-time, midsummer, and midwinter, Kioto has always remained to me foremost of Japanese cities.

Went for a trip to Otsu & then to Karasaki (Lake Biwa) where we saw a very large fir tree. Lunch at Otsu & then back to Kyoto in our rickshaws. Visited Nanikawa & bought one piece of cloisonne. Also went to Ikada where I bought a few things.

The pine tree at Karasaki is famous for its immense size and age and is considered sacred. Scidmore wrote of it:

'The greatest sight of Biwa, and one of the wonders of Japan, is the old pine-tree of Karasaki. Which has stood for three hundred years on a little headland a couple of miles above Otsu, with a tiny village and a Shinto temple all its own. Its trunk is over four feet in diameter, and, at a height of fifteen feet, its boughs are trained laterally and supported by posts, so it looks like a banyan tree. The branches, twisted, bent, and looped like writhing dragons, cover more than an acre of ground with their canopy.

The tips of the boughs reach far out over the water, and the sensitive Japanese hear a peculiar music in the sifting of the rain-drops through the foliage into the lake. High in the tree is a tiny shrine, and the pilgrims clap their hands and stand with clasped palms, turning their faces upwards as they pray. Under the branches a legion of small villagers, intimating by pantomime their desire to dive for pennies, untied their belts and dropped their solitary cotton garments as unconcernedly as one might take off hat or gloves. They frolicked and capered in the water as much at home as fishes and as loath to leave it.'

11th April 1897   Kyoto
Went to see temples in the morning. In one Chion-in there are fine paintings by the Kano family. In the afternoon I went to a lacquer shop & saw them making it. He also sold curios, but I bought nothing. I bought a Kimono and obis for Kathleen.

The Kimono is well known as the elegant Japanese gown with wide sleeves. An Obi is the sash worn with the Kimono. An obi worn by a woman is made wide and often ornamented with beautiful embroidery.

Kyoto 12/4/97
More temples, one very fine new one. Shopping in the afternoon. I bought a cut velvet picture of quail.

While in Kyoto, Bertie stayed at the Yaami hotel, one of the major hotels in Kyoto, founded in 1879 and which was also a favourite of Eliza Scidmore.

'Yaamis, the foreigner's Kioto home, with its steep terraced gardens, its dwarf-pine and blooming monkey-tree, its many buildings at different levels, its flitting figures on the outer galleries, is like no other hostelry. Yaami, proprietor of this picturesque hotel, is a personage indeed. He and his brother were professional guides until they made their fortunes. Their shrewd eyes saw further fortunes in a Kioto inn, where foreigners might find beds, chairs, tables, knives, forks, and foreign food, and they secured the old Ichiriki tea-house midway on the slope of Maruyama, the mountain walling Kioto on the east. …With it was bought an adjoining monastery, belonging to one of the temples on Mount Hiyeizan, and these two original buildings have expanded and risen story upon story, with detached wings here and there, until the group of tall white buildings, with the white flag floating high up in the midst of Maruyama's foliage, is quite castle-like…. In parts of the house you find relics of monastery days in dim old screens of fine workmanship, and there is a stone-floored kitchen with cooks serious as priests, wielding strange sacrificial knives, and who, in mid-summer, wear an apron only, apparently as a professional badge rather than a garment.

13th April 1897   Kyoto
Yaami Hotel. A glorious day. We started at 9 for the rapids (13 Miles). Half-way by rickshaw & then we walked the guide off his legs. Coming down the rapids was glorious, many cherry trees in flower & the maples

just coming out. Lunch at a large Japanese tea house at the bottom of the rapids.

Kyoto, showing the Yaami Hotel - photo from Bertie's album

According to Murray's Hand Book:

'Katsugama rapids are famed for cherry-blossoms and autumn tints. This expedition makes a pleasing variety in the midst of days spent visiting temples. ...The Rapids commence about 10 min below Hozu, ... the scenery is charming, the river at once enters the hills which rise precipitously on either hand, and continuing between them for about 13 miles to Arashi-yama. There are several good tea-houses at the landing stage.'

These rapids on the Hotsu-gawa river were originally used to transport timber for firewood, or to be used for building the cities downstream. The boats also transported rice, wheat and other farm produce. In the nineteenth century railways were constructed, so the need for river transport of goods declined, but the boatmen found they could make a good living by using their crafts to transport tourists instead.

Bertie was obviously having the time of his life when he wrote this enthusiastic letter to his sister, Kathleen:

Hotsu-gawa River rapids, Japan. Old postcard

Yaami Hotel
Kyoto
Japan
April 13th

Dear Kathleen,
I am having a rare time & enjoying myself thoroughly. It is still very cold here.

This hotel stands in a lovely situation high up on a hill, & from my balcony I get a splendid view of Kyoto. This is a lovely spot and the cherry blossom in
some places near is beautiful. I believe that there is very little fruit on the Japanese cherry. They grow it entirely for the flower. I am still travelling with Dr Otto & will probably do all of Japan with him. We had splendid weather while we were in the Inland sea. We went halfway in a Jap steamer with our guide from Nagasaki to a place called Hiroshima, visiting an island on the way, (Miyajima,) the most lovely place I have ever been in. At this place we sacked our guide, with whom we were disgusted – he had been robbing us all the way along. We were entirely in his hands as we could not speak Japanese & saw no Europeans during our trip. He used to buy the provisions for us and cook them – as an instance he

151

told us that he had to pay 2 dollars (4 shillings) for chickens.

From Hiroshima we came on to Kobe in another Japanese steamer by ourselves, arriving at 2 o'clock at night. We put our luggage on a truck & told the coolies to go to the Oriental Hotel. They took us to the most filthy Japanese hotel to start with, then we wandered about for three quarters of an hour before we found the one we wanted. There was not much to see in Kobe. We engaged another guide & came on to Kyoto, where we are staying for 10 days. This guide is like Edgar Tidd, on a very small scale, thinks too much of himself & has got a vile temper; he is a lazy as they make them, & always wants to ride in a rickshaw. We shall get rid of him as soon as we can & travel without one.

Today we have been for a lovely excursion. – 16 miles rickshaw & walking & then for one hour and a half, we came down some rapids in a boat amongst the most lovely scenery; it was very exiting at times & lots of water came into the boat. We had three men guiding the boat & they did it in grand style.

This trip would suit the Mater! This is the place where you can buy everything. I spent a whole afternoon in a second hand silk shop, with hundreds of "kimonos" & "obis" round me, choosing a costume for You. I think I have got a fairly good one. Some ladies at the hotel, (to whom I showed it,) say I have shown great taste. I also bought a lovely piece of embroidery. In the second hand curio shops I have also bought a lot of small things, a Japanese clock for Claude, amongst others. I could spend lots of money here if I bought everything I liked. One Englishman staying at this hotel spent 5,000 dollars (800 pounds) at one shop in one day.

Some of the Japanese costumes would make you laugh. They seem very fond of antiquated European hats & often you see one got up in the best Japanese style with a hat like an English poacher. One day I saw one in a topper which I am sure was 100 years old. I have seen the cherry dance here which is a great show. About 50 geishas perform. It is certainly very pretty.

There are 1000 temples in this town. I have seen a few of the best & do not intend to see any more. I thought when I saw 500 Buddha's in one temple at Canton, I should not see so many again, but here in one temple we visited yesterday there were 33,333 of some god, (life size)made of wood covered over with gold lacquer.

What I like at all these temples are the beautiful bronze lanterns of all shapes & sizes. I visited the shop here where they make the best cloisonne in Japan. We saw them making it & bought a small piece. The camellia trees grow to a great size here & are just now in full flower, also the magnolias & the wisteria will be out before I leave the island. I am not quite sure when I shall leave Japan, perhaps in the steamer "Peru" which starts on 13th May for Honolulu, where I many stay a week before going on to San Francisco. I shan't stay long in America.

Hoping that you are all well at home. I have had no letters for a long time now.

With best love to all, from your affect. Brother,   Bertie

૪૦૦૩

14th April 1897   Kyoto
Went to Nara by train & saw some lovely temples & hundreds of beautiful stone lanterns.   There were some grand old "Cryptomerias" in the park & lots of deer. We saw a sacred dance also a big bell & large bronze Buddha. In the afternoon we went to Osaka where we saw the castle with a fine wall on the moat.

Scidmore in her more poetic style, wrote of Nara:

'Nara! A mountain-side covered with giant trees bound together by vines and old creepers; an ancient forest seamed with broad avenues, where the sun-light falls in patches and deer lie drowsing in the fern; double and triple lines of moss-covered stone lanterns massing themselves together, their green tops dim in the dense shadow; temples twelve centuries old; the booming bells, and the music of running water.

Nara! The ancient capital, the cradle of Buddhism, and still a holy place of pilgrimages; its forest paths echoing the jingle of the devotees' ringed staffs, the mutter of their prayers, and the chink of their copper offerings at the temple gates. A place of stillness and dreams; an Arcadia, where the little children and the fawns play together, and the antlered deer eat from one's hand, and look up fearlessly with their soft human eyes. Old Shinto temples, where the priestesses dance the sacred measures of Suzume before the sun Goddess's cave; temple where Buddha and Kwannon sit in gilded glory on the lotus, and lights, incense, and bells accompany the splendid ceremonies of that faith....
The atmosphere of Nara is serene and gentle – the true atmosphere of Japan.

Cryptomeria trees are also called Japanese cedar, or in Japan, Sugi. They are a handsome variety of cedar tree native to Japan, but grown in many other parts of the world in gardens and forestry. In Japan, these trees have religious significance and are often planted around temples or shrines. They can live to a great age and grow up to seventy metres high. The *Cryptomeria* is the national tree of Japan.

15th April 1897   Kyoto
Went to the exhibition in the morning. I bought 3 fans, also bronze trays for 5 cents.

16th April 1897   Kyoto
More temples and Mikado Palace. Walked about in the afternoon. We are getting rid of our guide & do not intend to have another.

17th April 1897   Shizuoka
We left Kyoto by the early train 7.58. Met Mr. Raspe in the train. We saw the town with him in the evening.

18th April 1897   Miyanoshita Sunday, Easter day
We caught the 8.9 train to Gotemba & walked from there over the mountains to Miyanoshita. Raspe is fat & could not go fast uphill. We started before the coolies with our luggage, & went the wrong way. We did not get a good view of Fuji. The hotel (Fujiya) is full, mostly people from Yokohama.

After spending some years in the USA where he had been a Japanese delegate, Mr Sennosuke Yamaguchi returned to Japan and founded the Fujiya Hotel in 1878. He was determined to create a high class European style hotel in the Hakone area. The hotel was destroyed by fire in 1883, but was later re-built and enlarged. It remained under Yamaguchi family management for several generations. Over the years this beautiful hotel has been patronised by Royalty, and other notable people. After the Second World War, the hotel was taken over by the US occupying army and used for a Rest and Recreation centre until 1954. It still operates as a high class hotel, re-named Yumoto Fujiya and offering hot springs and luxurious accommodation.

In Murray's *Handbook for Travellers in Japan* that Bertie was consulting, it reports that:
'The Fujiya Hotel is a pleasant resort for many reasons – the purity of the air, the excellence of the hotel accommodation, the numerous pretty walks both short and long, the plentiful supply of "chairs" and of specially large and comfortable 'kagos' for those who prefer being carried, and the delicious hot baths, which containing but faint traces of salt and soda, may be used without medical supervision.'

Mr Basil H. Chamberlain, Emeritus Professor of Japanese and Philology at the Imperial

University of Tokyo, and one of the co-authors of the *Handbook,* must have really liked this hotel. So much so, that he took up residence there in 1891, and remained for the next 20 years.

The 'kago' referred to was a kind of reclining chair suspended from two long bamboo poles. These were placed on the shoulders of two coolies who carried the passenger in the chair. For longer trips, there were four coolies who would take turns.

19th April 1897   Miyanoshita
Rained the whole day and we did not go out.

20th April 1897   Atami
We walked to Atami having lunch on the way at Hakone, where we got a fair view of Fuji. We also had a good view of it from the hills. 16 miles to Atami. There are some lovely camphor trees just before you get to the village. Mr Hughes from Hong Kong also came today.

21st April 1897   Atami
A glorious day. We went to the top of the hill where a man is stationed to watch for fish. I went down to some small caves. In the afternoon I walked with Hughes along the road to Odawarra & came back with the switchback train. I see plenty of familiar wild flowers about, alder, dandelion, potentilla, milk thistle.

Between 1886 and 1898, the 'Switch Back train,' also known as Zusho Jinsha (Human Railway), ran between Atami and Odawara, a distance of 25 kms. The journey took four hours. It consisted of an eight-seater carriage which was powered by three men. They had to push the carriage up hills and on the flat, but when the track ran downwards, they would jump on board and operate the brake. Sometimes the train would get out of control and accidents occurred. It was considered a somewhat hazardous form of locomotion, so in 1898, steam engines were introduced.

22nd April 1897   Enoshima
We left Atami in the switchback for Odawara (4 hours,) then on to Kotsu, then by train to Fujisawa, then rickshaw to Enoshima. Japanese hotel. We had shell fish, (I kept the shells,) fish soup, hard boiled eggs, & rice. We slept on the floor. We borrowed kimonos & the " nesan" helped us on with them.

Scidmore described Enoshima as the '*Mont St. Michel of the Japanese coast*' and wrote:

'*Enoshima is an island at high tide, rising precipitously from the sea on all sides save to the landward, where the precipice front is cleft with a deep wooded ravine, that runs out into a long tongue of sand connecting with the shore at low tide. ...Enoshima's crest is a very Forest of Arden, and enchanted place of lovely shade. The sloping ravine which gives access to it holds only one street, or foot-path, lined with tea-houses and shell shops, all a-flutter with pilgrim flags, toys, ornaments, and banners. The fish dinners of Enoshima are famous, and the Japanese, who have the genius of cookery, provide more delicious fish dishes than can be named. At the many tateba set up in temple yards or balanced on the edges of precipices, conch-shells, filled with a black stew like terrapin simmer over charcoal fires. This concoction has a tempting smell, and the pilgrims, who pick at the inky morsels with their chopsticks, seem to enjoy it; but in the estimation of the foreigner it adds one more to the list of glutinous insipid preparations with which the Japanese cuisine abounds.'*

Friday 23rd April 1897   Kamakura/Yokohama
We got up early at Enoshima & went round the island. We had a splendid view of Fuji. We also gave 10 cents to see men dive into the sea for shells. - I believe they took them down with them into the water. There are plenty of shells for sale, but I saw no good ones. Went to Kamakura & saw Daibutsu. Had lunch at Kaihin in the Hotel. Scenery about rather like Bournmouth. In the afternoon, on to Yokohama. What a contrast! Dinner at the Grand Hotel, & Enoshima last night.

The Kamakura 'Daibutsu' is one of Japan's most famous colossal bronze statues of Buddha. It was originally housed in a temple but since 1495, has sat out in the open with a flight of steps going up to it. Murray's 'Handbook' said of it:

'No other gives such an impression of majesty, or so truly symbolises the central idea of Buddhism. The spiritual peace which comes from perfect knowledge and subjugation of all passion.'

This Daibutsu is thought to have been created in AD 1252, at a time when Kamakura was a major city in Japan. According to Scidmore, she had been told Kamakura had been the military capital of Japan in the Middle Ages and had once had a population of five hundred thousand. She was awed by the Daibutsu, but saddened by its state when she visited it:

'The light of Asia is seated on the lotus flower, his head bent forward in meditation, his thumbs joined, and his face wearing an expression of the most benignant calm. This is one of the few great show-pieces in Japan that is badly placed and lacks a proper approach. ... through an atmosphere thick with incense may be read the chalked names of ambitious tourists, who have evaded the priests and left their signatures on the irregular bronze walls, An alloy of tin and a little gold is mingled with copper, and on the joined thumbs and hands, over which visitors climb to sit for their photographs, the bronze is polished enough to show its fine dark tint. The rest of the statue is dull and weather-stained, its rich incrustations disclosing the seams where the huge sections were welded together....During his six centuries of holy contemplation at Kamakura, Dai Butsu has endured many disasters. Earthquakes have made him nod and sway on the lotus pedestal, and tidal waves have twice swept over and destroyed the sheltering temple, the great weight and thickness of the bronze keeping the statue itself unharmed.'

Kamakura Great Daibutsu (statue of Buddha) Old postcard

Bly only spent one hundred and twenty hours in Japan, since her aim was to get around the world as quickly as possible and to produce some sensational stories along the way. She visited the Kamakura Daibutsu and wrote:

'I went to Kamakura to see the great bronze god, the image of Buddha, familiarly called Diabutsu. It stands in a verdant valley at the foot of two mountains. ...I had my photograph taken sitting on its thumb with two friends, one of whom offered $50,000 for the god. Years ago at the feast of the god sacrifices were made to the Diabutsu. Quite frequently the hollow interior would be heated to a white heat, and hundreds of victims were cast into the seething furnace in honor of the god.

It is sad to hear so little respect being shown for this peaceful and spiritual monument.

Rudyard Kipling, who visited Japan in 1892 wrote a long poem about the Kamakura Daibutsu which was published in his book *The Five Nations* in 1903. These three verses demonstrate the respect he felt for the Daibutsu:

> O ye who tread the Narrow way
> By Trophet-flare to Judgement day,
> Be gentle when the 'heathens' pray
> To Buddha at Kamakura ...
>
> A tourist-show, a legend told,
> A rusting bulk of bronze and gold,

157

So much, and scarce so much, ye hold
The meaning of Kamakura? …

But when the morning prayer is prayed,
Think, ere ye pass to strife and trade,
Is God in human image made
No nearer than Kamakura?

Bertie's journey continued with his arrival at Yokohama which was the main port for ships travelling to and from the USA. Scidmore described it as: not Oriental enough to be very picturesque. It is too European to be Japanese, and too Japanese to be European. The hotel, where he was to stay, was definitely at the European end of the spectrum.

Yokohama harbour with Steam ships. Old postcard

The Grand Hotel at Yokohama was indeed very grand and was considered to be the height of Western culture. It was very popular with American tourists and was where many famous people stayed while in Yokohama. It was opened on 11th August 1873, just after the railway line between Tokyo and Yokohama had been constructed and was situated conveniently close to the harbour and the city centre. The hotel was renowned for its beautiful, hand-decorated menus which were much admired by all the guests. Besides Bertie, both Nellie Bly and Rudyard Kipling stayed at the Grand. They both commented on the grandness of the hotel, though they did have some reservations about it.
In her account, Bly wrote:

'I stayed at the Grand Hotel while in Japan. It is a large building, with long verandas, wide halls and airy rooms, commanding an exquisite view of the lake in front. Barring an enormous and monotonous collection of rats, the Grand would be considered a good hotel even in America, The food is splendid and the service excellent.'

Rudyard Kipling does not seem to have found the service to have been excellent.

'They are fine and large at the Grand, and they don't always live up to their grandeur, unlimited electric bells, but no one in particular to answer 'em, printed menus, but the first comers eat all the nice things, and so forth. None the less, there are points about the Grand not to be despised. It is modelled on the American fashion, and is but an open door through which you may catch the first gust from the Pacific slope'.

Bisland was also a guest at the hotel, when she stayed there on arrival at Yokohama after travelling from San Francisco. She had never left the USA before, so she was filled with joyful anticipation.

'I move in a joyous dream. Can this be I? . . . I, to whom Japan had seemed as fair and vague as heaven – a place to which only the excessively virtuous and fortunate ever went? . . .And, lo! I, in the fullness of earthly imperfection, am permitted to see it! . . .

Mediaeval folk in blue stand about on the stone pier and welcome us with friendly smiles, and we charter their jinrickishas to take us to the hotel. Now, the jinrickisha is exactly the vehicle in which one would expect to ride in this land of fairy children – large perambulators that hold one person comfortably; but instead of being trundled from behind by a white-capped nursemaid, one of the Henry II gentlemen, who wears also straw sandals and an enormous blue mushroom hat on his head, ensconces himself between the little shafts in front and prances noiselessly away with it. He has legs as light and muscular as a thoroughbred horse, and can spin along with the 'rickisha at a rate of five miles an hour. He can, with a few intervals for rest keep this up all day; he will charge you seventy-five cents for the whole; he will not be winded at all, and will be in a gay and charming temper when the day is done. . . .

Our way lies along the Bund, a broad and handsome street on the water-front, with a fringe of slim pine-trees strange of outline as are those one is familiar with upon fans. Other jinrickishas are scampering about. Tonsured doll-babies in flowered gowns, such as one buys at home in Oriental shops, are walking about here alive, and flying queer-shaped kites, with a sort of unconscious elfishness befitting dwellers of fairyland. Two little Japanese ladies with pink cheeks, and black hair clasped with jade pins, toddle by on wooden pattens that clack pleasantly on the pavement. Their kimonos are gay crape, and their sashes tied behind like bright-tinted wings. Everyone – even the funny little gendarme who stands outside his sentry-box like a toy soldier – gives us back smile for smile.

The Grand Hotel is at the upper end of the Bund, and here another specimen of the "Moyen-age in his stocking feet shows us into beautiful rooms facing the water – rooms with steam heat and electric bells! . . . The darkness closes down swiftly, but charming things are still to be seen

159

from our veranda. The air is crisp and keen; gay cries and clinking pattens tinkle in melodious confusion from the street below. The 'rickishas have swinging from their shafts now crimped pink and white paper-lanterns, and flit by in the dark like fire-flies. A broad yellow moon rises up from the other side of the water and turns the bay to wrinkled gold against which the ships and junks show delicately black, as if drawn with a pen; and a few clear black lines of clouds are etched across the moon's path. . .

Sadly, the whole of the Grand Hotel was destroyed by the 1923 earthquake and fire. This also devastated much of Yokohama and Tokyo. The hotel was later replaced by the New Grand Hotel.

24th April 1897   Yokohama
The Grand seems full of Americans.
Went shopping & had a walk in the afternoon along the coast.

While staying at the Grand, Bertie wrote a letter to his father to report on his progress:

Grand Hotel
Yokohama
April 24th

Dear Governor,
I arrived here yesterday & found a letter from the Mater (March 3rd) & one from you sent on from Singapore by G. Paterson. We (Dr. Otto & I) have been travelling for the last week without a guide & find it much better fun. The last one we had was such a lazy little beggar; always wanting us to ride in rickshas & preferring to take us to shops (where he got a commission) to going elsewhere. We find ourselves much more free now & get on very well with "Murray's Guide to Japan" & " A Hand Book of Japanese Language."

We went from Kyoto to Gotemba where we got a fair view of Fuji. (the mountain of Japan) It was covered in snow & looked grand with the sun on it. I got into conversation with a gentleman in the train & found that I had an introduction to him from Kleinwort. His name is Raspe, (a German), he has stayed on Denmark Hill at the Kleinworts' & knows the Martins also. We travelled together for two days.

From Gotemba we walked over the mountains to Myanoshita, a lovely place, but we had bad weather while we were there. Then we walked 18 miles to Atami, a pretty little place on the coast where there are hot springs. From there we had a four hour ride on s switchback railway to Odawara, (about 18 miles). You go in a little carriage that holds 4 & have four coolies who push you up the hills, & then you go down the other side at a rare pace. It is up and down-hill the whole way along the coast. I was told it was very dangerous and advised not to try it, but we got to our destination in safety. The night before last, we stayed at Enoshema in a Japanese hotel where we lay on the floor & eat our dinner, (rice, fish & eggs) with chopsticks in pyjamas & a "kimono" with all the attendants sitting round & watching, & when we finished our dinner our beds were made on the floor in the same room. I put plenty of flea powder down, but all the same was attacked during the night. I did not have a bath in the morning, as I did not fancy entering the same tub of water into which about 20 Japs had already had theirs. What a change yesterday! When we sat down to dinner, with about 100 Europeans in evening dress & the band playing.

I shall call on Flora when I go to Tokyo & ask her to dinner. I am going up to Nikko soon where I shall probably stay some time. I am ashamed to say that I have done hardly any painting as I have been rushing about from place to place. I come across lots of wild flowers here which are almost identical with the English ones. One hears lots about the lovely scenery in Japan. I consider as far as I have seen yet, that England is far more beautiful. This does not mean that I am not enjoying myself. One thing I miss greatly in the country is birds. I have seen hardly any. I shall probably be sending a large box home from here with curios, as I don't want to take it across America.
I am afraid that business must be very bad on the S.E. & that you must have had a big drop in prices now war is declared. I shall probably leave Yokohama in the "Coptic" on the 24th May, perhaps I shall stay a few days in Honolulu. I might get a letter if you write to the Post office San Francisco. I shall probably be home about the end of June.

With best love to all & hoping that you are all well.
Your affec. Son
        Bertie
P.S. I don't think I shall want any more money.

The Greco Turkish war began on 5th April 1897, but it only lasted until 8th May and was sometimes referred to as the Thirty Days War. It was a conflict over the status of Crete which was ruled by the Ottoman Empire. The Cretans were fighting to gain the right to become part of Greece and were supported by mainland Greek forces. The Turkish army was much stronger and better equipped than the Greek army, which was defeated in 1897. However, in 1898, the Ottoman Empire was forced by the other great powers of Europe, to declare Crete an autonomous self-governing state and Prince George of

Greece and Denmark was made its first High Commissioner.

25th April 1897   Yokohama
Went out with Dr. Otto Seitz & Pickenpack. Bought my first piece of
Makudsu porcelain. Also a "Daibutsu."

Monday 26th April 1897   Tokyo
Imperial Hotel. Not many people staying here. Went to call on Flora. I
am asked to dinner there on Wednesday. The trees are coming out now &
the country is looking very pretty.

Another Victorian traveller who commented on the attractive scenery between Yokohama and Tokyo, was Marianne North, when she was there in October 1877. She wrote:

'The railway went alongside the famous Tokada Road, and was full of interest. The rice and millet harvest was then going on, and the tiny sheaves were a sight to see. They piled them up against the trees and fences in the most neat and clever way, some of the small fan-leaved palm trees looking as if they had straw petticoats on. There was much variety in the foliage; many of the trees were turning the richest colours, deep purple maples and lemon-coloured maidenhair trees (Salsiburia), with trunks a yard in diameter. The small kind of Virginian creeper, (Ampelopsis) was running up all the trees. These seemed generally dwarfed, except around the temples, which were marked all over the country by fine groves of camphor, cryptomeria, cedars and pine trees, as well as a small variety of bamboo.'

The Imperial hotel, where Bertie stayed, was built at the request of several Japanese people of influence in the government, who felt there was a need for a prestigious hotel in Tokyo where visiting foreigners could stay. It first opened in 1890 and was designed by Yuzuru Watanabe, who had been sent to Germany to study. It was situated close to the Imperial Palace and had 60 rooms. During its first years of operation, the hotel tended to have low occupancy, but business improved later. The building was destroyed by a fire in 1922. It was, at the time, fully occupied by dignitaries, staying in town in order to attend the Imperial Garden party held in honour of HRH Prince Edward, Prince of Wales, who was making an official visit to Japan. Luckily the fire occurred while all the hotel guests were across the road at the Royal Palace enjoying themselves at the party, so there was no loss of life. Later, the hotel was re-built.

27th April 1897   Tokyo
Did some shopping & went to the Exhibition where I bought a "Kakemon"
(5 dollars.) Mr and Mrs Ablar came over today. We met them first at
Kyoto.

28th April 1897   Tokyo
Museum, temples & shopping.

29th April 1897   Tokyo
Temples at Shiba Park.

Shiba Park is Japan's oldest public park, having opened in 1873. The park was originally the gardens attached to the Zojoji temple. It also contained other temples, shrines and tombs of the Shoguns. It is still a popular park in Tokyo and is one of the few open spaces in the city with beautiful trees and is especially spectacular at Cherry blossom time.

Scidmore wrote of it:

'*Under the shadow of century-old pines and cryptomeria stand the mortuary temples of the later Shoguns, superb edifices ablaze with red and gold lacquer, and set with panels of carved wood, splendid in color and gilding, the gold trefoil of the Tokugawas shining on every ridge-pole and gable. … On a rainy day, the green shadow and gloom, the cawing of the ravens that live in the old pine-trees, and their slow flight, are solemn as death itself; broken only by the droning priests at prayer, and the musical vibrations of some bell or sweet-voiced gong, invite a gentle melancholy.*'

30th April 1897   Tokyo
Went over to Yokohama, a lovely day, went to the factory of the Makudzas (Kozan) pottery & bought a pretty white vase with blue dolphins. In the evening went with Dr. Seitz in a rickshaw to the "Yos."

Miyagawa, (Makuzu Kozan), was one of Japan's most gifted potters of the Meiji era. He came originally from Kyoto, where his family had been making and decorating pots for many generations. Miyagawa opened a workshop in Yokohama in 1870 and continued there until early in the 20th century.

Saturday 1st May 1897   Nikko
Left Tokyo in the afternoon, arriving here for dinner. The Criptomerias on the old road, near which for a long time the railway runs are beautiful. We are in the Japanese part of the hotel.

Isabella Bird, an intrepid Victorian spinster lady, wrote a series of books about her adventures while travelling to various parts of the world. In her book '*Unbeaten Tracks in Japan*' (1879), she wrote of her visit to Nikko:

'*Nikko means 'Sunny Splendour,' and its beauties are celebrated in poetry and art all over Japan. Mountains for a great part of the year clothed or patched in snow piled in great ranges round Nantaizan, their monarch, worshipped as a god; forests of magnificent timber; ravines and passes scarcely explored; dark green lakes sleeping in endless serenity; the deep abyss of Kegon into which the waters of the Chiuzenjii plunge from a height of 250 feet; the bright beauty of the falls of Kiri Furi; the loveliness of the gardens…a gorgeousness of azaleas and magnolias; a luxuriousness of vegetation perhaps unequalled in Japan.'*

2nd May 1897   Nikko
Went in the morning to the temples. In the afternoon we walked to a waterfall Kirifuri-no-taki. There are lots of azaleas out in the hills.

Besides the waterfall and the flowers that entranced Isabella Bird, Nikko is renowned for its beautiful buildings. Murray's *Handbook* says of the shrines there:

'In the 17th century, … Japanese wood carving and painting on wood being then at their zenith, the result was the most perfect assemblage of shrines in the whole land. But though there is gorgeousness, there is no gaudiness. That sobriety, which is the key-note of Japanese taste, gives all the elaborate designs and bright colours its own chaste character.'

3rd May 1897   Nikko
Rain the whole day and we did not go out.

4th May 1897   Yumoto/Chuzenji
Walked to Chuzenji where we had lunch & then on to Yumoto (in a thunder storm) where we stopped the night. Dr. Otto had a dip in the public bath. We had a good dinner & slept on the floor. We had trout both here & at Chuzenji, but they were rather tasteless.

There is a beautiful lake at Chuzenji and another lake at Yumoto which has hot springs which sometimes colour the lake with their minerals.
Scidmore also travelled to Yumoto and wrote:

'Yumoto has two streets and a dozen tea-houses, whose galleries are hung with red lanterns, as if in perpetual fete, and the atmosphere nearly all sulphuretted Hydrogen. One of the hot springs bubbles up at the entrance of the village, filling a tank about ten feet square, covered by a roof resting on four corner pillars. The sides are all open to the air, and an Arcadian simplicity of bathing arrangements prevails. Citizens and sojourners stroll hither, because the site commands a view of the thoroughfare, remove and fold up their garments, and sit down in the pool. When sufficiently boiled, they cool off occasionally on the edge of the tank, and then drop into the pool again. If the company proves agreeable, the bath occupies hours. … To a new-comer this extraordinary simplicity is startling, but if he stays long enough, he finds that the childlike innocence and unconcern of the people make a new code of the proprieties.'

5th May 1897   Nikko
A lovely morning at Yumoto. There is still plenty of snow on the

mountains. We started at 8.15 & walked back to Nikko.

6th May 1897   Nikko
Went painting in the morning, in the afternoon I went to see the 100 stone
Buddhas.

Scidmore, in her description of Nikko said of the Buddhas:

'A hundred stone representatives of Buddha sit in mossy meditation under the shadow of the river bank, long branches trailing over them and vines clambering about their ancient brows. Time has rolled some from their lotus pedestals, beheaded others, and covered them all with white lichens and green moss, the Gamman, as this row of Buddhas is named, is the strangest sight among the many strange sights of the river bank. Custom ordains that one should count them, and no two persons are believed to have ever recorded the same number of images between the bridge and the Kobo Daishi's open shrine.'

7th May 1897   Tokyo
Wet all day. In the afternoon we left for Tokyo & arrived soon after 8pm. The trees along the railway had come out wonderfully during our short stay at Nikko, especially the Azaleas.

8th May 1897   Tokyo
Went shopping in the morning & to the bazar at Ueno Park in the afternoon, also to the bazar at Shiba Park where I bought some pretty red lacquer from the "Loo Choo" islands.

Ueno Park is still one of Tokyo's most beautiful and famous parks. There are over 1,000 cherry trees there, which look breathtaking during March and April.
The Loo Choo islands, also known as Lieu Chieu, or Ryukyu are a chain of thirty-six volcanic islands, the largest of which is Okinawa. They stretch out in a chain south of Japan towards Taiwan. Their climate is sub-tropical, and their inhabitants, though governed by Japan, have their own Ryukyuan dialect and consider themselves to be somewhat independent from the centre of government.

9th May 1897   Yokohama
Bought a piece of wood carving at Yackertakeys (Kenko.) We left for Yokohama in the afternoon & I bought some photos.

10th May 1897   Yokohama
I took my berth on the "Gaelic" for the 10th June (52 pounds.) Went for a walk to Mississippi Bay. Saw the Irises coming out on the roofs of the houses.
Mississippi Bay was named after a ship which was one of the fleet that US naval

Commodore Mathew Perry sailed into Yokohama in 1854 for a spot of gunboat diplomacy. His aim was to persuade the Japanese government to open up their ports to United States merchants and allow trade to commence between the USA and Japan.

11th May 1897   Yokohama
Went to see Yamada in the morning and took my curios there. Went out with Otto in the afternoon. We dined out & Simons turned up at the Grand. This has upset my trip to Atami, as I have promised to go with him to Miyanoshita.

GRAND HOTEL LTD
11th May 1897

Dear Mater,
I have not had one of your newsy letters for a long time. I came back here from Nikko two days ago & found a letter from Kathleen waiting for me, which I was glad to get. I hope Lewis has done the right thing, & kept the prize for the billiard tournament in the family. Nikko is a lovely place but we were a little too early in the season to see it at its best. We had some fine walks amongst the mountains. There is still snow in some places. There is a red lacquer bridge over the river near the hotel, which is over 260 years old; and the temples at this place are the finest in Japan. We walked to a place called "Yumoto" about 17 miles from Nikko & stayed the night. There are sulphur baths there & my friend, (Dr. Otto) had one in the public bath, I had mine in the hotel. The japs stay a long time in the bath, sometimes for hours at a time. At one place, (Kawanaka) they stay in the water for a month at a time, & I have read that the caretaker, an old man of seventy, spends the whole winter in the bath.

I am getting quite good at Japanese bowing. When they come into your room, or meet you in the hotel, they put their hands on their knees & bow very low two or three times - I do the same - but when they kneel & almost touch the ground with their foreheads, I don't know what to do, so stand on my head and kick my feet in the air, it amuses them greatly. Dr. Otto leaves on 13th May for America, so I shall be alone for a bit. I am going back to Atami again, as it is a nice, warm & pretty place. I have bought a lot of photos. They are coloured beautifully & very cheap. I have taken a berth on the "Gaelic" which sails from Yokohama on the 10th June for San Francisco via Honolulu.

The peonies are coming out now, they are really beautiful, also the wisteria, for which they make a kind of scaffolding. The flowers hang down, the flower stems are sometimes over four feet long. I don't fancy you would care for me to go in for flower decoration in the Japanese style? How would you like me to cut large branches off the fruit trees, when in flower, & stick them in pots in the rooms?

When in curio shops, I always look for "Dr Nikola's magic stick" - to bring home to Guy - but I can't find it. The nearest approach is a curious box made out of one joint of bamboo, carved, & with Chinese writing all over it. I showed it to a Japanese gentleman, he tells me it is very old & a good curio. The cabin trunk I brought out is all coming to pieces, so I have bought a Jap one which I hope will last till I get home.

I think Kathleen would call me a "pink nosed bounder" if she could see me just now - it is not drink, but the sun. I shall probably be home about the end of July. Please notice! Being such a good sailor, I have taken the longest route to America, namely via Honolulu.

Hoping that you are well again & that all the others are in good health. With best love to all at Durlstone,

Your affect. Son
                    Bertie

In this letter, Bertie jokingly claims to be seeking a Dr Nikola's 'magic stick'. Dr Nikola, with his mysterious black cat, was a fictional character with occult and magical powers in the extremely popular books written by his Australian born brother in law, Guy Boothby.

At this stage of his journey, Bertie started collecting art works in earnest and arranging to have them sent home.

12th May 1897   Yokohama
Went in the morning with Abear and Yamada to the porcelain factory. In the shop I saw some lovely bronze geese. Bought photos & a book at Yamamura's.

Kozaburo Tamamura, (1856 – 1923), was one of Japan's photography pioneers. He first opened his shop in Yokohama in 1883, where he prospered by selling Albumen and collotype photographs and albums to the tourists. These were often hand tinted, and he employed over 100 colourists in the 1890s.

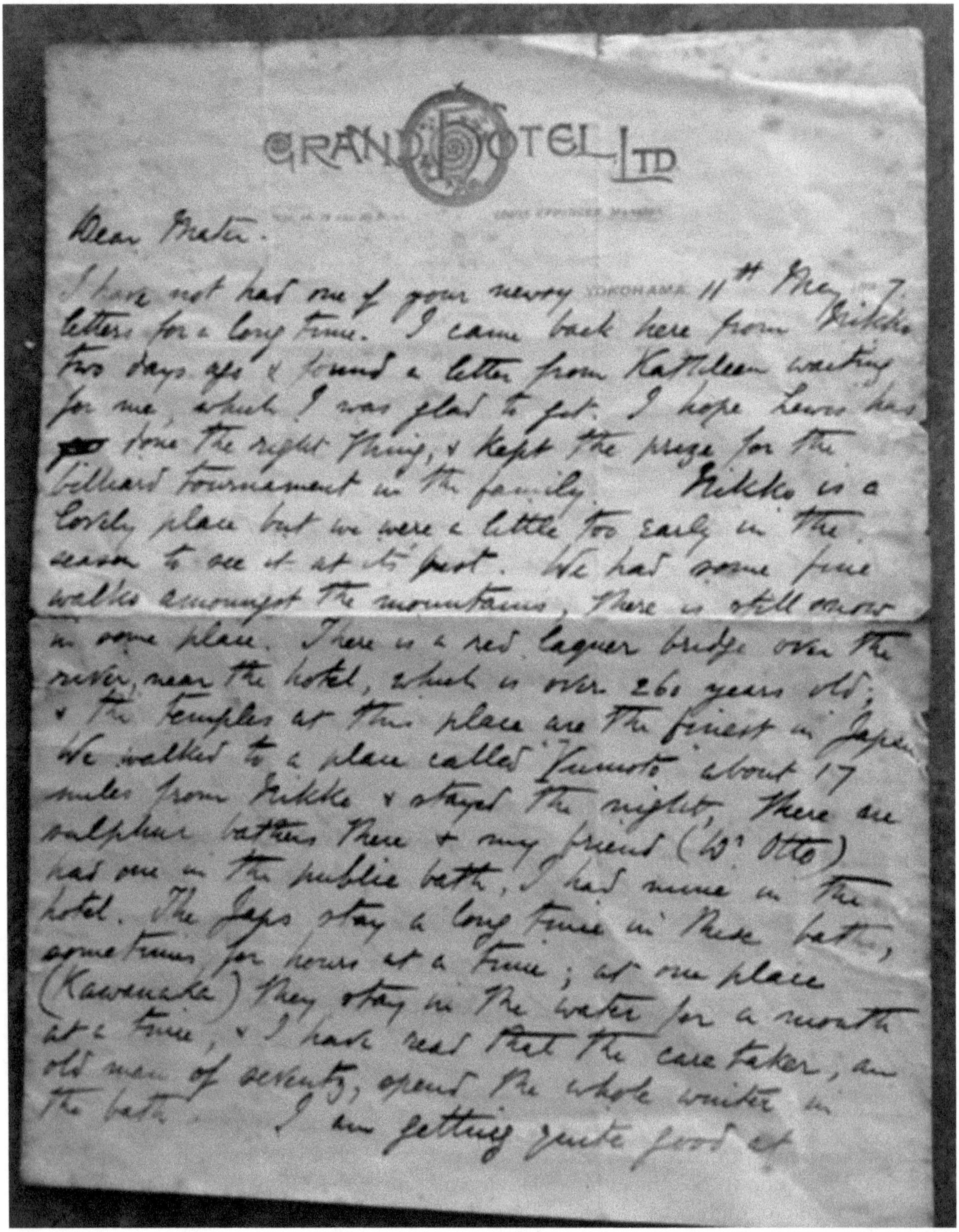

GRAND HOTEL LTD

Dear Mater,

I have not had one of your newsy letters YOKOHAMA 11th May 190 7.
letters for a long time. I came back here from Nikko
two days ago & found a letter from Kathleen waiting
for me, which I was glad to get. I hope Lewis has
done the right thing, & kept the prize for the
billiard tournament in the family. Nikko is a
lovely place but we were a little too early in the
season to see it at its best. We had some fine
walks amongst the mountains, there is still snow
in some place. There is a red laquer bridge over the
river, near the hotel, which is over 260 years old;
& the temples at this place are the finest in Japan.
We walked to a place called "Yumoto" about 17
miles from Nikko & stayed the night. there are
sulphur bathers there & my friend (W. Otto)
had one in the public bath, I had mine in the
hotel. The Japs stay a long time in these baths,
sometimes for hours at a time; at one place
(Kawanaka) they stay in the water for a month
at a time, & I have read that the care taker, an
old man of seventy, spend the whole winter in
the bath. I am getting quite fond of

168

13th May 1897   Miyanoshita
Fujiya Hotel. Simons and I left Yokohama in the afternoon after saying goodbye to Dr. Seitz, Otto with whom I have travelled for 5 weeks. He left on the Peru. We met Murray Mumford for the first time.

Friday 14th May 1897   Miyanoshita
Simons, Mumford & I went to Hakone where we had lunch. We had some shooting with bows and arrows on the way.

While Bertie chose to walk to Hakone, Scidmore was carried in a 'Kago.' She wrote of this experience:

'From Miyanoshita's comfortable hotel the two foreign women and the Japanese guide started on the first stage of the Tokaido trip in pole-chairs, carried by four coolies each. The 'danna san,' or master of the party, scorning such effeminate devices, strode ahead with an alpen-stock, a pith helmet, and russet shoes, while the provision-box and general luggage, filling a kago followed after us. We were soon up the hill in a bamboo-shaded lane, and then over the grassy uplands to the lake of Hakone. The singing coolies strode along, keeping even step on the breathless ascents, past the sulphur baths of Ashunoyu and on to the Hakone Buddha – a giant bass-relief of Amida sculptured on the face of a wall of rock niched among the hills. The lonely Buddha occupies a fit place for a contemplative deity – summer suns scorching and winter snows drifting over the stony face unhindered. A heap of pebbles in Buddha's lap is the register of pilgrims' prayers.

At Hakone village, a single street of thatched houses bordering the shore of Hakone lake, the narrow footpath over the hills joins the true Tokaido, a stone-paved highway shaded by double rows of ancient trees. … The chrysanthemum-crested gates of the Emperor's island palace were fast shut, and Fuji's cone peeped over the shoulders of encircling mountains, and reflected its image in the almost bottomless lake – and ancient crater, whose fires are forever extinguished.

The Tokaido road, which Scidmore referred to, is the ancient thoroughfare running from Osaka and Kyoto to Edo, (the old name for Tokyo.) This comprised 303 miles, or 488 kilometres and had 53 stations along its length for travellers to rest, obtain refreshments, or lodge for the night. In old Japan, most people travelled on foot, except the high-class people who might be carried in Kagos. Much of the route was lined with beautiful old trees and the Tokaido has often been the inspiration for works of art.

15th May 1897   Miyanoshita
Went with Simons and Ross to the shops. In the afternoon I went for a short walk with Mumford. It rained.

16th May 1897   Miyanoshita
It rained all the morning so we did not go out. Ross tells me that Lombok is a lovely island.

169

17th May 1897   Miyanoshita
A lovely day. Lots of people have gone to Atami. One American girl from Honolulu in a short dress, (velveteen) down to her knees only, with brass buttons, brown top boots, short hair & a sailor cap with Boston on it in gold letters. Ross, Simons, Mumford and I went to Hakone. Went in a boat to the north end of the lake, & home by the Sulphur springs.

Murray's Japanese handbook says of Hakone: 'Hakone…has a picturesque lake where one may bathe and boat and go on water picnics, and the reflection of Fuji in the lake are great attractions.'

The sulphur springs are also mentioned:

'Ashinoyu is famous for its sulphur springs, whose efficacy in the treatment of skin diseases and rheumatism attracts crowds of Japanese patients, and not a few foreigners, despite the bare uninviting appearance of the locality.'

18th May 1897   Miyanoshita
I caught some fine butterflies today, mostly in the "Goldfish" tea house garden where I went with Mumford and Simons. Ross has left for Yokohama. In the afternoon I went with Simons, Mumford & Capt. Parsons to the top of the mountain. I found Alder growing, also Osmunda & Pulmonaria.

Murray's Japanese handbook gives descriptions of walks around Miyanoshita. In one it says:-

'To Kiga (distance 9 cho, say 1/4 hour) :- no climbing, tame fish at the favourite "Gold-fish Tea-house." – The ravine spanned by a bridge soon after starting is called Jakotsu-gawa, lit. "Stream of Serpent's Bones," from some white stones popularly believed to be the bones of dead serpents. A little way up is a waterfall, and the hot water which supplies the village can be seen issuing from the rocks in several places.'

The three plants Bertie was surprised to find growing in Japan also grow wild in Britain. Alder is a common bush, Osmunda regalia, a tall growing fern, and Pulmonaria, is a herb with blue flowers.

Wednesday 19th May 1897   Miyanoshita
Went to the Goldfish tea house after butterflies in the morning. In the afternoon walked to Yumoto to see Mr. Simons off.

FUJIYA HOTEL
Hot mineral Spring
MYANOSHITA,
Hakone, 20th May

Dear Kathleen,
My friend, the Hungarian left in the 'Peru" on 13th for America. Two days
before he departed, Mr Simons from Singapore, (Paterson & Simons Co.)
turned up at the Grand, Yokohama. He is on his way to England, where
he will remain for a year or two. He is staying in Japan till the 28th May.
As he was travelling alone & wanted to see Miyanoshita, I volunteered to
go with him.... The hotel is quite full & the place is much prettier than
when I was here before. A Mr Parsons is staying here with his wife. He
comes from Dulwich, & is the son of old Colonel Parsons, with whom
I have played tennis. The old boy used to go to the political dinners that
uncle Tom gave. We have no guide. I am glad to say, & we go for splendid
walks with a coolie to show us the way. ...I have been very busy the last
few days catching butterflies & have secured a nice lot. There are plenty
of Americans here, I am sick of their twang. One young thing of about
25 started off for "Atami" – short hair, a sailor cap with "Boston" in
gold letters on it, with brass buttons, & brown top boots. I guess she
looked fine! – you bet.

I shall stay here another week as it is a very comfortable hotel & there
are lots of places worth seeing round about, besides I am well away
from the curio shops. I enclose a bad photo which was taken by Mr.
Simons at one of the sulphur springs in the mountains near here.

Hoping that you are all well, and with best love
          Your affec. Brother
                    Bertie

                    ଐଔ

20th May 1897   Miyanoshita
Walked up the hill near the hotel with Mumford & Mr. Kirby, caught a
few butterflies.   In the afternoon went out again with Mumford to the
short cut to Yumoto: a very pretty place where there are lots of little
iris out.
21st May 1897   Miyanoshita
In the morning to "Otometoge Pass." A good view of Fuji, lunch at the

pass & then back to Mi by the cattle farm (very smelly) & Ojigoku Pass A glorious day.

According to Murray's *Handbook*:
To the top of the Otometoge, or "Maiden's Pass", distance 3 ri (7 ½ miles), whence can be gained the nearest and most complete view of Fuji and of the plain at its base. The path is not steep excepting 11 cho of stiff climbing at the end…. The labour entailed is amply repaid by the view from the gap forming the pass.

Ojigoku, or Big Hell, alternatively named Owaki-dani, i.e. The Valley of the Greater Boiling. … Neither name is a misnomer. The whole gorge reeks with sulphurous fumes, vegetation decreases as one ascends higher, and the aspect of the scene becomes weird and desolate. It is advisable to keep to the path and tread carefully after the guide, as more lives than one have been sacrificed by a false step on the treacherous crust. The scene at the top differs as widely in its charms from the scene of desolation just traversed as can well be imagined. In the centre Fuji towers up in perfect beauty, to the right is tooth shaped Kintoki-zan, then Otome-toge, the Nagao-toge, and to the left the more imposing slopes of Ashitaka.'

22nd May 1897   Miyanoshita
In the morning I went with Mumford past the Goldfish tea house to the bamboo forest & caught a few butterflies. "Short cut" in the afternoon, a pretty moth like a large "Prunaria," one "Taminata" and found some pretty orchids.

23rd May 1897   Miyanoshita
Caught a fine lot of butterflies and moths.

24th May 1897   Myanoshita
Rained the whole day. Billiards with Parsons in the afternoon. They have two excellent tables here made by Thurston.

It is not surprising that Bertie was impressed that the Fujiya Hotel had two Thurston billiards tables. These tables were first made in 1799 by John Thurston of London. He was the first to introduce rubber cushioning around the tables to protect the balls and ensure an even bounce, also slate beds for a smooth surface. Thurston billiard tables won the highest awards at the Great Exhibition in 1851. In 1892, the Thurston table was accepted as the official standard for billiard tables. The company has been the proud recipient of no less than five Royal Warrants in the 19th and 20th century. What better way to while away a rainy afternoon in Japan, than to play a game of billiards on a Thurston table.

25th May 1897   Miyanoshita
After butterflies in the morning. "Short Cut" (Happy Valley) in the

172

afternoon with a lady & her daughter & Mumford. Found some pretty ferns & saw a Japanese wedding procession.
Miyanoshita 26/5/97
Walked to Saijoji & saw the temple "Doryo." Capt. and Mrs. Parsons walked to the top of the hill with us. We nearly ran all the way down to the valley as two thunder storms were coming up & we got there just in time. The carving in the temple is beautiful. I think the best I have seen. Walked back the same way after the storm, put up a pheasant & found some large orchids (Cypripediums.)

Cypripedium japonicum is the Japanese version of the Slipper orchid. It is a terrestrial orchid which used to be wide-spread throughout the islands of Japan, but now has become scarce. The wild form is usually pink, but under cultivation, other colours have been developed.

Murray describes the expedition to Saijoji as:

'Perhaps the most delightful of all; for it alone includes architectural beauties as well as beauties of nature. ... The path leads up to a grassy plateau near the summit of Myojin-go-take. ...whence may best be seen the superb view... From this point is a descent, Saijoji being even lower down on the other side of the mountain than Miyanoshita....Before reaching it, the open moorland of the hillside is exchanged for a fine grove of pines and cryptomerias, with an undergrowth of flowering shrubs, - deuzia, azaleas, pyrus, japonica, aucuba etc., according to the season.

The temple of Saijoji ..was founded by a hermit named Ryo-an who died in 1401, but it owes its special reputation for sanctity to his successor Doryo who was held to be one of the many reincarnations of Kwannon, the Goddess of Mercy. To Doryo's memory is dedicated the finest of shrines ... It is called Myokwaku-do... The fan of feathers which forms so striking a feature of ornamentation, was Doyo's crest. The winged figures with large noses represent goblins (tengu) who dwell in the mountains. Do not fail to notice the elaborate wood-carvings... and the perfect taste and beauty of the scene.'

27th May 1897 Myanoshita
After butterflies in the morning with Mumford. I gave a net to a little boy staying here & he is very busy.

28th May 1897 Yokohama
Left Miyanoshita at 1 o'clock for Yokohama. Found the Chamberlins had just left the Grand for Nikko. Met Hill who I had met at B. Bressey's in Ceylon. Two letters, one from Tom Hilder & one from the Governor.

29th may 1897 Yokohama
Went to Yamada's (Bishansha), but he had no more china.

Bought the geese & silver tea set. In the afternoon it rained, so I went and had a chat with Yamada.

Yokohama 30/5/97
Went to see wrestling with Yamada & his son. 1 o'clock until 6. Very good and most interesting.

Yokohama 31/5/97
Played tennis with Parsons. Won two sets out of three.

The Bristowe family were obviously excellent correspondents, and with the reliable sea-mail service, Bertie was able to keep in touch with family members.

Bronze geese bought by Bertie in Yokohama on 29 May 1897

Grand hotel
Yokohama
June 1st

Dear Kathleen,
I have just been to the post office & found a batch of letters for me. One from the Governor, two from the Mater & one from Ethel. I am sorry to say my stay in Japan is drawing to an end. I am off for a last trip to a place called Gifu, so see the fishing with cormorants that goes on there. I have taken a guide for this trip as I am by myself. I had a grand time at Miyanoshita where I stayed 15 days at the hotel with Mr Mumford. While there, I caught a fine lot of butterflies & moths. There was a jolly little English boy of 6, (staying there with his mother) with whom, of course, I made friends. I gave him a spare net I had. The day after I left, he went up to Mr Mumford & said - "What will you do now Mr Bristowe has left? You can't have dinner by yourself! You must go & sit at the table with my Mamma". - I had some splendid games of tennis yesterday with Capt Parsons & also played in some fours - I have not forgotten my cunning. There is a beautiful tennis ground here, which

174

reminds me of the one at Bournemouth. I went to see the Japanese wrestling on Sunday afternoon. I had been told once or twice that it was not worth seeing. I went and enjoyed it thoroughly, sitting watching it for 5 hours straight off. There were some enormously fat chaps & one veritable giant, the biggest Jap I have seen. He must have been 6 feet 3 or 4.

The Americans have a fashion in boots of their own. It is called the tooth pick boot & is at least 3 inches longer than the foot coming to a wonderful point & turning up. It looks awful. I am not looking forward to the sea voyage & do not think I shall have my brass buttons put on my blue suit & get my sailor hat till I get home. I have just been round to see about my second batch of curios. They tell me that there will be about a ton of it. I shall be home before this lot. I hope the box I sent from Hong Kong has arrived safely.

I am very sorry to hear that Edith Puckle is so seedy.
Hoping that you are all well at home & with love to all.
Your affec. Brother   Bertie

ℰℭ

1st June 1897   Yokohama
Went for a walk to Mississippi Bay. Counted 9 English plants in one small waste piece of ground. Dock. Potentilla, Goosefoot, shepherd's purse, coltsfoot. Tennis in the afternoon.

2nd June 1897   Nagoya
Started at 8 o'clock from the "Grand" and arrived at Nagoya 8.15.

3rd June 1897   Nagoya
Wet.   Had intended to go to Gifu today, but owing to the wet, shall not go till tomorrow.   Went to the curio shops, bought some nice "curios," also red and gold lacquer dishes.

4th June 1897   Gifu
Went to see a temple at Nagoya in the morning. In the afternoon off to Gifu. I left the hotel at 6.30 to see the cormorants. They were in baskets, partitioned off to hold four. They have, (the man told me) 14 tail feathers as a rule, but sometimes 15 or 16.

5th June 1897   Shizuoka
Left Gifu in the rain.   If fine, I should have stayed at Nagoya again &
gone to Seto to see the pottery. Got to Shizuoka at about 5 o'clock.
Went to see a temple a little way out, saw some fine old lacquer boxes
there. The "Lotus" leaves are coming out fast in the moat round the
castle.

6th June 1897   Yokohama
Arrived here about 4 o'clock & found Mumford is staying here at the Grand.
7th June 1897   Yokohama
Went to see Yamada, bought another piece of "Makuza." Yamada showed
me some cloisonné, & told me the prices they export it at. Very fine
pieces for 2.50.

8th June 1897   Yokohama
Bought a few butterflies at a Japanese shop. They asked as much as $2
for one large "Dannais!"   Did a little packing in the evening.

During his last week in Japan, Bertie spent much of his time shopping for art works and 'curiosities' to send home. He would have found plenty of shops catering to tourists in Yokohama and other popular cities.

Japan had been closed to western visitors for hundreds of years, so it came to be regarded as a country of mystery. When the Meiji regime eventually opened the ports and allowed western technology and visitors to enter the country, people were keen to explore the land and acquire beautiful oriental artefacts to adorn their homes.
At first, the passenger ships to Japan were few and far between, the hotels did not cater to western people, who wanted chairs, tables and proper beds with no fleas. Land transport was difficult with virtually no roads and the food was unappealing. In the latter half of the nineteenth century, more ships were scheduled, including regular services between Japan and the USA and many more travellers arrived.

The Japanese quickly adapted to the needs of westerners. Comfortable hotels were built in the major cities, railways were developed and a thriving tourist industry supplying guides, transport, entertainment and of course, shopping.

Previously Japanese artists and artisans who created paintings, carvings, pottery and porcelain, had as their customers, the temples and monasteries, the aristocracy and Japanese moneyed classes, but with the arrival of the western tourists, they quickly realised there was a new demand for their goods, so enterprising businessmen set up factories and shops in the main cities to supply them with items of great beauty which were totally unlike anything they could obtain at home. In addition to the traditional art works, other popular souvenirs were photographs. Dutch traders had introduced photography to Japan and many studios were set up. Images were skilfully hand tinted and showed romantic scenes with cherry blossom, geishas or samurai artfully posed and possibly mounted in ornate albums. Ownership of personal cameras was not universal, so people were prepared to pay well for photographs.

Most of the visitors to Japan at the end of the nineteenth century, like Bertie, were middle class and the fashion was for their houses to be filled with artworks, sculptures, wall hangings and other artistic items. There was a huge hunger for things from the orient which differed from the usual. Other services offered were by agencies which would pack up purchases and ship them back to their customers' country safely.

Grand Hotel
Yokohama
June 9th

Dear Governor,
This is the last letter I shall write from Japan. I go on board the "Gaelic" tomorrow morning. I have had a glorious time in Japan & am really awfully sorry to leave. I have just returned from my last trip, which was to Gifu, where I saw the cormorants fishing. It was most interesting! It took place at night. There were 5 boats, each with a long pole in the bows with an iron cage tied at the end, in which was a fire. The fish are attracted by the light. The cormorants had string around their throats to prevent them swallowing the fish, & also a kind of harness, (made of string), with a bit of whalebone sticking up in the middle of the back. This is used as a handle to take them out of the water. To the whalebone, is attached a string about 12 feet long. A man stands in the bows of each boat & manages 12 of these birds, all at once, in a marvellous manner without letting them get into a tangle. When the bird has got its throat full, he pulls it in & makes if disgorge into the boat, keeping an eye on the others all the time. The five boats go down stream abreast. I was between two of these in a hired boat, so close that I was often splashed by the cormorants when they dived!

I think of sailing from New York on the 21st or 28th July in a White Star steamer. They go to Liverpool. I shall not decide till I get to San Francisco, (when I will telegraph for a berth.) I will then write & let you know. With regard to the case I sent from here on 26th April. I expect you will be advised by Davies Turner and Co., 52 Lime Street E.C. when it arrives in London. I do not think you will be able to get it, as I have not sent you the receipt. I suppose it will have to remain at their place till I come home. If you do get it, be very careful when you open it, as there are lot of things that would break easily. The German I met at the Raffles Hotel, Singapore & the American with whom I travelled in Java are both sailing in the "Gaelic"....

Hoping that the Mater is in better health, (I think she must be as I had two very newsy letters from her) & that you & all at Durlstone are well.
    Your loving son,
        Bertie

P.S. The enclosed is my bill at the Jap hotel, Gifu. I send it just to show you what a bill here is like.

ഇ൪ഇ

9th June 1897   Yokohama
Bought a chair, also some pretty little lacquer cups at Biskusha's. I have been to see the "Gaelic." She is very full & there are 600 stinking Chinese in steerage.

By this stage of his journey, Bertie's thoughts had turned to home. He had arranged for his estimated one ton of purchases to be shipped back to England. He made his reluctant farewell to Japan and embarked on the last lap of his journey. Once again he faced the prospect of more sea sickness while sailing across the Pacific Ocean for fourteen days, with only one brief respite at Honolulu, before reaching his next destination, the great city of San Francisco.

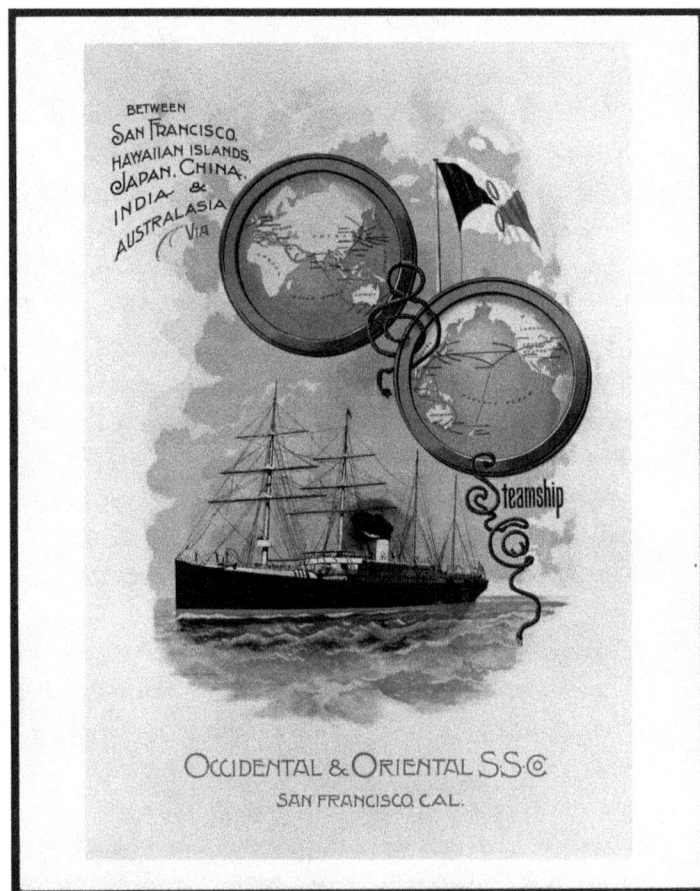

Occidental and Oriental Steam Ship Company Poster [Stanford University Library]

Chapter Eight

The Journey to Hawaii, San Francisco, USA and Across the Atlantic to Home

SS Gaelic (owned by White Star Line, chartered to O&O Steamship Co.)
Photo from Stanford University Library

10th June 1897   Gaelic
Left Yokohama about 12 o'clock. A good lunch, but at dinner it was rough & I could eat little. Cole Watson & Saubolle in my cabin. The former has been 14 years in Japan.

Gaelic was a ship owned by the White Star Line, but she had been chartered to the Occidental and Oriental Steamship Company (O&O) since 1885. She was a popular ship used in the Pacific on the passage between Hong Kong, Yokohama, Honolulu and San Francisco until 1904.

The O&O originated in 1874 as a partnership between the Central Pacific Railroad Company and the Union Pacific Railroad Company. It was based in San Francisco and provided a reliable service transporting passengers and freight between Asia and the west coast of the United States. This linked up with their railroad service to the east coast. The company policy was not to purchase their own vessels, but to charter them.

In 1874 Captain George Bradbury was sent to England to negotiate with shipping companies willing to charter ships to O&O. He made an agreement with the directors of the White Star Steam Ship Company that they would provide several of their vessels: the first being *Oceanic*, then *Arabic* and *Coptic*, and later, *Gaelic* and *Belgic*. These ships flew an O&O house flag, but also the White Star Line flag. The officers were British, appointed by White Star and the crew were mainly Chinese. During its years of operation, O&O was a profitable venture, but eventually other shipping companies introduced larger, faster vessels. O&O could no longer compete, and the company ceased to operate in 1905.

Gaelic was built in 1885 by Harland and Wolff at their Belfast shipyards as a passenger and cargo liner. She was 420 feet (128.12 metres) long, and her gross registered tonnage was 4,206 tons. She had two compound steam engines with a single screw, but also four masts, two of which were square rigged with sails, so with a fair wind the sails could be used to supplement the steam engines. Her speed was about thirteen knots (twenty-four km/h,) so she could travel around 300 miles a day.

Bertie mentioned the ship was very full, with sixty-eight first class cabin passengers, and hundreds more in steerage. The steerage passengers were generally Chinese, Japanese or Korean men going to the USA or Hawaii. Those heading for the USA went in search of employment, or if travelling to Hawaii, they were mostly destined to be labourers in the sugar, rice or pineapple plantations.

Most of the freight carried by O&O ships was to the USA from China and Japan. Bisland, who travelled between San Francisco and Japan on one of the O&O ships, wrote:

'These ships, like those of the merchant Antonio. voyage to the East for cargoes of tea, silk, and spices. There are three lines between China and America; two, The Pacific Mail and the Oriental and Occidental – controlled by the Central Pacific Railway magnates, Huntington, Crocker, and Stanford - have their termini in the United States, and the Canadian Mail from Vancouver. They carry out to China returning subjects of the yellow emperor, passengers for the East, flour, Connecticut clocks, hats, shoes, and such select assortment of Yankee notions as are required by the Barbarian.

Returning, they fetch hundreds of bales of raw silk, worth $700 apiece, which must be rushed across the continent immediately upon arrival, and have left the ship and are on their way across the country to the Eastern mills before the passengers have landed. The usual cargo is from 1200 to 1300 bales, and in June the tea trade begins, 1700 to 2700 tons in every ship – the whole of the Formosa crop, some 6,000,000 tons come to us. The English will not drink the light perfumed Oolong. They demand something coarser and stronger. Spices, pepper and tapioca come from Singapore, and gamibier in great quantities for coloring American beer, with thousands of bales of gunnysacks from Calcutta for American wheat, and, from Manilla, hemp and jute.'

Gaelic's charter to O&O ceased at the end of 1904. She was sold by White Star Line to the Pacific Steam Navigation Company in 1905 and was re-named Callao. She was then transferred to the service between Liverpool and South America, but was retired and scrapped in 1907.

Since the ship was so full, Bertie had to share his cabin with two others. They were Mr Cole Watson and Mr Saubolle. Mr Watson was mentioned in Harold William's book Shades of the Past: Indiscrete Tales of Japan, where he was described as being the 'Taipan' of a Scottish mercantile and agency firm, Findlay Richardson and Co. in Yokohama. Apparently in 1897, he was on the jury of a notorious murder trial in Yokohama when Mrs Edith Carew was accused and convicted of using arsenic to poison her husband and she was sentenced to death. After a sensational trial, questions were raised as to whether the verdict had been unbiased and fair since there were only five members of the jury and they had all been close friends of Mr Carew. Eventually the sentence was commuted to life imprisonment and Mrs Carew spent thirteen years in a British prison.

Mr Saubolle came from a family which had been in India for several generations that had French and Portuguese origins.

11th June 1897   O & O SS "Gaelic"
Sea sick

12th June 1897   "Gaelic"
Sea sick

The journey continued, but once again Bertie was sea-sick and it was several days before he showed interest in his fellow passengers. He made a list of those he had met which indicates the variety of nationalities who had visited Japan and were travelling with him on the ship....

13th June 1897   Gaelic
Mr. & Mrs Baker (New Zealand,) The Miss Ballons, Miss Clifford (Tonbridge,) R.P. Duncan (Manila,) S.E. Murray & Ewer (England,) Gillespie , Hall (Siam,) Joshua & Purvis (Australia,) Mr. & Mrs. King (Hawaii,) Kirkwood (Ireland,) H. Kopoch (China,) Mr. and Mrs. Thoms (America,) Mr. & Mrs. Scottowe (Shanghai,) Saubolle (India,) Cole-Watson (Japan,) one Chinaman & several Japanese.

14th June 1897   "Gaelic"
Rough

15th June 1897   "Gaelic"

16th June 1897   "Gaelic"
We crossed parallel 180 today, so gain one day. Tomorrow will also be Wednesday 16/6/97 for us. There are two very nice girls on board from Boston U.S.A. named Ballon.

Things had definitely improved if Bertie was able to notice pretty girls. He was later to confide in a letter sent to his sister from San Francisco, that he became 'quite pally' with one of the Misses Ballon. He was sorry they disembarked at Hawaii.

16th June 1897   "Gaelic"

17th June 1897   "Gaelic"

There is a Mr. Duncan on board who comes from Manila where he has been for 14 years. He knows J. Whitehead. The fighting between Spaniards and the natives began near his house. He tells me the rich half-casts get up tiffin parties & go after butterflies on horseback. Some of them have very fine collections.   It is good exercise & they catch sometimes as many as 20 or 30 "vars" in a morning.   We saw Venus today at 10.30 in the morning.

The fighting in the Philippines occurred in 1896 when there was a revolt against the Spanish who had ruled the Philippines since 1565. In 1898 the Spanish American war occurred and the Filipino revolutionaries hoped the US would assist them in their struggle for independence, but all that happened was that the Philippines were ceded to the United States and they were not attain independence until 1946.

Bertie was surprised that Venus was visible at 10am, but this phenomenon is not unknown. Several astronomers have reported observations of the planet at different times of the day when conditions are right. One occasion when it seemed especially bright, was on 4th March 1865 at the inauguration ceremony of President Abraham Lincoln in Washington just after mid-day. The planet was observed by many people, including the President himself.

19th June 1897   "Gaelic"
Sports. We had " Chalking the pig's eye" & the Americans showed their business-like way of playing games. We arrived at Honolulu at Midnight.

Chalking the pig's eye was a game commonly played on board ships in the days when passengers were expected to organize their own entertainments. A blackboard was set up with the image of a pig drawn on it. The contestants were given a piece of chalk and were blindfolded. They had to draw in the pig's eye and the winner was the person who drew it closest to the correct position. A particular attraction of this game was that it was suitable to be played by both male and female passengers together.

The Hawaiian, or Sandwich Islands as they were still named in 1897, were in the process of being taken over completely by the United States. They were to be annexed as a USA territory in 1898, but did not become the fiftieth USA state until 1959.

This group of islands resulted from a series of eruptions which pushed several volcanic mountains up out of the sea. Over millions of years, these became covered in vegetation and eventually were colonised by humans. Archaeological evidence suggests that the first settlers may have come first from the Marquesas Islands and also later migrations from other Polynesian islands. They brought with them useful food crops, pigs, and their dogs. They lived for thousands of years as independent small social groups ruled by their chiefs. The people of the Hawaiian Islands eventually became united under King Kamehameha in 1795 after much conflict. One of the last and bloodiest battles was at Nu'uanu Pali on the island of Oahu where Kamehameha conquered the Oahu defenders, many hundreds of whom were driven over the Pali precipice to their death on the rocks below.

The Spanish claim to be the first Europeans to have discovered Hawaii. They sailed across from their colonies in South America, but did not settle there. Captain Cook arrived in 1778 and at first, had friendly contact with the Hawaiians. They were under the mistaken impression that the white people were gods and immortal, but unfortunately on his second visit, a dispute occurred, when he and several of his crew were killed. Cook named Hawaii as the Sandwich Islands in honour of his patron, Lord Sandwich, but recorded that the locals called it Owyhee.

Following Cook, the islands were visited by other sailors, most of whom were whalers. Unfortunately, they often treated the indigenous Hawaiians very badly and introduced alcohol and diseases which decimated and demoralised the Hawaiian society. Missionaries also arrived, most of whom were Protestants from New England, USA. They had good intentions, but did almost as much harm to the Hawaiian culture as the whalers had. They disapproved of the care-free Hawaiian way of life and condemned Hula dancing, surfing, sex outside marriage and the exposure of bare flesh. All were declared sinful. Whilst they were converting the Hawaiians to Christianity, and curbing their morals, the American missionaries became extremely rich and powerful politically. Laws were passed to allow foreigners to acquire land, and the planting of sugar, pineapples and rice made the white settlers even more prosperous. They also imported large numbers of Chinese, Japanese and Koreans to work in the plantations, since the Hawaiians, very sensibly, were reluctant to labour all day in the hot sun to benefit the white land-owners.

Until 1893, the Hawaiian Islands still had a monarchy, but their powers had gradually been eroded by the dominant white government, which passed laws to disenfranchise the Asians and Hawaiians. Therefore seventy-five per cent of the people entitled to vote were white. In 1893 Queen Lili'uokalani, who had tried to resist the disempowerment of her people, was deposed, and in 1894 a Republic of Hawaii was created with the first President being Stanford Dole, a lawyer and son of US missionaries. These actions were considered illegal, and disapproved of by many, including USA President Grover Cleveland.

Hawaiians, who were loyal to their queen and wanted to retain their independence protested, but US Marines were brought in to restore order. The Hawaiian Islands were considered to be of strategic importance as a place to keep an American naval base.

This was mainly due to the conflict at that time between the USA and Spain, which had colonies in the Philippines and Mexico. President McKinley, who had succeeded President Cleveland, signed a joint resolution to annex the islands in 1898.

20th June 1897   Honolulu

I went for a drive in the morning to Pali (a precipice.) Saw plenty of mangoes, quinces, palms, hibiscus, oleander, Poinciana, & many other tropical trees. There is one tree (Argiroba,) a kind of acacia, growing all over the island. It was introduced in 1807 by a Roman Catholic priest. It is the only instance of a useful tree being introduced & spreading over the island that I have come across. I went to lunch with Gillespie at the Hawaiian Hotel & then went to Waikiki & saw a fine bathing place & there were turtles swimming near the header board. We went to hear the band play. The native ladies wear loose Mother Hubbard gowns like night dresses. They also ride on mens' saddles. The Misses Ballons are getting off here I am sorry to say. The missionaries here, as in Yokohama, have some of the best houses. We had to pay $8 (gold) for our trip to "Pali" in the morning - 16 miles. We took on a lot of fruit here, grapes (that have a taste of strawberries,) mangoes, pines, oranges.

The influence of the missionaries on the islanders was evident from the modest mode of dress worn by the women that Bertie observed. He also mentioned in a letter home, that due to it being Sunday, no one was swimming at beautiful Waikiki beach, nor were floral leis presented to welcome the visitors off the ship, and also all shops were closed when they arrived at Honolulu.

'Argiroba' is also known as *Algarroba* or *Kiawe*, or its botanical name, *Prosopis pallida*. This is a tree which was introduced to the islands by Hawaii's first Catholic priest, Father Alexis Bachelot in 1828. It is a tropical legume from South America, which can grow in very harsh conditions. It produces good quality timber for construction or firewood with seed pods containing a sweet nutritious pulp, useful for human or animal consumption. As an added bonus, its flowers are beloved by bees and produce high quality honey. It is also a useful tree for stabilizing sand dunes. However, because it is so robust and reproduces rapidly, it is now classified as an invasive weed species in Hawaii.

22nd June 1897   Gaelic

22nd June was the day of Queen Victoria's Diamond Jubilee which was enthusiastically celebrated with church services, parades and elaborate parties by her loyal subjects, not only in Britain, but also throughout the British Empire. Many Victorians idolised their Queen, which was something the Americans found difficult to comprehend. Bertie mentioned in a letter to his sister that the British on board had provided champagne for all the passengers at a gala dinner, with loyal toasts to mark the occasion. Unfortunately this resulted in some people having too much to drink which almost led an international brawl when one of the young British passengers took exception to the fact that some of the Americans were drinking beer, which he felt was an insult to his Queen.

Nellie Bly, travelling on a P & O ship, observed the loyalty the English passengers held for the Queen with amazement. She wrote:

The passengers endeavoured to make time pass pleasantly … The young women had some 'tableaux vivants' one evening, and they were really very fine … Another evening we had a lantern slide exhibition that was very enjoyable.

The loyalty of the English to their Queen on all occasions, and at all times, had won my admiration. Though born and bred a staunch American, with the belief that a man is what he makes of himself, not what he was born, still I could not help admiring the undying respect the English have for their royal family. During the lantern slide exhibition, the Queen's picture was thrown on the white sheet, and evoked warmer applause than anything else that evening. We never had an evening's amusement that did not end by everyone rising up to their feet and singing 'God Save the Queen'. I could not help but think how devoted that woman, for she is only a woman after all, should be to the interests of such faithful subjects.

With that thought came to me a shamed feeling that there I was, a free born American girl, the native of the grandest country on earth, forced to be silent because I could not in honesty speak proudly of the rulers on my land, unless I went back to those kings of manhood, George Washington and Abraham Lincoln.

23rd June 1897   Gaelic
There is a young chap on board with his wife, Mr.McNear, son of a millionaire in San Francisco, great corn shippers.

This young man must have been one of the four sons of George McNear whose company, G. W. McNear was well known in every grain market of the world. In 1880 he had established extensive warehouses and docks in San Francisco, where he was able to load up to ten ships at one time with wheat or oil, which he also shipped. In addition, he had business interests in flour and milling works. Also G. W. McNear was president of the first electric street train company in Oakland and was President of the First National Bank.

24th/25th July 1897   Gaelic
A lovely day. Rather rough in the afternoon. We arrived at San Francisco about 10pm.

Sunday 27th June 1897 San Francisco

The city of San Francisco has Spanish origins. The first Europeans to explore the area were

Market street, San Francisco. From an old postcard

Spaniards who travelled up the coast from their colonies in Mexico in the sixteenth century. They did not settle at that time, nor did Francis Drake, who sailed past the bay in 1579 mapping the coast, which he named 'Nova Albion'.

The first European settlement was established in 1774 when the Spanish decided the bay had strategic importance, and set up a military outpost there, which they named Yerba Buena. The missionaries, who arrived hoping to convert the local Ohlone population to Christianity, founded a mission, known as San Francisco de Assisi. Later, the name of the town was changed to San Francisco. Thus, California was a Spanish territory until 1821, then Mexico broke away from Spain and it became Mexican until 1848, when USA claimed California as a territory in the Treaty of Guadalupe Hidalgo.

In1850 California became an American state.

Statehood was granted largely because in 1848, gold was discovered   in California and the gold rush began. This led to a rapid growth in the population of San Francisco. People flocked there from all over the world, including China, all hoping to make their fortunes. In the early days, San Francisco became a very rough, and at times, dangerous town to live in. It was not until the 1860s to 1880s that it gradually became a more settled city.

In 1889 Bisland travelled by train from New York and passed through San Francisco at the beginning of her trip round the world. It was the first time she had seen the West Coast of USA. She had to wait a few days before her ship left for Japan, so she had time to look around the city. In her account Bisland wrote:

'*To my eyes accustomed to the soaring loftiness of New York architecture, this city seemed astonishingly low. Three of four stories at the most the average is. Because of earthquakes they say, but latterly these had almost entirely ceased to occur, as if the land had grown to realize that civilization would not tolerate such impulsive ways, and had gradually abandoned them shame-facedly, as being in very bad taste. Consequently a few of the more recent buildings have begun to climb, Babel-like into the dripping skies.*

One gets a remarkable impression of newness here, such as a Londoner might feel on his first landing in New York…All the buildings look new and fresh and the whole atmosphere of the place is charged with vigorous disrespectful sort of youth….

The hotel at which I stop was built in 1875. It is a huge caravansary, built around a square and enclosing a vast asphalted court adorned with palms and ferns. There is an arcade within the court where the typical American hotel frequenter tips back his chair, reads the paper and smokes. On the outer side of the arcade are shops of every description, so one may purchase all the ordinary needs of life, without leaving ones lodging place.'

Her rival in the race round the world, was on the last lap of her journey when she reached the city. Miss Bly had a specially chartered train waiting for her when she disembarked from her ship, to convey her by the southern route to avoid snowdrifts in the mountains, which may have delayed her. This was arranged by her sponsors at the 'New York World' and it was claimed that this cost more than the whole of the rest of her journey.

At the time of Bertie's visit, James Phelan was Mayor of San Francisco. He managed to raise funds to develop schools, hospitals, parks, libraries and other necessary infrastructure, which improved the city immensely. His ambition was to transform San Francisco into 'the Paris of the West'.

On arrival, one of the first things Bertie did was to send off letters to his family. These would have been transported across the continent by train to connect with a mail ship to cross the Atlantic. He was also able to communicate by telegraph. This method was quicker, but charges were so much per word, so messages needed to be short.

STEAMSHIP GAELIC
June 26th

Dear Kathleen,

We sailed on June 10th. The steamer is quite full - three in my cabin - It was rough for the first few days & of course I was ill, but I soon got over it & we had a good time all the way to Honolulu. The 68 first class passengers represent many nationalities. The majority are Americans, there are also Germans, French, Danes, Chinese, Japanese, Australians, New Zealanders & English. We had some sport on board & I won the bucket quoits with a Miss Woods.

We arrived at Honolulu late on Saturday night June 19th.   We had the whole of Sunday on shore.   This is the last peep I shall have at the tropics! It is a lovely place & I believe the most expensive to live in in the world. I went for a drive in the morning with an American, a German, & a chap from India to a precipice where one gets a glorious view of one side of the island. It was the scene of a great battle years ago, the defeated side being driven over the cliffs. Being Sunday, all the shops were shut, so in the afternoon I went for another drive to a noted bathing place. There was nobody in the water, but I saw some turtles swimming about.   I hear that 90% of the natives speak English.   The usual costume of the native ladies is a loose " Mother Hubbard" sort of dress, like a night gown, & they are very fond of decorating themselves with flowers. I also saw two men riding with flowers round their hats. Sunday is kept very strictly here, or the passengers would have been covered with flowers when they returned to the steamer – it is the custom – as it was a few of the ladies & gentlemen had flowers round their hats, & one old fat chap had flowers round his hat & also a large chain over his shoulders.   I should have liked to have stayed for some time as the country is beautiful, & besides an American girl I was rather pally with got off here.

We have got a fine lot of fruit on board that we took on at Honolulu, plenty of a small kind of grape that has a decided flavour of strawberries, also mangoes, oranges & pineapples.

We kept the Diamond Jubilee on board. The English people standing champagne. We had a few speeches after dinner & a small dance. There was nearly a row between the English & Americans. Some of both nations had had rather too much by 12 p.m. Some Americans were drinking beer & a young English chap told them it was an insult to drink it on such a day & knocked all their glasses over. One of them jumped up, took off his coat & wanted to fight & they were kept apart with difficulty.   If they had started, it might have led to a general row – Although the English were in the minority I think we could have knocked corners off them.

The weather has been delightful lately & the sea as calm as a mill pond. We shall arrive at San Francisco on June 27th & I have almost made up my mind to take a berth on the " Britannic", a White Star Steamer!   She sails from New York on July 28th, so I shall be home about the 3rd August.

Hoping that you are all well & with best love to all

Your affect. Brother,
Bertie

P.S. I shall stay at the Brunswick Hotel New York & shall expect to get a letter before I sail for England.

൧൩

San Francisco Sunday 27/6/97

They took a long time examining our luggage at the custom house. I had to pay $7.80 on my silver boxes & pins. They luckily did not come across my photos. Murray had to pay $12 on his. Went to the Golden Gate Park & saw a large crowd listening to the band. We then went to the Cliff House where we saw lots of seals & cormorants on a rock close to the shore. We also went to the swimming bath. My room at the Palace Hotel is $2.50 & the meals on the American plan $2.

169 San Francisco, California, Cliff House and Seal Rocks from Parapet, Sutro Heights.

Cliff House, San Francisco. Old postcard

Golden Gate Park was established in 1870 as a recreational park for the people of San Francisco, and was named after the Golden Gate Strait. It was developed by engineer, William Hammond Hall and his assistant, John McLaren, who was a horticulturist, trained in Scotland. McLaren supervised the planting of hundreds of beautiful trees from all over the world, and he continued to be Superintendent of the park for over 50

189

years. He lived there until his death in 1943 at the age of 93. There was no Golden Gate Bridge in 1897, as this was not constructed until 1937.

Sutra Baths at the Cliff House, San Francisco. Old postcard

Golden Gate Park was established in 1870 as a recreational park for the people of San Francisco, and was named after the Golden Gate Strait. It was developed by engineer, William Hammond Hall and his assistant, John McLaren, who was a horticulturist trained in Scotland. McLaren supervised the planting of hundreds of beautiful trees from all over the world, and he continued to be Superintendent of the park for over 50 years. He lived there until his death in 1943 at the age of 93. There was no Golden Gate Bridge in 1897 – it was constructed in 1937.

The Cliff House mentioned was the third to stand on the site. The first was a wooden structure built in 1858 from timber salvaged from a ship, which had been wrecked at the base of the cliff. The second Cliff House was built in 1863. This was extensively damaged by an explosion in 1887 when another ship, carrying dynamite, foundered on the rocks below; though repaired, the building was completely destroyed by a fire in 1894. The third Cliff House, built in 1896 by Adolf Sutro, was a very ornate seven storey mansion, sometimes known as the 'Gingerbread Palace'. He also built the famous Sutro baths which included six indoor heated pools, a skating rink and a museum.

During her two days in San Francisco, Bisland's friends took her to the Cliff House for lunch:

'We lunch, jovially and sumptuously, upon the sea's edge. Already the day is declining as we finish. The rain has ceased, and in the west the curtain of cloud lifts. On a balcony that overhangs the water we watch the sunset. Three great crags stand up sharply two hundred yards away –

Seal Rocks – covered with grumbling, barking sea lions, the city's pets, whom the law protects. They look much like fat pigs from this distance. At the last moment the sun flames out gloriously; reddens all the heavens, and gilds a rippling road for me across the watery world I must traverse. It is a sign of promise, they tell me.'

In a brochure about the hotel patronised by Bertie and also Elizabeth Bisland it states:

'THE PALACE HOTEL
Is the largest and most magnificent structure ever dedicated
to the needs of the travelling public of the world.
It justly stands pre-eminent --- the leading caravansary of the world.
Located in the heart of the city, it is accessible to every commercial enterprise,
as well as every pleasure resort.'

This Hotel was the brainchild of William Ralston, a colourful and very rich entrepreneur who had many business interests and had founded the Bank of California. Ralston was determined to build a hotel which was equal to the best in Europe, so no expense was spared. It had 775 guest rooms, each with its own bathroom, extensive public rooms, restaurants, and bars, all with flamboyant decorations. Unfortunately just as the hotel was nearing completion in 1875, Ralston's business empire collapsed, including the Bank of California. A few days later his dead body was found floating in the Bay. Suicide was suspected, but luckily for his widow, who would not have been able to claim his life insurance had he taken his own life, it was found he had died of an apoplectic stroke. The hotel opened and was dubbed the 'Bonanza Inn' by the locals. In 1906, following the great San Francisco earth quake, a fire started, and the whole magnificent structure burnt to the ground, as did many other buildings in the city.

Bertie continued with his exploration of the city, but also decided to see more of the country.

Palace Hotel, Market Street, San Francisco, from an old postcard

191

Monday 28th June 1897   San Francisco, Palace Hotel
I have taken a ticket for Yosemite Valley & start on Wednesday. Looked about town & went to the music hall in the evening (Orpheum), where we saw some very clever acrobats. Murray borrowed $ from Saubolle, Pickenpack has got the $200 he lent the Warrens.

The Orpheum Theatre, a popular place of entertainment, was another building completely destroyed by the 1906 earthquake and fire.

Bertie wrote the following letter to his sister, Ethel with his first impressions of San Francisco:

Palace Hotel
San Francisco
June 30th

Dear Ethel,
I arrived safely in San Francisco on the 27th (Sunday.) All the passengers had to go to the Customs House & have their luggage examined. They make you pay duty on everything. I had to pay 7 dollars (1.8 pounds) on two small silver boxes I had & should have had to pay highly on my photos if they had found them. A Mr. Murray who has been travelling round the world like me & buying photos of places he visited, had to pay 12 dollars (2.8 pounds).

There are some very large buildings in San Francisco but they are not beautiful. There are 1,000 rooms in this hotel. The first afternoon I went to the Golden Gate Park, the gardens are very pretty & there was a large crowd there listening to the band. This is the first American crowd I have seen & I am not favourably impressed. I think that if you were to dress up the people you see at the Crystal Palace on Easter Monday in fine clothes, & they behaved decently, they would look much the same. The type of face is certainly similar. I went later on in the day to a place called Cliff House (on the coast.) There are some rocks about 100 yards out on which were lots of large seals basking in the sun, also cormorants nesting. Near this place there is a splendid swimming bath – said to be the finest in the world – It is certainly very fine.

There are electric trams & cable tramways by which you can go all over the city. I saw plenty of humming birds buzzing round the flowers in Golden Gate Park. I tried to knock some down with my stick but they were too nippy.

Lots of girls ride bicycles here; mostly in bloomers.

I am going to a place called Yosemite Valley with some friends I made on the "Gaelic". This trip will take about a week. I have not wired for a berth in the "Britannic" yet for July 28th but am nearly certain to leave by that boat. I stop at the Brunswick Hotel, New York.

Hoping that you are all quite well at Durlstone.
Best love to all,
*   Your affect brother*
*   Bertie Bristowe*

Americans always start their breakfast with fruit, & they don't use egg cups. The eggs being broken & turned into a wine glass by the waiter.

ജ

Tuesday 29th June 1897   San Francisco, Palace Hotel
Went to the Golden Gate Park with Pickenpeck and Pervis (an Australian.) The latter told me that the Australian boys, when ducks are flying over, imitate the cry of a hawk & they immediately fly to the ground. We saw lots of humming birds in the park.

30th June 1897   On the way to Yosemite
We left S.F. 4.30 for Raymond, Pickenpeck, Saubolle, Mr. and Mrs Baker, a French lady & her manservant, & a young American & his wife. It was awfully hot and dusty in the train. Dinner and tea at Lathrop.

When Bertie visited the Yosemite Valley, it was an area which had been ceded to the state of California by the Federal government since 1864 for 'public use, resort, and recreation'. Originally it had been the territory of the local Ahwahneechee people. Unfortunately their hunting ground was increasingly invaded by outsiders, such as trappers, or those in search of gold. This resulted in conflict which escalated into the Mariposa War in 1851 and led to the dispossession of the Native Americans.

Part of the valley was declared a National Park in 1890, and later the whole area was incorporated; even though the total size was decreased to allow the building of a dam and logging, the park now is 3,081 sq. km (1,169 sq. miles), about the same size as the State of Rhode Island. It is one of the best loved and most frequently visited national park in USA to this day.

1st July 1897   Wawona
We started from Raymond on the coach at 6.30 after breakfast ($1.)
Parched up country with many kopjes & evergreen oaks, awfully dusty.
Saw lots of ground squirrels, hares and quail. One grouse of sorts. I
had a box seat. Had lunch at a small rest-house on the way. Saw lots
of wood-peckers hawking for flies, blue jays, yellow pine, balsam fir.
The natives I am told use the gum in the blisters on the top shoots
for all kinds of wounds. After lunch the most of our journey was
through pine woods. The undergrowth was principally a small kind of
rose (white.) The most graceful pine I have seen is the sugar pine, the
cones of which hang in festoons at the end of the branches. I saw
mistletoe growing on many kinds of trees, among others "Arbor Vitae."
It is rather different to ours with round small leaves.

Sugar pines, *Pinus lambertiana,* are the largest pine species, often growing forty to sixty
metres high. The tallest ever recorded was one known as the Yosemite Giant which was
eighty-two metres. Their hanging pine cones can reach a length of 30 cm and the seeds
are edible, as is their sweet tasting resin which gives the tree its name. Unfortunately a
foreign disease known as White Pine Blister Rust was accidentally introduced in 1906.
This decimated the Sugar pines and almost wiped them out, but rust resistant trees are
being developed and introduced, which hopefully will save this magnificent tree.

Arborvitae are evergreen trees, which are a kind of Cyprus, in the genus *Thuja*. These trees
occur naturally on the North American continent and in Asia. They are cultivated widely
in gardens where they make beautiful specimen trees, or may be kept trimmed as hedges.

2nd July 1897   Yosemite
We left Wawona at 7 o'clock for Yosemite. A long drive mostly through
pine forests. I saw lots of jolly flowers. A vivid brick red columbine,
a pretty "Mariposa Lily" (3 petals, 6 stamen,) azaleas, a pretty pink rose,
a wallflower, & a lupin. I also saw lots of quail, one grouse of sorts.
Arrived at Yosemite for lunch and saw the Bridal Veil Falls. On a drive in
the afternoon we saw the rainbow on the Bridal falls on our way home.

The Mariposa lily is a beautiful lily with three petals, of the genus *Calochortus*, which
occurs in California's Sierra Nevada mountains. There are up to seventy species and
they may be white, pink, yellow or purple. Their bulbs are edible and were eaten by the
Native Americans.

3rd July 1897   Yosemite
Up at 5.30. Went to Mirror lake & saw the sun rise there. Then we drove
to the foot of the trail for Nevada falls. Mr & Mrs. Baker & I walked. We

Glacier Point Yosemite National Park. From an old post card

saw the Vernal falls & had lunch at the top of Nevada falls.

Marianne North also visited California on two occasions and both times created beautiful paintings of the trees, flowers and the spectacular scenery. On her second visit she noted with regret, how many of the large trees had been felled, but found plenty still to admire and paint. She wrote:

'The whole road was beautiful, through the biggest trees of the fir kind I ever saw, till I saw "The Trees," All the world knows their dimensions, so I need not repeat them; but only those who have seen them know their rich red plush bark and the light green eclipse of feathery foliage above, and the giant trunks that swell enormously at the base, having no branches up to a third of their whole height.... There are about seven hundred in that one grove of Mariposa alone, and the three other groves within a day or two of them. They stood out grandly against the other trees, which in themselves would have been worth a journey to see – sugar pines, yellow pines and arbor vitae, hung with golden lichen. The forest was full of strange trails of big bears and other wild animals'.

4th July 1897   Wawona
We left Yosemite valley & walked up to Glacier Point. Pickenpeck and I took 2 hours ¾, Mr. and Mrs. Baker and Saubolle 3 hours 20 minutes. Had lunch there & saw some bombs exploded near Glacier Point. We took the coach from here to Wawona. Three American ladies & one man who had ridden up the trail also got on the coach. One turned out to be a cousin of the Misses Duff. (Mrs Watson.)

In 1870, James McCauley, a hotel owner at Yosemite, lit a bonfire at the top of Glacier Point and later kicked the burning logs over the point. The people below were so impressed at the display of flames and sparks cascading over the precipice, that it became a regular event for the tourists. Sometimes, to make the show more dramatic, real bombs were included. After some years this practice was discontinued since it was deemed to be harmful to the environment.

5th July 1897 Wawona, Big trees
Went to see big trees. The "Grizzly Giant" 285 feet high, 105 in circumference. We drove through two in the coach.

We had lunch in a log hut. Mrs. Baker made a sketch & we drove back.

On the way back to San Francisco 6th July 1897
Coach drive back to Raymond. I heard today that the Bakers had the same guide in Japan that I had, Yasuda.

A Horse carriage passing under a Great Tree at Wawona Mariposa

7th July 1897 San Francisco
Back for lunch at the Palace Hotel.
Gillespie turned up. He had a very rough passage from Honolulu.

Palace Hotel
San Francisco,
California July 7th

Dear Mater,
I have just returned from Yosemite Valley where I have had a glorious time. I went with a party of 8 (all from the "Gaelic".) We started on 30th June, one night in the train & then a coach drive from 6 in the morning till 6 at night through dust the like of which I have never experienced before. We were simply smothered by the end of the day. We stopped the night at a place called Wawona where they made us pay

through the nose for everything, as they did all through this trip; 50 cents (2 shillings) for a cold bath for instance. The following morning we started in the coach again at 7a.m. & got to Yosemite Valley at 1p.m. It is certainly a wonderful valley & our two days there compensated for all the discomforts we went through. The valley is 7 miles long, & not more than a mile in width anywhere, 4000 feet above the sea, & there are perpendicular granite cliffs on both sides from 3000 to over 5000 feet high. There are 5 beautiful waterfalls, (the Yosemite falls).

We caused quite a sensation when we arrived at the "Sentinel Hotel" because our party of 9 represented 6 countries - England, America, New Zealand, India, Germany and France. We made some lovely excursions, some of the party riding on mules & the others walking. I walked & nearly always got up the hills as quickly as those who rode. At one place, "Glacier Point" you stand on a rock that projects from the cliff & look straight down 3250 feet into the valley below.

Going up to this place there were three American ladies riding on mens' saddles. (They had loose knickers with a skirt over.) I saw many others riding in this way I am told that it is the only way they can ride on the Mexican saddles. These three got into the coach in the afternoon & drove to Wawona. We got into conversation with them & one, (Mrs Watson) turned out to be a cousin of the Duffs - She had stayed with them on Champion Hill - Her home is in San Francisco.

The following day we went to see the big trees. (These are of the species we call "Wellingtonia's" at home, but the Americans won't know them by that name & call them "Washingtonia's". They are enormous, one called the "Grizzly Giant": being 104 feet in circumference & 275 feet high. We drove through two of these giants in the coach and four, through holes cut, as you must have seen them in their advertisement for Californian Wine in London. I saw many other sorts of fine pine and fir trees, the prettiest I thought was one called the "Sugar Pine". I also saw lots of pretty flowers. The "Lupin" that we have in our gardens grows wild in many places. Also lots of pretty birds and butterflies. California quail, here very plentiful, also blue Jays & Woodpeckers.

I have just received a letter from the "Governor" dated 7 June. Of course I shall be glad to find you all at Durlstone when I get home, but am sorry that you are staying away from Scotland on my account. I expect Kathleen is swearing away at me like a trooper, also Alec & Lewis.

197

I leave here tomorrow for Salt Lake City. From there I intend to go to Chicago, Niagara, Montreal, Quebec, and New York if I have time. I shall be home probably 4th August.

Hoping that you all are well.
Your affec. son,
Bertie

P.S. Ethel's letter I carried about with me for 6 days thinking I had posted it. I have just seen Mr Chamberlin & party who I have not seen since the trip from Colombo to Singapore. They are just starting on the trip to Yosemite Valley.

The advertisements featuring the Wawona trees that Bertie referred to were for 'Big Tree Wines.' This was the main brand exported to England and Australia by the Californian Wine Association. This was marketed in flat sided flagons of brown glass and sold at Harrods from 1895 at a cost of eighteen shillings a dozen. Their advertisements showed scenes of the Yosemite Park, including one of a coach being driven through a huge tree. The wine was described as: '*Zinfandel good table wine … very soft and round and free from acidity, most wholesome and blood-making*'.

8th July 1897   San Francisco
Got a letter from the Governor. After lunch went with Gillespie to China town, also through St. Mary's Street. Left by the 6 o'clock train for Salt Lake City. Our train & another at the same time were taken across an arm of the sea in a steam boat.

It is the custom in America to give the waiters a tip at each meal.

The Transcontinental rail road linking California to the rest of the USA was completed when the lines being built from the east and west met at Promontory Summit, Utah on the 10th May, 1869. This rail road ran for 1,907 miles (3069 km). Its construction used about 20,000 men, many of whom were Chinese or Irish immigrants. It took 6 years to complete.

The rapid rise in the population of California during the Gold Rush was an added incentive to construct this rail link and it had an enormous effect on the prosperity of California, as goods and people could be transported much more cheaply and in a few days, rather than weeks or even months.

At first, trains still had to be transported across San Francisco Bay by steamer. In the mountains, the tracks passed through the 'snow sheds', which were long tunnels constructed of wood on the Donner Pass to protect the railway line from the heavy snow drifts, which form there every winter.

A train emerging from Snow Sheds in the Rocky Mountains. An old postcard

9th July 1897   On the train on the way to Salt Lake
For forty miles the train went through snow sheds.

10th July 1897   Salt Lake City

Arrived at Ogden too late (3 hours) for the local train to Salt Lake City,
so waited till 2.30.   The Tabernacle & the Temple (Morman) are splendid
buildings. The roof of the former is 250 feet long, 150 broad, 70 high –
there are no pillars. Went to Douglas Fort in the electric train, through
the Eagle Gate, and saw a fine regiment of negro & half-casts.
Treated children to the round-about.

Salt Lake City was founded in 1847 by a small group of Mormons (Church of Jesus Christ of Latter Day Saints). They were led by the visionary prophet, Brigham Young, in search of a place where they could live without being persecuted because of their beliefs. The first arrivals consisted of 143 men, three women and two children.

Brigham Young had seen the land they were to settle in a vision and when the group reached the site of Salt Lake City, he was moved by God to declare; 'This is the right place.' Within days they started planting crops and laid out plans for a town-site. They were later joined by other settlers and soon the city took shape.

1016. Eagle Gate, Salt Lake City, Utah.

Eagle Gate, Salt lake City: Entrance to Brigham Young's property. Old postcard

The famous Mormon Tabernacle was completed in 1867 with its huge dome constructed of pine joists and covered in wooden shingles. Its organ had 800 pipes, which was considered a phenomenon in 1867, but the organ today has 11,623 pipes, making it one of the largest in the world.

The Temple was completed in 1893 after forty years of construction. The site was chosen by Brigham Young four days after they arrived and was dedicated in 1853. The stones used to build it had to be transported thirty miles by ox carts until 1869, when they were carried on the newly built railway and then construction could proceed more rapidly.
  Eagle Gate is a large archway built in 1859 over the road to commemorate the entrance to Brigham Young's property. It was topped by a large wooden carving of an eagle with outstretched wings. Later this was replaced by a metal sculpture.

Fort Douglas, originally named Camp Douglas, was first established in 1862 to protect the overland mail route. By 1897 it was a regimental post, and of course the mail was more safely transported by rail.

Sunday 11th July 1897 Salt Lake City
Went to Saltair for a bathe. 22 per cent salt. It is very hard to swim. We had the key of our rooms round our necks on a string. We were to have seen a gold mine belonging to Mr. Schenk. I saw "Camberwell Beauties" here.

200

Saltair was a resort and amusement park opened in 1893. It was situated on the shores of the Great Salt Lake and was a respectable and popular place for the city people to go to swim, dance or amuse themselves. It was run as a partnership between the Mormon Church and the Salt Lake and Los Angeles Railway Company. It lay about 15 kilometres outside the city, but had a convenient train service running there every forty-five minutes.

Saltair Pavillion at Salt Lake City, Utah. Old Postcard

Saltair Pavilion was destroyed by fire in 1925, and even though a new pavilion was built, it never became quite as successful as the first one, even though it had what was claimed to be the largest dance floor in the world.

Bertie recognised the Camberwell Beauty (Nymphalis antiopia) butterfly because of his interest in Lepidoptera, but it is unlikely he ever saw one alive in England. They are only very occasional migrants there, but are more common in Northern Europe, Asia and North America, so it was not surprising he spotted some flying around Salt Lake City. In North America they are known as the Mourning Cloak butterfly.

In the train for Chicago   12/7/97
We missed the 7 o'clock train in the morning & had to wait till 6.30pm. There is an amusing conductor on the train. He has been to England and had a suit made at Poole's which he offered me cheap. He says we can't make clothes or boots. He also said that although America has only a standing army of 25000, they could raise one of 3,000,000 in 10 days.

It was bizarre to be offered a genuine Henry Poole suit by a railway conductor in the middle of America. Henry Poole had been an exclusive bespoke tailoring company in London since 1806. The firm started with the first Henry Poole, who specialised in military tailoring. He prospered during the Napoleonic Wars. After he died, his son, also Henry, moved the business to 15, Saville Row, to become the first of many tailors in that famous street. He extended his client base to the cream of society, both in Britain and overseas. This included royalty, and the firm has been granted a large number of royal warrants by crowned heads from many countries.

It was Henry Poole, in consultation with the Prince of Wales (later to be Edward V11), who in 1865 invented the 'Dinner Jacket'. The Prince required something suitable to wear at Sandringham at less formal dinners. This garment was later adopted by some of Poole's rich American clients who introduced it to the exclusive Tuxedo Club in New York City. This mode of dress became popular and the term Tuxedo, or Tux, was coined in the USA.

Denver and Rio Grande train with multiple engines needed to surmount the Rocky Mountains
Old postcard

In the train for Chicago 13/7/97
The collector told me today about the Civil War. He also told me an anecdote about Lincoln & the little girl who came a long way to save her brother from being shot (for sleeping while on duty.) Also that Cleveland has not got a friend, & drinks.

The legend of the sleeping sentinel was based on a true event. A young soldier from Vermont, called William Scott, was condemned to death for sleeping while on sentry duty during the Civil War and it was believed that President Lincoln did issue a Presidential pardon. It became a famous case in the USA, with the story being featured in a popular epic poem and later, a silent film. William Scott did not have a sister, so that part of the story may have been invented for dramatic effect.

President Cleveland was not a popular figure with railway attendants in 1897. In 1894, there had been a strike of 125,000 railway workers demanding better pay and improved work conditions, but as this threatened to cripple the transport system and cause great damage to the US economy, the President had mobilized the army and the workers were forced back to work.

Bertie made little mention of the landscape the train was passing through, but Bisland was more observant. She was travelling from east to west and since she considered her fellow passengers to be not very interesting, so she spent much of her time gazing out of the window at the passing scene.

'. . . Soft undulations, full and tender as the bosom of a sleeping mother, rose and fell far beyond the eye's reach, and melted into the sky. No tree or thicket broke the suave outlines, but where the thin silver veins of the streams slipped through the curves of the plain, slim, leafless willows hung, like glistening fringes. . . . In the night a hoar frost had fallen that was to snow as sleep is to death; and the pale reaped fields, the sere meadows, and silent uplands were transfigured by the first gleam of day to a mystery and glory of silver and pearl. As the light grew, nacreous tints of milky blue and rose flushed the argent pallor of the land, and when the yellow disk rolled up over the horizon's edge I travelled for some brief space in a world of intolerable splendor, where innumerable billions of frost crystals flashed back to the sun the reflection of his shining face. Even the engine-driver was moved, I fancy, by this marvellous morning vision, for though we were far from any stopping-place, there suddenly thrilled through the silence a long, keen, triumphant blast, and we trailed as we flew floating golden plumes of steam. . . .'

In the train for Chicago (Omaha) 14/7/97
We had to spend most of the day at Omaha, so went over Hammond's packing establishment. Left again at 4.30 for Chicago.

The G H Hammond packing plant covered 30 acres where large numbers of cattle, pigs and sheep were slaughtered and processed ready to be transported to all parts of the USA. George Hammond, in partnership with Marcus Towle, first started business in 1868 at Detroit where chipped ice from the Great Lakes was used to chill meat for shipment to Boston by rail. The Hammond plant at Omaha opened in the 1980's and closed in 1901.

Chicago 15/7/97
We arrived here at 7.45 this morning & I went straight to Victoria Hotel. I am glad to get a bath. We had a drive round Jackson Park & saw the

Field Museum, also Washington Park & Drexal's boulevard. We went in the afternoon to a variety entertainment at the top of the Masonic Building 22 stories. We then went to the art gallery.

Chicago, Ill., Masonic Temple.

Masonic Temple building Chicago. Old postcard

Bertie found there was much to see and do in his one and a half days in Chicago. This city, in 1897, was one of the most up-to-date and sophisticated in the United States. It had magnificent museums, shops, parks and concert halls, to house the world-famous Chicago Symphony Orchestra which was founded in 1891. During the nineteenth century, it was probably one of the fastest growing cities in the world. In 1829 the number of people living in the fledgling town of Chicago was 100 and when it was incorporated in 1833, there were 350 residents. By 1840 this had risen to 4,000 and in 1890 it was the second largest city in the USA with a population of 1,099,850. This was to increase to 1,698,575 in 1900.

The reason for this great city's meteoric growth was largely because of its geographic position on the banks of Lake Michigan in the middle of the USA. This made it ideally placed to be the major transportation hub in the country. Initially goods were transported via the Great lakes and using portage overland to the River Mississippi, and thence to the Atlantic. Later, improvements occurred when, in 1848, firstly, a canal connected the city to the Mississippi, and then the railroads were constructed, opening up new areas. By the 1850s there was a vast web of rail lines entering Chicago from all over America, and after 1869, this included a line to the west coast and the Pacific.

In addition to transportation, Chicago became an important centre for manufacturing industries, commerce and retail businesses. It was also well placed to have access to many valuable natural and agricultural resources such as timber, grain crops and farm animals. All were processed and shipped to the rest of the USA. Chicago became a Mecca for businessmen and entrepreneurs. Working men and women in search of employment flocked to Chicago: initially from the eastern states of the USA, then in the 1840s, immigrants from Ireland fleeing the great famine, and later many from European countries, some escaping persecution, all seeking the dream of a better life in the USA.

In October 1871 Chicago was partially destroyed by a catastrophic fire in which 300 people lost their lives and 17,000 buildings were burned, leaving 10,000 homeless. This was a major tragedy, and the damage was made all the more significant because so much of the city consisted of wooden houses. When re-building occurred, flammable materials were replaced with bricks, stone and steel. The new Chicago rose from the ashes to become a much grander place. In 1885 the first sky scraper in the world was built there, with the new method of construction using a steel frame allowing it to rise to ten storeys. Later many much taller structures were built.

By 1893, Chicago was deemed a suitable venue to hold the Great Columbian Exposition, a huge event to commemorate 400 years since Columbus discovered America. This attracted over twenty-seven million visitors to Chicago during the six months it was open. People marvelled at the exhibits and the elaborate decorations when they attended the Exposition at Jackson Park by the lake. This was the park with the beautiful gardens Bertie visited and admired four years later.

Union Railway Station. Chicago, old postcard

The Field Museum Bertie referred to was an offshoot of the Columbian Exposition, and originally was to have been named the Columbian Museum of Chicago. The plans for this venture were running into difficulties due to lack of funds. Marshal Field, who had come to Chicago as a young man and made a large fortune, generously donated one million dollars, so when this wonderful museum was opened in Jackson Park in June 1894, it was named the Field Columbian Museum. It still exists, but in 1921 was moved to new premises in Grant Park.

The Victoria Hotel was built in 1878 on the corner of Michigan and Van Buren Street. Originally it was named 'Beaurivage Bachelor Apartments' with luxury apartments. In 1882 it was damaged by fire, but was rebuilt, and in 1892, was converted into a hotel, and re-named The Victoria Hotel, with 278 rooms. This conversion was probably undertaken in preparation for the influx of visitors anticipated in Chicago for the 1893 Grand Columbian Exposition. In 1908 the hotel was demolished and a 20 storey skyscraper, the McCormick building, was constructed on the site.

The Masonic temple was built in 1892. This was twenty-two storeys high, making it the tallest building in Chicago. It contained offices and apartments with the top floor reserved for the Masonic rooms and a theatre. It was demolished in 1939 because the offices were considered old fashioned, the elevators were inadequate and also there were plans to build a subway under it, which would have necessitated expensive modifying of the foundations.

Victoria Hotel Chicago, old postcard

VICTORIA HOTEL July 16th
CHICAGO
Miligan & Upman, Props

Dear Mater,

We had a very hot and dusty railway journey to Salt Lake City. The only incidents worth mentioning were - 1st - The whole of our train & another one besides were taken on a steamer across an arm of the sea. - 2nd - We went for 40 miles through a covered passage (made of wood) put up to keep the snow off the line In winter. The country through which we passed during the day light was very uninteresting. Salt Lake City is the headquarters of the "Mormans" & they have a beautiful temple & tabernacle there. A monument is put up to one of these "rascals" who had 26 wives. We had a bath in the Salt Lake, quite a new experience. There is 22 per cent of salt in the water. (There is only 3 per cent in the sea) & consequently you can't sink if you take your feet off the ground they come to the top of the water at once. It is hard to swim well as your feet will come out of the water behind. I think that even Ethel could manage to keep up without putting one foot on the bottom. There is a regiment of negro soldiers quartered near the city. We saw them drilling; they are certainly fine fellows.

From Salt Lake we took the train to Chicago, but had to change at Omaha. Having about 5 hours to wait, we went over the packing establishment of "Hammonds." It was certainly very interesting. They kill nearly 500 head of cattle a day, besides sheep and pigs. It was a disgusting sight, but I am glad that I have seen it. We arrived here yesterday morning. We went for a drive through Jackson Park, where the exhibition was held, also through Washington Park. They are both beautifully laid out & I really think the finest I ever saw.

In the afternoon we went to the theatre at the top of the "Masonic Building". (22 stories high) & heard a concert It was rather foggy so we could not get a very good view of the city. We leave here this afternoon for Niagara. I might possibly leave New York on the 21st July in the White Star steamer "Adriatic" as the chaps I am travelling with will depart at about that time. As soon as I have taken my berth I will cable the name of the ship only & you will know that I am coming in that steamer. It will be the Adriatic on the 21st, or the Britannic on the 28th July from New York.

Hoping that you are all quite well at Durlstone, & with best love to all Your affec. son,
Bertie Bristowe

∞∞∞

16th July 1897   On the train to Niagara
Went to the Museum again & caught the train at 3pm for Niagara.

7th July 1897   Niagara Saturday
Arrived 6.30 am.   We wanted to get out at Clifton House on the Canadian side, but passed the station without knowing it. Went to Prospect House. Took a drive round (4 hours for 6 dollars - a swindle) We took 6 hours & had to pay another 2 ½ dollars. Was robbed over a satin stone brooch on the Canadian side.

A train passing the Niagara Falls, old postcard

Things did not go very well for Bertie at Niagara, nor does he write much about his impressions of the falls; Marianne North, on her visit, painted several pictures of the falls. She was more enthusiastic and wrote:

The falls far outstretched my grandest ideas. They are enormous, the banks above and below wildly and richly wooded, with a great variety of fine trees, tangles of vine and Virginian creeper over them, dead stumps, skeleton trees, and worn rocks white with lichens; the whole setting is grand, and the bridges are so cobwebby that they seem by contrast to make the falls more massive. …The Horseshoe Fall tempted me much, standing close to its head, with the rapids like a sea behind, and the rainbow dipping into its deep emerald hollow; the tints were endless in their gradation, and delicious, but I got wet through in the mist."

18th July 1897   In the train Niagara to New York
Went again with Pickenpack to see the falls from the Canadian side.
Thunder storm in the afternoon.

The last city Bertie visited before embarking on the ship to cross the Atlantic was New York City. This great city had a colourful and turbulent past.

New York City showing horse drawn traffic at the junction of Broadway and 23rd Street, old postcard

The site of New York City was originally the territory of the Lenape people and the first recorded visit by Europeans was in 1524 when a French ship, La Dauphine, explored the area, but did not stay long. The first settlement was credited to Henry Hudson who arrived on his ship Half Moon in 1609, while employed by the Dutch East India Company. He was actually searching for a passage to the East Indies, but discovered a wonderful harbour and a river containing thousands of beavers. Their pelts were highly prized by the fur traders. The first settlers were mainly Dutch with their African slaves, they named the town New Amsterdam.

In 1664 the British supplanted the Dutch and changed the name to New York. British rule, with their regulations and taxation, was generally resented by the residents and in 1765, there was a revolt which led up to the War of Independence. When George Washington arrived in New York in 1783, the British were finally driven out.

From 1785 to 1790 New York was the capital of the United States. Even though this honour was transferred to Philadelphia and then Washington, New York City has always been the major commercial centre, and by 1835, became the largest city in the United States. This was largely due to the great number of immigrants arriving by ship at New York harbour. During the nineteenth century, world events caused a huge rise in the numbers of people seeking a better life. One was the terrible Irish potato famine (1845 – 1850), which led to an influx of migrants, and later many migrated from various European countries, fleeing poverty, persecution and political upheavals. In 1886 the Statue of Liberty was erected at the mouth of the harbour as a symbolic welcome to immigrants. This iconic monument was a gift from the Citizens of France.

New York City in 1897 was a prosperous and cosmopolitan city, and in the short time he was there, Bertie was able to pursue his interests in natural history and art, by visiting the world class Natural History Museum, the Art Gallery, and also to stay at a very classy hotel.

New York 19th July 1897
Hoffman House Hotel. Took my berth on the "Adriatic." White Star for the 21st July.

In 1897 Hoffman House was one of the best and most opulent hotels in New York City. It was opened in 1864 and was situated on Broadway, adjacent to Maddison Square Gardens, across the road from the famous Delmonico's restaurant. The hotel was famed for its modernity, comfort, and the elegance of its internal decor. It became the New York headquarters of the Democrat party, sometimes to the inconvenience of the other guests when they had rowdy parties.

We can only speculate as to whether Bertie indulged in the elaborate cocktails being dispensed in the strictly men-only Grand Saloon Bar in the hotel. This was a place of carved mahogany, shining brass, red velvet, with colourful tapestries and oriental carpets. It was also famous, or infamous, for its art works, which included near-naked bronze statues of Eve and Bacchus, but most shocking of all were several paintings of luscious nude ladies. One in particular scandalized 19th century society. It was an eight foot high, very beautiful painting by the French artist William-Adolphe Bouguereau called Nymphs and Satyr. This painting, with its gold frame, draped by a red velvet canopy, was hung on the wall opposite the bar behind which was a very large mirror, so the gentlemen could discretely admire the painting from all angles. It shows a bevy of nude nubile nymphs cavorting with a half man, half beast satyr beside a woodland pool and now is displayed at the Clark Institute in Williamstown, Massachusetts.

The art works in the bar belonged to one of the hotel's partners, a colourful character named Edward (Ned) Stokes, who in 1872, shot dead his friend and business associate, James Fisk. They had fallen out over deals that had gone wrong, and, to add insult to injury, Stokes ran off with Fisk's mistress, the voluptuous actress Josie Mansfield. Stokes was sentenced to death, but appealed. After three trials, the sentence was commuted to seven years in prison, of which he served only four years at Sing Sing jail. When he was released, he returned to the hotel and resumed his business as usual.

The hotel continued to operate after 1897, with various renovations and enlargements occurring, but it was finally demolished in 1915 to be replaced by a sixteen storey office and loft building on the site.

20th July 1897   New York

Hoffman House.   Went to the Natural History Museum in the morning. American "Colias" Eurytheme with Var. alba, also yellow Colias philodice with white var.   A small Orange Tip "Authocaris genutia" the size of our Wood White with slightly hooked wing, something between our "Cardamines" & the Japanese Authocaris scolymus. Bats with wings spread out on glass. The Cat bird is rather like a large Black Cap. It has chestnut coloured feathers under its tail.

I went to the Museum of Art & saw the Horse Fair by Rosa Bonheur.

Museum of Natural History, New York City, old postcard

Bertie must have found the butterfly exhibits at the museum extremely useful to his studies. The species he mentioned, Colias eurythme and Colias philodice butterflies are widespread throughout the American continent. They are commonly known as Clouded Yellows, Sulphurs or Alfalfa butterflies, because sometimes they can become a pest to Alfalfa crops. Anthocaris genus butterflies may be found in many countries of the world and are generally white with yellow of orange tips to their wings. Bertie could have collected similar specimens in England, Japan and the USA.

After some busy days in New York, Bertie was about to embark on the last leg of his journey; the crossing of the Atlantic and home to England.

For another nineteenth century traveller, the Atlantic crossing was the beginning of his adventures. On 8th June, 1867 Mark Twain set sail from New York on the 'side-wheel steamship', *Quaker City*. This ship had been launched in Philadelphia in 1854 as a commercial vessel, but was aquired by the US Navy in 1861. It saw active service during the American Civil War. After the war it returned to civilian service and in 1867 was chartered to transport a large group of US citizens on an expedition to Europe and the Holy Land. At this time, Twain was a young newspaper correspondent and persuaded the newspapers he worked for to sponsor his trip. He wrote a series of very amusing articles about his experiences, which were published as a very popular book in 1869, titled *Innocents Abroad*. Bertie was lucky to have good weather and a smooth crossing. This was not so for the *Quaker City*.

Metropolitan Art Museum, New York City, old postcard

Twain wrote in his description of the commencement of his trip:

'In the fullness of time the ship was ready to receive her passengers. I was introduced to the young gentleman who was to be my roommate, and found him to be intelligent, full of generous impulses, patient, considerate and wonderfully good-natured.... We selected a stateroom forward of the wheel, on the starboard side, 'below decks'. It had two berths in it, a dismal dead-light, a sink with a washbowl in it, and a long, sumptuously cushioned locker, which was to do service as a sofa – partly – and partly as a hiding place for our things. Notwithstanding all this furniture, there was still room to turn around in, but not to swing a cat in, at least with entire security to the cat. However, the room was large, for a ship's stateroom, and was in every way satisfactory.

The vessel was appointed to sail on a certain Saturday early in June. A little after noon on that distinguished Saturday I reached the ship and went on board. All was bustle and confusion. {I have seen that remark before somewhere.} The pier was crowded with carriages and men; passengers were arriving and hurrying on board; the vessel's decks were encumbered with trunks and valises; groups of excursionists, arrayed in unattractive travelling costumes, were moping about in drizzling rain and looking as droopy and woebegone as so many moulting chickens.... Finally, above the banging, and rumbling, and shouting, and hissing of steam rang the order to 'cast off.' – a sudden rush to the gangways – a scampering ashore of visitors – a vevolution of the wheels, and we were off – the picnic had begun!...

We steamed down to the foot of the harbour and came to anchor. It was still raining. And not only raining, but storming. 'Outside' we could see ourselves, that there was a tremendous sea on. We must lie still in the calm harbour, till the storm should abate....We were alone on the deep. On five fathoms, and anchored fast to the bottom. And out in the solemn rain, at that. This was pleasuring with a vengeance.

It was an appropriate relief when the gong sounded for prayer meeting. The first Saturday night of any other pleasure excursion might have been devoted to whist and dancing; but I submit it to the unprejudiced mind if it would have been in good taste for us to engage in such frivolities, considering what we had gone through and the frame of mind we were in. We would have shone at a wake, but not anything more festive.

However, there is always a cheering influence about the sea; and in my berth that night, rocked by the measured swell of the waves and lulled by the murmurs of the distant surf, I soon passed tranquilly out of all consciousness of the dreary experiences of the day and damaging premonitions of the future.

All day Sunday at anchor. The storm had gone down a great deal, but the sea had not....We must lie still till Monday. And we did....The next morning we weighed anchor and went to sea. It was a great happiness to get away after this dragging, dispiriting delay. I thought there never was such gladness in the air before, such brightness in the sun, such beauty in the sea. It was breezy and pleasant, but the sea was still very rough....By some happy fortune I was not seasick – that was a thing to be proud of. I had not always escaped before. If there is one thing in the world that will make a man peculiarly and insufferably self-conceited, it is to have his stomach behave itself, the first day at sea, when nearly all his comrades are seasick.

213

On this last leg of his journey, Bertie makes no mention of seasickness, so he must have had a calm passage on *Adriatic*. This vessel was one of the White Star Line ships which plied the route between Liverpool, to New York, with a stop at Queenstown in Ireland. She carried passengers and freight to and from the New World.

The White Star Line originated at the port of Liverpool in 1845. It was then a company that operated sailing ships, mainly taking emigrants to Australia. By the 1860s, the company was in major financial difficulties, caused by over-extending themselves buying ships. The final straw was the collapse of their bank.

In 1868 Thomas Ismay made an offer of one thousand pounds to buy the rights to use the White Star name, its flag and the company's good will. When this was accepted, he made his headquarters at Albion House in Liverpool. His plan was to operate a service running large passenger steam ships between Liverpool and the American Continent. The official name of the company was the Oceanic Steam Navigation Company, but it was generally known as The White Star Line. An advantageous deal was agreed with the ship building company Harland and Wolff of Belfast that they would build the White Star fleet. This was commenced in 1869 with the first four ships: *Oceanic, Atlantic, Baltic,* and *Republic.* These were followed by the slightly larger sister ships, *Celtic* and *Adriatic.*

In 1870, the Liverpool business man, William Imrie joined the company, the first passage was undertaken in 1871 between Liverpool and New York; and so began the weekly service. This became a highly successful venture, but with its share of disasters. In 1873, *Atlantic* was wrecked with a loss of 535 lives, then in 1912 the great ship, *Titanic* was lost on her maiden voyage, her sister ship, *Britannic* hit a mine and sank during the First World War while serving as a troop ship. Also several other vessels were sunk by enemy action during the war. White Star Line continued to operate through difficult times, but in 1934 White Star merged with the Cunard Line when both companies were struggling during the Depression. At first the company was known as Cunard White Star, but later, White Star was dropped, and by 1950 White Star Line had ceased to exist.

Adriatic was built by Harland and Wolff in 1871 and made her first voyage in 1872. Being the largest in the fleet, she became the White Star Line flag ship. She was 437 feet (138.1 metres.) long and of 3,888 gross tons. She had accommodation for 166 passengers in first class, and one thousand in third class. Later in 1884 she was re-fitted to accommodate 2nd class passengers as well. There had been plans to light the ship with gas, which would have made her the first Atlantic liner to do so, but they had to revert to oil lamps when dangerous gas leaks occurred in rough seas.

The rivalry between the shipping lines operating the lucrative trans-Atlantic crossing was intense. Speed and comfort for the passengers was paramount. During her second voyage, *Adriatic* won the 'Blue Riband' for the fastest crossing of the Atlantic in seven days, twenty-three hours and seventeen minutes at an average speed of 14.53 knots.

This record had been previously held by the Cunard ship Scotia since 1866.

Possibly because of the emphasis on traveling at speed, during her twenty-seven years of operation *Adriatic* was involved in four collisions, the first in 1874, being with *Parthia*, a Cunard ship. Not too much damage was done on this occasion, though *Adriatic* had to return to New York for repairs. In 1875 *Adriatic* collided with a US ship named *Columbus* and sank her. Later in the same year, she completely destroyed the sailing ship, *Harvest Queen* off the coast of Wales. None of *Harvest Queen's* crew survived. The fourth incident also occurred off the Welsh coast in 1878 when *Adriatic* collided with a small brig, *G. A. Pike*. Five of *Pike's* crew were killed. In an enquiry, it was suggested that *Adriatic's* excessive speed in the foggy conditions was the cause. Ships did not have the benefit of radar to assist navigation in 1878.

When Bertie was a passenger, there were no collisions and a mercifully smooth seas, but *Adriatic* was reaching the end of her days of steaming across the Atlantic. She was retired from service later in 1897 and laid up at Birkenhead. She was scrapped in 1899.

22nd July 1897   SS Adriatic
Beautiful weather.   King and Busch from California. The latter has also been 7 years in Dutch Guiana. He tells me that the natives cut a sort of Rattan, squash it & throw it into the river to kill the fish. They also have a preventive for snake bites. He has caught sharks on the pacific coast which when cut open had live young inside. One can hear the baboons roaring 6 miles off. The natives wrap tough birds in "Paw Paw" leaves to make them tender.

SS Adriatic (White Star Line), from the Ian Farquhar collection

SS Adriatic   23/7/97
A chap from Canada tells me that there is fine salmon fishing (spoon)
off Victoria (Vancouver.) He has also been to S. America where he one
day saw on the river Parana, 7 large kind of white storks with black
heads & red necks. He had an easy shot, but missed them. Potropolis is
the place to go for humming birds & " Morphos."

As he was a keen lepidopterist, Bertie knew about Morpho butterflies. The genus has beautiful iridescent blue wings and is one of the largest species of butterflies in the world. Specimens have always been much prized by butterfly collectors.

24th July 1897   SS Adriatic
Busch told me today a tale of the Tapir eating a certain plant & catching
fish, also that pigs when too fat eat a plant that makes them able to run
again. There is a small fish with very strong jaws in Guiana which bites
ducks' feet off. Get your scatter gun, smell dog & come & hunt quail or
tumbledoodle (woodcock.) Please wipe your gun on the doormat.   Do
you like -----any?   Some.   Out of sight.

It sounds as though Bertie was spending most of his time at the bar swapping tall travellers' tales which seemed to be getting more and more wild and garbled. By this stage in his journey. He may also have taken part in the deck games, but his enthusiasm for recording his experiences in his journal had dwindled, so after this last bizarre entry, there was nothing more recorded during the last five days of the crossing except the dates. On the other hand Mark Twain on his Atlantic crossing, which was obviously on turbulent seas, recorded some of the day to day activities of his fellow ship-mates more fully. He wrote:

'We ploughed along bravely for a week or more. ... The Passengers soon learned to accommodate themselves to their new circumstances, and life in the ship became nearly as systematically monotonous as the routine of a barrack. I do not mean that it was dull, for it was not entirely so by any means – but there was a good deal of sameness about it. As is always the fashion at sea, the passengers shortly began to pick up sailor terms – a sign that they were beginning to feel at home. Half-past six was no longer half-past six to those pilgrims from New England, the South and Mississippi Valley, it was 'seven bells'; eight, twelve and four o'clock were 'eight bells'; the captain did not take the longitude at nine o'clock, but at 'two bells'. They spoke glibly of the 'after cabin', the 'for'rard cabin', port and starboard and the 'for'castle'.

At seven bells the first gong rang; at eight bells there was breakfast, for such as were not too seasick to eat it. After that all the well people walked arm-in-arm up and down the long promenade deck, enjoying the fine summer mornings, and the seasick ones crawled out and propped themselves up in the lee of the paddle-boxes and ate their dismal tea and toast and looked wretched. From eleven o'clock until luncheon, and from luncheon until dinner at six in the evening, the employments and amusements were various. Some reading was done, and much smoking and sewing, though not by the same parties; there were the monsters of the deep to be looked at and wondered at; strange ships to be scrutinised through opera-glasses, and sage decisions arrived at concerning them; and more than that , everybody took a personal interest in seeing that the flag was run up and politely dipped three times in response to the salutes of those strangers; in the smoking room there were always parties of gentlemen playing euchre, draughts and dominoes, especially dominoes, that delightfully harmless game; and down on the main deck, 'for'rard' – for'rard of the chicken-coops and the cattle – we had what was called 'horse billiards'. Horse billiards is a fine game. It affords good active exercise, hilarity, and consuming excitement. It is a mixture of 'hop-scotch' and shuffleboard played with a crutch....

On several starlight nights we danced on the upper deck, under the awnings, and made something of a ballroom display of brilliancy by hanging a number of ship's lanterns from the stanchions. Our music consisted of the well-mixed strains of a melodeon which was a little asthmatic and apt to catch its breath where it ought to come out strong, a clarinet which was a little unreliable on the high keys and rather melancholy on the low ones, and a disreputable accordion that had a leak somewhere and breathed louder than it squawked – a more elegant term does not occur to me just now. However, the dancing was infinitely worse than the music. When the ship rolled to starboard the whole platoon of dancers came charging down to starboard with it, and brought up in a mass at the rail; and when it rolled to port they went floundering down to port with the same unanimity of sentiment....The Virginia reel, as performed on board the 'Quaker City' had more genuine reel about it as any reel I ever saw before, and was as full of interest to the spectator as it was full of desperate chances and hairbreadth escapes to the participant. We gave up dancing, finally.'

The Landing Stage at Liverpool, old postcard

Bertie might have enjoyed playing Horse-billiards with Mark Twain and his friends, but possibly he may have attempted to introduce them to the game of deck cricket.

Finally, Bertie's journey was coming to a close, when he arrived at Liverpool eight months after leaving Tilbury on 27th November 1896. In the last entry in his journal, he merely wrote:

Friday 30th July 1897   Liverpool

There is no record of whether any of the family met Bertie at Liverpool, but if not, there was a convenient train service to transport him back to London. Boat trains were provided by the shipping companies for passengers embarking, or disembarking from their ships. Liverpool Riverside railway station opened in 1895 and was situated at the Ocean Liner Terminal on the docks. Passengers could then board a London and North Western Railway (LNWR) express train to Euston Station.

Family members may have waited to greet him at Euston and escort him back to Camberwell. His parents, brothers and sisters no doubt were eager to see the traveller safely home again and to hear all he had to tell them about where he had been, and what he had done while he was visiting fascinating places around the world.

Bertie Bristowe, home (Bristowe papers)

How did the experiences they had while roaming the world affect the future lives of our nineteenth century explorers? Some, who enjoyed wandering around exotic landscapes, found it irksome to return to their narrow lives at home and continued travelling. A number of them wrote accounts of their adventures. Sometimes their journals or letters were purely for their own, or their family's consumption, but others wrote published works. Newspaper or magazine articles and books of travellers' tales became a popular form of literature in the nineteenth century. These could earn their authors a comfortable income.

Isabella Bird, Eliza Scidmore and Marianne North continued to travel and write, until ill health and age curbed their activities, as did Nellie Bly, who returned from her record-breaking journey round the world as a celebrity. She later wrote as a war correspondent while in Austria in the First World War. Elizabeth Bisland had no desire to court publicity, so soon after her arrival back in New York, she escaped to England for a year to concentrate on her serious writing. She was to marry when she finally returned home. After marriage, she did not travel extensively, but continued to write, for the rest of her life.

Sir Samuel Baker returned to England from Ceylon, but did not linger long before setting out on more adventures in Europe, where he acquired his second wife. He later made several expeditions to Africa. He wrote a number of books about the exiting explorations he and his wife undertook in darkest Africa and other countries. These were widely read by the Victorian general public, who had a thirst for knowledge about the more exotic parts of the world.

Rudyard Kipling and Mark Twain became two of the most respected and popular authors of their era and both continued to travel throughout their lives, partly for pleasure, but also in relation to their vocation.

When he had finished his term as Governor of Ceylon, Sir William Gregory married again and returned to his estates in Ireland, but he continued to travel, including return visits to Ceylon. He wrote books about his journeys and also his memoirs, which were published posthumously by his wife.

Major Thomas Skinner spent nearly fifty years in Ceylon, during which time he survived many bouts of fever and hazardous encounters with wild animals. He achieved much and became a highly respected figure there. When the time came for him to retire, he was happy to return to England where he took up salmon fishing, arranged his extensive collection of shells and wrote his memoirs which were published by his daughter after his death.

His Highness Raja-i-Rajgan Jagatijit Singh always returned to his palaces in Karpurthala, but continued to travel extensively and write of his experiences. His books were published as limited editions, mainly for his family and friends to read. He was to circumnavigate the world twice in his life and was welcomed as a popular guest by monarchs and presidents everywhere.

Even today, travellers in tropical countries can be struck down by various maladies, but, with benefit of modern medicine, these are rarely life-threatening. This was not so in the nineteenth century. Old cemeteries in tropical countries record the huge numbers of European young men, women and children who died of the various tropical diseases and disorders which were prevalent then. Both Sir William Gregory and Sir Stamford Raffles lost their first wives while in the tropics. By the time he was in his forties, Sir Stamford Raffles and his second wife were in extremely poor health and they had lost all but one of their children to various diseases, making it necessary for them to return to the cool climate of England, but he was to die quite soon afterwards.

John Still took pleasure in travel, but it was to result in severe consequences to his wellbeing. He spent years in the jungles of Ceylon which he loved, but it was there he contracted malaria, which severely compromised his health. He was compelled to return to England, but later could not resist returning to Ceylon and then married there. Unfortunately he enlisted in the army at the beginning of the First World War. His health, both mental and physical suffered while a prisoner of war in Turkey. He did, however write two books during this time. He and his wife were to return to Britain, where he wrote more books while living on a farm in Wales. On his wife's death, he joined his son, John in Rhodesia, but his health was poor and he died there soon after hearing the terrible news that his son had been killed in actionat the beginning of the Second World War.

The two scientific travellers, Alfred Russel Wallace and Frederick Burbidge spent years in wild places collecting specimens, but did not travel widely after their return. Neither were rich men, so the main aim of their collections was to obtain specimens be sold and generate income. They also had a keen scientific interest in their subjects. In both cases what they discovered had enormous significance and they both brought home many creatures and plants never seen before. In addition Wallace developed his own theory of evolution independently of the more famous Charles Darwin.

Wallace developed an interest in entomology as a boy in England and had embarked on a collecting expedition to the jungles of South America before his years spent in the forests of the Malay Archipelago. Nineteenth century museums were willing to pay well for insects, birds, mammals or any other creature for their collections, so Wallace's many thousands of specimens made him a considerable amount of money. When he returned to England, he also wrote his famous book, *The Malay Archipelago*, which he dedicated to Charles Darwin. This was to become one of the best known scientific books of the century. He was later to write more books and scientific papers about his discoveries and became a revered figure in the field of zoology and the study of biogeography. Once he returned to England he married and seemed to lose his desire to travel the world.

Burbidge came from a horticultural background and his collecting expedition to Borneo was commissioned by the famous Veitch and Co. nursery gardens. During the nineteenth century, as many people became more affluent, it became fashionable to have large gardens, shrubberies and heated glass houses, so the demand for exotic and colourful plants was huge. Collectors were sent to all parts of the globe in search of novelties in the garden world.

Burbidge had not been married long when he set off in 1877 and he was away for over two years, but during that time he collected a vast number of plants, seeds and specimens. He also made many meticulous botanical paintings of flowers. Many of these were new to science and quite a number, when formally classified, were named after him. In 1880 his book *Garden of the Sun* was published and he was to write several more books on horticulture and botany. Like Wallace, once he returned, he remained contentedly in the British Isles and worked for many years as curator of the botanical gardens at Trinity College, Dublin, where he became highly respected in the area of horticulture and botany.

Some people, though they have the sense of adventure and courage which leads them to travel, do not feel the urge to continue wandering once they reach their journey's end. Both William Mawson and Gertrude Bindloss led comparatively settled lives once they reached their final destinations.s They both wrote lively and entertaining accounts of their experiences which have been enjoyed by their families and friends, but have never been published.

Bertie, too returned to England apparently with no desire ever to travel far from home again, but was he a changed man after the experience of world travel and how did he adjust to normal life?

His son Bill Bristowe, in his memoirs, implied that before his father left, life had been at low ebb for Bertie, both physically and mentally. His work had been stressful and he was disappointed in his love life, but Bristowe wrote of his father that: *He came home completely fit, with a mind enriched by his experiences.*

Daibutsu statue bought by Bertie in Yokohama on 25 April 1897

There was a joyful family reunion on his return, but he had certain things that needed to be done before he returned to his routines of day to day living. He needed to organise the collection, or delivery, of all the beautiful art works he had purchased and had shipped to London, and then would come the excitement of unpacking the large crates to reveal the treasures within. This would have been a task his sisters Kathleen and Ethel might have enjoyed helping him with.

Also, mention had been made in his letters home of a family holiday in Scotland. This had to be postponed, so everyone would be at home when he arrived on 30th July. Perhaps he accompanied them when they travelled north. The close-knit Bristowe family enjoyed each other's company and made a habit of going on holidays as a group. Members of the London Stock Exchange often used to take time off when business was slow in the summer months, and head to the countryside for recreation.

Soon after his arrival back home, Bertie resumed his employment with his father and brothers in their family firm at the Stock Exchange. This was expected of him and perhaps, after his travels, he returned with renewed enthusiasm and enhanced knowledge of overseas investment opportunities. Also he made some useful contacts among the business men and potential investors he encountered. He continued in this occupation for the rest of his working life.

He soon had strong motivation to have a secure job with a reasonable salary for Bertie's circumstances changed. He now had responsibilities, since he became engaged to be married.

Whether or not it was true that Bertie left England to heal his broken heart because he believed he had failed to gain the love of Mary Johnston, he must have wasted no time in renewing his acquaintance with her. With his new-found confidence and savoir faire acquired from his travels, he was much more successful in his suit this time. Soon after his homecoming, their letters indicated they were in love, and by April 1898, he had proposed to her and been accepted.

Mary Rosa Johnston lived with her family not far from the Bristowes in Camberwell Green. Her father, John Brookes Johnston, was born in 1819 and worked as Company Secretary of the Royal Insurance Company. He was an astute businessman and was very erudite, with a love of art, books and the cultivation of exotic plants. He travelled widely throughout the world in connection with his work, but another side of him was his fervent religious beliefs. He was an extremely devout member of the Catholic Apostolic Church. The Johnston family moved to Camberwell Green so they would be within walking distance of the new ornate Church there. Their sizeable residence was called Tudor House at the top of Grove Lane which had a garden of one acre.

Four of the Johnston sisters and family in 1927. Henderson family album

In his autobiography, Harry Johnston wrote slightly tongue in cheek of his father:

He believed unshakably that 'the Lord' might come at any time; that at His Second Coming those of the Elect who had held their faith would be caught up into the air to meet Him, would, without dying, be subtly changed into immortal beings, and – apparently – would return to earth with the Son of God, to assist Him in governing the planet for the Millennial Period; after which this poor world would be destroyed by fire, or at any rate cease to interest the Creator of all things.

John Johnston earned a generous salary and also had inherited a private income from his father derived from various properties and investments. This was just as well, as he had a large family to support, having fourteen children: two by his first wife, and twelve more by his second wife, Esther Laetitia, whom he married in 1857. Mary, being born in 1873, was the third youngest child in the family. By all accounts, as a child, she was a spirited young thing.

In her memoirs, her older sister Annette (Nettie) wrote:
I was very fond of my younger sisters & can remember much admiring my sister Mary for her spirit and daring – when my father corrected her for some childish misdemeanour – she cried defiantly 'Naughty Pa-boy'. She was a bonny little pet with closely cropped hair. Lilian was playing at being a hair dresser & set little Mary on a stool and started cutting her hair. Alas! It ended in the hair being jaggedly clipped quite close to the head in some places & a fair length in others! They were both so frightened at the result that they started howling. When Mother came to see what was wrong, she decided that the only thing to be done was to take Mary to the hairdresser & have a complete crop. When she came back she looked like a nice little boy & was promptly christened 'Tom', & 'Tom' she remained, even after her marriage, & her letters were signed 'T'.

The Johnstons were an unusual and lively family. As children they loved to spend their evenings playing and singing Gilbert and Sullivan's songs and Nettie recorded how excited they were when a new opera came out. Mr. Johnston forbade the playing of frivolous songs on Sundays, but Harry managed to circumvent this edict by playing naughty ditties on the piano very, very slowly so they sounded like hymns to their father who was in his study reading serious religious works.

Many of the Johnston family had a keen interest in the arts and science. Harry, (later to be Sir Harry Johnston) the oldest of Laetitia's children, was a brilliant artist, but also a distinguished African explorer and administrator. He was a naturalist of some note and it was he that discovered the Okapi. This strange animal was found deep in the equatorial forests of the Congo. It looks like a cross between a zebra and a giraffe and the species was named *Okapia johnstoni*, in his honour.

Mabel, Mary's younger sister, married the gifted musician, Arnold Dolmetsch. Together they founded a remarkable family dynasty of musical virtuosi specialising in early music. They not only researched and played the music, but also constructed authentic musical instruments. They inaugurated the Hazelmere Festival of Early Music in 1926 which still continues today.

Mary was to lose both her parents when she young. She was only four years old when her mother died in childbirth in 1877, and her father in October, 1896 when she was 21. John, her step brother, being the oldest in the family and about twenty years older than Mary, then assumed the role of head of the family and looked after his younger siblings' affairs.

Because they lived quite close to each other, Bertie and Mary had no need to write many letters, but when either of them went on holiday, they were devoted correspondents. Some of their little notes have been preserved by the family. They are letters with all the sweet sentimentality of a Victorian engaged couple, but reading between the lines, they give interesting insights into their personalities, way of life, interests, recreation, and relationship with their families. They are included in this narrative, as they reveal how Bertie's life was to continue after his journeys abroad, when his travels were closer to home.

During the nineteenth century, it became commonplace for city-dwellers to travel to the countryside or seaside to escape the grime and bustle of town. Some, who could not afford accommodation, would only take day trips and the railway companies provided cheap day return tickets for them. Others could spend more time and stay in the lodging houses or hotels which sprang up in the popular resorts.

The popularity of taking holidays by the sea-side and bathing in the sea first came about in the eighteenth century when it was mainly embarked on for health reasons, rather than for pleasure. Just as doctors recommended that their patients 'take the waters' at various spas with mineral springs, they also believed that immersing the body in sea water, and even drinking it was a cure for many ills.

In the early days, bathing was strictly segregated with the men in one area and ladies, in another, out of sight of each other. The ladies wore voluminous clothing covering them from neck to ankles out of modesty and also to shield their skin from the sun. They also wore stockings, lace up slippers and a bathing hat. Men, on the other hand bathed naked until the 1860s, when new laws were passed dictating that they wear bathing costumes. These were either one piece or two with long pants, sleeves and covered up to their necks. It was considered indecorous to be seen on land in swimwear, so bathing machines were provided on each beach. These were small huts on wheels which could be pulled by a horse. These were parked on the beach, so bathers could enter them fully dressed and change inside. When ready to enter the water, the horse pulled the equipage into the sea, so they could climb down the steps provided into the water in privacy.
  By the end of the nineteenth century, the ladies were bathing in dresses, sometimes with a sailor collar, bloomers and bathing slippers and cap. The men wore baggy bathing suits covering them from neck to knee, and the segregated swimming rule was beginning to be relaxed.

During the nineteenth century when sea-side towns became accessible by train, more people discovered the pleasure of frolicking in the waves and the associated pleasures such as making sand castles and shrimping. In addition the local traders soon found they could make good money from the visitors by providing accommodation, selling food such as jellied eels, winkles and whelks, or hiring donkeys to ride on the beach. Punch and Judy shows and other entertainments were popular and deck chairs could be hired. Since many visitors wanted to take something home to remind them of their holiday, souvenir shops appeared selling items made of shells, or chinaware with crests or pictures of the resort on them, as made by WH Goss. Local products or handiworks were also popular. Picture postcards started to be sold after 1894.

To attract more visitors, hotels were built and promenades were constructed where people could walk, meet their friends and take in the sea air. Also at many seaside resorts, piers were erected which contained places of entertainment such as theatres, dance halls and sideshows.

The seaside towns, which may have originally been small fishing communities, prospered hugely from the influx of visitors brought by the new railway service. Some, which were in easy reach of large towns, became popular with the large crowds of working class people. These included Margate and Ramsgate which were close to London and Blackpool and Scarborough in the north. It is noticeable that Bertie and Mary's families preferred to holiday in smaller and quieter towns, where they could enjoy the countryside and avoid large crowds of people. Bertie pursued his hobbies of butterfly collecting and bicycling and Mary loved country walks and looking at historical buildings. They both enjoyed sketching and painting beautiful scenes.

Bertie Bristowe and Mary Johnston at the time of their engagement in 1898

It seemed cruel that Bertie and Mary were separated so soon after they had become engaged, but while Bertie stayed in London and worked at the Stock Exchange, Mary was away in the country with family members. The first letter was written by Mary to Bertie in April 1898 when she was in Bournemouth, staying with her brother Harry and his wife at the house of his mother-in-law. She wrote this short note soon after they became engaged.

Tanheim
Wimbourne Road
Bournemouth
April 20th 1898

My dearest,

I was so pleased to get your sweet letter, and it quite, quite satisfied me. I am so glad you love me. It makes me so happy to think of it, and I want to be quite worthy of your love.

I am so glad your father and mother and brothers and sisters are pleased, and I hope we shall soon know each other very well.

I have had several very nice letters, which I'll show you.

I am coming home tomorrow, Thursday, by train arriving at Vauxhall 4.37 and shall love to see you there.

With love, dear Bertie. Hoping to see you soon.
Yours ever,
Mary

I suppose you went to see John yesterday. I hope everything went off all right. I shall see you tomorrow and you can tell me -- Au revoir!

When Mary wrote this letter she was staying with Lady Anderson, who was the widow of Sir Percy Anderson.

William Louis in the English Historical Review wrote of him:

Anderson was the great and only African power of the Foreign Office. He was the African thinking machine of the British Government. He was a civil servant immune to the vicissitudes of political fortune, a permanent fixture at the Foreign Office valued by Conservatives and Liberals alike.

Between 1883 and 1896 in his position as Head of the Africa Department in the Foreign Office, Sir Percy was almost entirely responsible for ensuring that Britain got the lion's share of colonies in the 'Scramble for Africa' that went on among the European powers at that time. He was also Harry Johnson's patron, friend, employer and step-father of his future wife. His sudden and unexpected death in 1896, had an adverse effect on Harry's career.

More letters were written in July when Mary was in Seaford with her brother, Sir Harry Johnston, and his wife Winifred. They had just returned from Tunisia where Harry had been appointed British Consul. It is obvious by then that plans for the marriage were well advanced:

Seaford , showing the church mentioned in Mary's letter

The Esplanade Hotel
Seaford, Sussex
July 13th 1898

My dearest boy,

I received your letter by the second post, and many thanks for it dear. I like to think that you miss me, and I hope you really do love me, darling, with the best kind of love. But I know you do. I know that you will always love and respect me. We have had a very quiet day and done nothing particular.

Harry went off soon after breakfast on his bicycle to Eastbourne, and we took a windy walk in the direction of Newhaven, which looks quite close, but is really miles away, as you have to go a good deal inland to get to it, the beach being marked off Private Property, at intervals.

This is a very small place; there is a little old church with a square tower, and a few primitive shops. The hotel is very nice. We have a private sitting room looking over the sea, with a nice little balcony, where we sat yesterday evening. There are very few people in the hotel, strange to say, and what there are, are harmless and uninteresting. There is a poor old doddering man, who walks up and down outside. His one last interest seems to be in dress, for he appears in three or four different costumes a day. He has a dreadful valet, who swaggers about, smoking a pipe all over the hotel, and has been trying to pump Winnie's maid about us. Then there is a married couple who bicycle, several mothers with children, and a clergyman.
I wonder if Leonard will go to dinner with you tomorrow. I doubt it.

I am just going out a little before tea. They have such enormous meals here. Harry likes such funny messy things for tea, shrimps, and jam and cakes and cherries, then we have table d'hôte soon afterwards.

Goodbye, dearest. You must write to me tomorrow, and you must think about me in the meantime, and you must love me for ever and ever.

Dear Bertie I am yours,   Mary

Leonard was one of Mary's older brothers, who never married.

Seaford was a small coastal town in East Sussex between Brighton and Eastbourne. In medieval times it had been one of the major Cinque Ports on the south coast, but its fortunes dwindled when the port became silted up and the town was attacked on several occasions by the French. Its inhabitants eked out a living from fishing and by the sale of items they could salvage from the occasional wrecked ship. It was even rumoured that some wrecks had been caused by unscrupulous locals placing lights up on the cliffs to confuse the mariners and lure the ships onto the rocks below. They earned themselves the nick-name Seaford Cormorants or Shags from their habit of plundering the cargoes washed up on their beaches.

The Esplanade Hotel, Seaford - photo by H Ewing

During the nineteenth century the economy of the town was improved by the fashion for sea bathing and the arrival of the railways, so Seaford became a small resort. The Esplanade Hotel where they stayed was built in 1891 and contemporary photographs show it was a splendid Victorian 'gingerbread house'. Mary's brother, Harry, did not mention his bike rides, but wrote of this holiday in his autobiography:

We went for a fortnight to a hotel at Seaford in Sussex, and I spent enjoyable days painting its wonderful cliff scenery, or sailing along the coast between Newhaven and Cuckmere Haven. Seaford in those days was a delightful place for quaintness and scenery, but I believe long since then it has been spoiled and made ugly by building lodging houses and establishing golf clubs.

The next letter from Bertie to Mary must have crossed with the previous one. In this letter, it can be seen that he has adopted Mary's family pet name, Tom.

Durlstone
Champion Hill, S.E.
Thursday

Sweet Mary,

I must write to you darling, to tell you what I am doing.

The General is in here this evening, we have been playing tennis; and now he is playing billiards with the boys.

You little know how I miss you dear Tom, and how lonely I feel tonight. I look forward very much to your letter tomorrow.

I saw Frank this morning and he says that he would like to give us dessert or fish knives and forks, if nobody else does? (That means silver ones darling)

Leonard is coming here to dinner tomorrow.

We are doing no business on the Stock Exchange and I think darling, that perhaps I shall be able to have a day or two with you at Littlehampton next week.

I have nothing more to tell you sweet, except that I love you.

Yours for ever
Bertie

Members of Bertie's family were keen tennis players. They had their own tennis court at Durlstone and used to play spirited games with their cousins and friends, as well as playing in matches at the local tennis club. Bertie was awarded various trophies, among which was a little silver coin holder, (now owned by the author,) which could be attached to a watch chain. He won this when he was twenty-three. On it is inscribed TENNIS TOURNAMENT CHAMPION HILL 1887 and on the other side, an elaborate rendering of his initials.

Lawn Tennis is a game which is now played world-wide, but it is claimed to have had its origins at a garden party in Wales in 1873. A retired army officer, Major Walter C. Wingfield invented it and later patented the rules and marketed its equipment. He named it 'Sphairistikè', which is Greek for the art of playing ball. Neither the name, nor the Major's original rules survived. The court he devised was hour-glass shaped and the net was higher, and perhaps nobody knew how 'Sphairistikè' was pronounced.

A Good Return. [Illustration in Young ladies' Treasure Book]

Nevertheless the modified game was adopted by the late nineteenth century 'smart set' in many countries, including the USA and the first tennis championship was played at the All England Croquet Club at Wimbledon in 1877. This was an all-male affair, the first ladies' official competition there occurred in 1884. One of the major reasons that tennis became so popular, was that it could be played by men and women together, and sociable tennis parties were enjoyed by many. Ladies were expected to wear long skirts and white stockings when playing, which must have hampered their activities somewhat.

In the *Young Ladies' Treasure Book*, a comprehensive guide to all activities suitable for young ladies in the late nineteenth century, it states in the chapter on Outdoor Amusements, that:

Never has such an enjoyable game as lawn tennis been invented for the delight of our countrymen and women. Other games of strength and activity have their special excellences, but none so completely falls in with our humour as this one. Lawn tennis is all that a pastime for men and women should be. It is an outdoor game; it is pleasant to play at, and pleasant to see played; and there is room in the game for almost any degree of skill and judgement, strength and activity.

The dessert and fish knives and forks Bertie referred to were a nineteenth century invention. They came about as dining habits changed with large meals being served in courses whereas previously all the dishes of food were placed onto the table at once. Each course required a different set of cutlery. Fish knives were generally made of silver, since steel knives could absorb fishy odours, but the knives were also conveniently designed with a pointed tip to make it easier to pick out the bones. To own fish knives and forks became a symbol of middle class gentility, indicating that you could afford to have several sets of cutlery on the table and knew what to do with them. Other people preferred to use the traditional method of dealing with bony fish by using two forks.

Durlstone
Champion Hill, S.E.
July 15th

This is the hottest day we have had this summer, and I am glad sweet that you are not in London, you would find it very trying.

I have been 21 miles on my bicycle today and feel very well. I think it is because I am so very, very happy.

Dearest Tom, I long to see you again and the time passes so slowly.

I sat in the garden after dinner and thought of you. Do you know that it is less than seven weeks to our wedding day?

I hope that curious tea of shrimps, jam and fruit did not upset you.

The garden is looking beautiful now, and there are lots of sweet peas, and plenty of mignonette ready for you when you come home.
I look forward to one of your sweet letters tomorrow darling.

I have no news to tell you except that I had a note from John asking me to go and see him, I went and we had a chat about money matters.

Darling Mary I love you and shall do so always.

Bertie

Claude Bristowe at Durlston on his safety bicycle - Bristowe family album

One aspect of life made obvious from his letters, is how keen Bertie and his family had become on the new universal craze of bicycling. He mentions his rides frequently in his letters and boasts of how far he had ridden. Also, his brother-in-law to be, Harry Johnston, wrote in his autobiography of a holiday in England, when he was staying with a party of family and friends in the country:

It was the real sunrise of the bicycle. A year or two previously the Safety bicycle had been perfected, and all the world was on wheels. My comparatively large house-party ... was all mounted on bicycles, and we went on expeditions of astounding length and variety: all over Dorsetshire, Wilts, and much of Hampshire.

Durlstone
Champion Hill, S.E.
July 16th

My darling Mary,

Thank you so much for the sweet letter you wrote me, it has made me very happy. I received it by the first post this morning.

I have done twenty two miles on my bicycle today. Leonard came to dinner and I think he enjoyed himself, he stayed till 10.35.
Claude is nearly well again.

I shall probably go for a long bicycle ride on Sunday with Alec and Lewis round Dorking and Leatherhead.

Mind you let me know, sweet Mary, what train you are coming home by on Monday and I will meet you. Darling I look forward to Monday when I hope to see you again.

I read a few chapters "About Roses" but I can't read much as I am always thinking of you, darling.

Hoping to see you again soon, Sweet.
Yours for ever and ever,

Bertie

Claude, mentioned in this letter, was the youngest in the Bristowe family and seems not to have had good health. He was only 25 when he died in 1904.

Later in July, Mary moved further along the Sussex coast to continue her holiday at Littlehampton. This town had its origins as a Saxon fishing community, but developed into a small port where there was also a ship-building industry in Tudor times. Littlehampton became a popular holiday destination in the eighteenth century, and even more so in the nineteenth century, when the railways made access easier. There was also a ferry from Littlehampton to Honfleur in France.

Littlehampton Pier, lighthouse and windmill, old postcard

Bertie must have been able to take time off from his work to visit her there, because on the 26th July he wrote:

> *Durlstone*
> *Champion Hill, S.E.*
> *July 26th*

Sweet Mary,

I arrived home safely tonight at 11.15.

I think of you always darling, and I can't go to bed till I have written to say how happy I have been at Littlehampton in your company. Your sweet face and fascinating manner have a charm for me which I can't describe.

Sweet Tom, I long for the time when I can call you my wife and be with you always. I shall write to you again tomorrow evening, and hope to get a letter from you, darling, about that time. Good bye, my own sweet Mary, I have nothing more to tell you now.   *Bertie*

In his next letter, Bertie mentions another of his favourite pastimes, which was playing or watching cricket. He was a keen player and was a member of several local amateur cricket clubs throughout his life and also liked to attend Test matches with his friends and family.

Durlstone
Champion Hill, S.E.
July 27th

Sweet Tom,

I love you and am longing for a few lines from you darling. Your letter has not arrived yet, I expect I shall get it by the first post tomorrow. I did not get up early this morning as I was too sleepy. I went today to get seats for the 'Ambassador', but am sorry to say, darling, that St. James's theatre is closed. I enclose a list of entertainments, so please, sweet Mary, choose what you would like to see next Thursday, and let me know.

Ernest Bristowe tells me that his wife and children are staying at Littlehampton.

Mr Francis is very anxious for me to play cricket again for Orpington next Saturday. Would you mind darling, if I go? Of course I told him I could not in any case stay for dinner.

Dearest Tom, if you want me to do anything or go anywhere with you, please say so, as you must know that I will do anything for you with pleasure, as you are always first in my thoughts.

Darling Mary, I feel very lonely tonight, and shall go to bed when I have finished this letter.

I long for Friday when I shall see your sweet face again.

It has been very hot in the city today.

Good bye, sweet Tom, I think of you always

Yours for ever,
Bertie

P.S. I shall write again tomorrow.

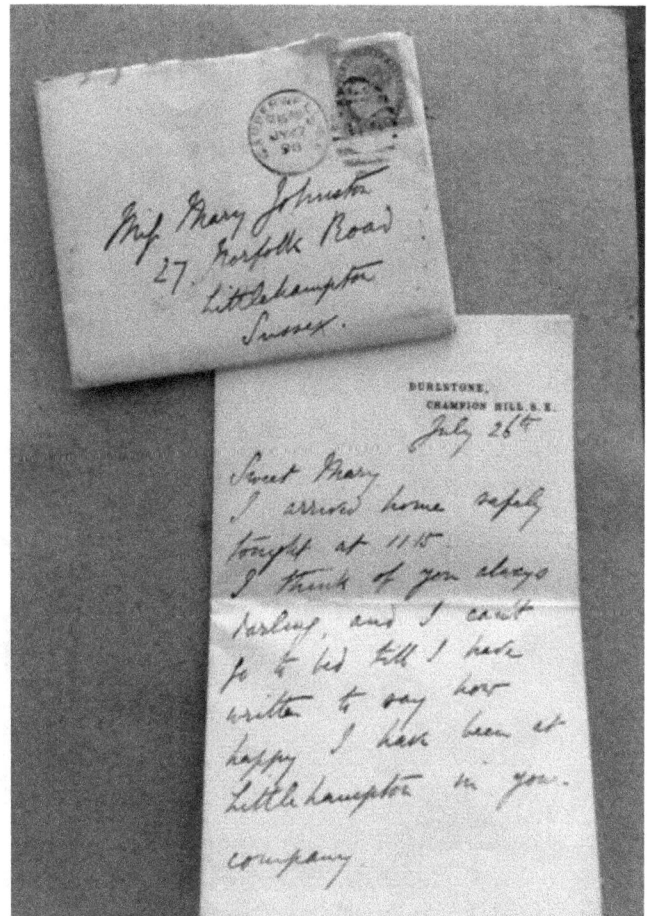

The plans for Mary to accompany Bertie to the theatre would have been an exciting experience for her. Her brother Harry recorded in his autobiography that throughout her youth, their father forbade his children to attend public theatres because of his religious beliefs.

27 Norfolk Road
Littlehampton
July 28th 1898

My own dear boy,

I am coming home tomorrow! Are you glad? Yes, I know you are, and I am looking forward so much to seeing my dear, precious boy again at London Bridge.

I have told Lily that we shall arrive at Tudor House about 5 o'clock and that we should both like some afternoon tea.

I believe a box has arrived for me marked 'Fragile. With Care'. It must be either my dressing bag or the salt cellars. We shall have to unpack it.

I wonder if you have seen the Registrar yet. I hope it is all right and that he can come on the 1st of September.

We are going over on the ferry this morning and afternoon, as I should like to do a sketch of the black mill. I hope I shall be able to bring home something. We couldn't go yesterday afternoon on account of the thunder storm, but took a walk across the fields inland to a little place called Toddington where there are a lot of old cottages, and a charming Elizabethan farm house, very picturesque.

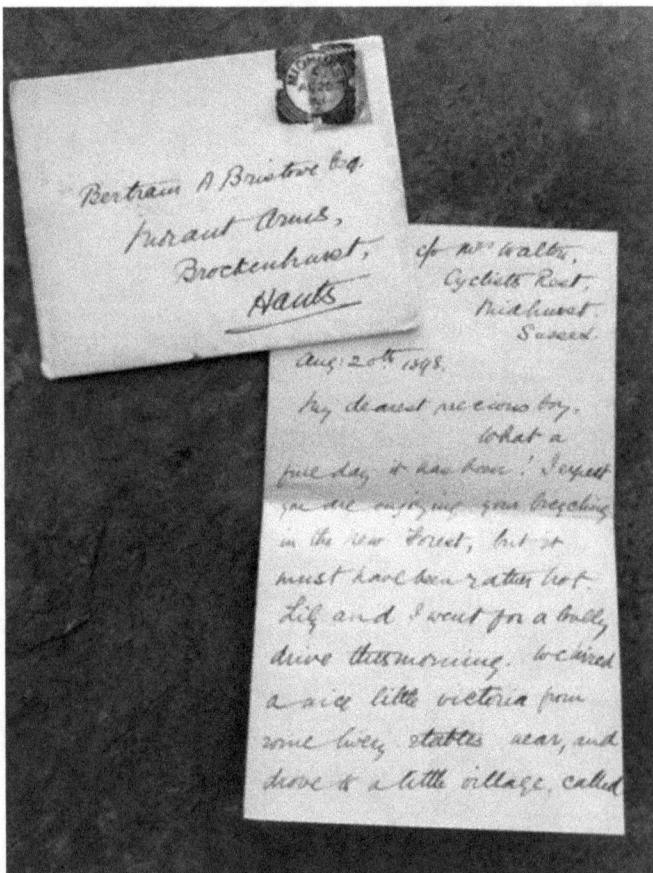

Mabel will arrive this afternoon. It is rather heavy and misty just now, the remains of the storm, I suppose. I hope it is going to clear up.
Goodbye my dearest, I shall look out for you tomorrow at London Bridge.

Don't forget me, think of me till then. Au revoir! Your loving Tom

From this letter, we can deduce that the wedding was set for 1st September 1898, which incidentally was the date their second child, William was born in 1901. Lily was the family name for Mary's older sister Lilian, who was still living at the family home, Tudor House. Mabel, was Mary's younger sister, who was later to marry Arnold Dolmetsch.

Durlstone
Champion Hill, S.E.
July 26th

My own sweet Tom,

Many thanks for your letter, it has made me very, very happy.

I am afraid that I am very selfish, but I am so glad that your holiday is nearly over and that I shall see you again, sweet Mary tomorrow.

It seems ages since I saw you and I want that kiss you promised me in your letter.

I forgot to tell you that I went about the banns on Wednesday night, they don't publish them as we are to be married at the Catholic Apostolic Church.

After receiving your letter I went to the Registrar this morning and will tell you all about it when I see you tomorrow.

Lewis, Alec, and Claude have gone to the Palace theatre tonight, so I am at home alone: I like it! As I can sit in the armchair, undisturbed, and think of you my sweet Mary; my heart is at Littlehampton and I don't care to go anywhere without you.

I went this afternoon to Kennington Oval with Charles Paton to see the cricket after business, but the rain stopped play when we had seen very little.

I have received a present from Mrs J. Bristowe, a Silver flask, I did not expect much from her, as I know that she is not well off.
I am not likely to forget that you are coming by the 2 o'clock from Littlehampton tomorrow, and shall be at London Bridge to meet your train.

Darling Tom, I long so much to see you again.

Yours for ever and ever.
Bertie

P.S. I hope Loulou is getting on well with the accounts? Have you paid yourself the 9d yet?

Charles Paton, mentioned in this letter, was a friend and colleague at the London Stock Exchange who was later to marry Bertie's sister, Kathleen. Loulou was Mary's sister, Louise.

In August Mary and Bertie were to be separated yet again. This time he was out of town, at Brockenhurst in the New Forest with his bicycle, while she was spending time with her family in the town of Midhurst. She and her brother, Alick joined their sister, Lily and brother, Phil, who had some sort of an accident. Maybe, he fell off his bike?

Though missing 'her own precious boy', Mary was able to enjoy the beautiful summer weather in the company of her family exploring the countryside around Midhurst. She did not seem to have taken up the bicycle craze, but explored the countryside with long walks and a hired horse carriage. She also had time to write an affectionate letter each day to Bertie telling him what she has been doing.

c/o Mrs. Walton
Cyclist's Rest,
Midhurst
Sussex
August 19th 1898

My own precious boy,
This is where I have finally pitched my tent.

No telegram came from Littlehampton, so after lunch, I sent off a telegram to Lily, then packed my bag, and left the house at 3 o'clock. Alick came with me and we did it very comfortably.

He took his bicycle, but apart from that we had no boxes, only our two bags which we took with us in the carriage.

This is a most charming and beautiful old town, with no end of old houses. I have not seen much of it yet, only having just walked through it from the station. We have just had our Tea/supper, (which is the meal most usual in this sort of place) and we are now going out for a stroll.

There is a post at half past 8, so your letter will go by that.
Phil is getting over his injuries gradually. One hand is all bound up, and there is a piece of cotton wool and plaster over the bridge of his nose, and a patch on his chin, but in spite of it all he is very cheerful and looks well.

He is pointed out here by small boys as "the person who's been fighting."

Do you know, dearest, I saw your train going off this morning as I was coming towards the station, and I saw you putting your bicycle into the train!
Darling, I suppose you are down at Brockenhurst now, and I hope you are thinking of me.
With my best love, dearest. Yours for ever,   Tom

ℰℭℛ

c/o Mrs Walton
Cyclist's Rest
Midhurst
Sussex.
August 20th 1898

My dearest precious boy, what a fine day it has been!

I expect you are enjoying your bicycling in the New Forest, but it must have been rather hot.

Lily and I went for a lovely drive this morning. We hired a nice little Victoria from some livery stables near, and drove to a little village called Treyford, a forgotten sort of spot buried away in the downs. We stopped there a few minutes to look at an old church and church yard, which are all over grown and in ruins. It was like some sleeping beauty's garden, a tangled mass of weeds, ivy and climbing plants.

The church yard was all over-grown and desolate, some of the tomb stones, lying flat on the ground, but the little church was a most curious sight, for though the walls are perfect enough, there is no glass left in the windows, and door and roof have fallen in. Strong saplings are growing up inside, and it is simply a tangle of weeds, yet the old frescoes are still quite distinct, and all the carvings. It is a beautiful little church, and it is a great shame that it should be left to go to ruin, like that, but I suppose it is out of the way and nobody cares.

We came home in time for lunch, then Lily left by an afternoon train, and I saw her off. Afterwards I had a very nice walk with Alick. It is the most glorious country round here. Lots of lovely sketches, so I really must do something before I come home.

There is a most picturesque ruin called Cowdray Castle quite near.
Goodbye my dearest, and write to me soon, Ever your loving,   Tom

The Victoria horse carriage that Lily and Mary hired was an elegant French design based on the phaeton. It was named in honour of Queen Victoria and was first imported into England in 1869 by the Prince of Wales. It had a hood which could be raised, if it rained.

Treyford is an isolated little village in the Downs south of Midhurst and the ruined church Mary wrote of was the thirteenth century Saxon Church of St Mary. This was abandoned, when in 1849, St. Peter's, a grand new church with a tall spire, was built. This was sometimes called the cathedral of the Downs. Unfortunately the new church was constructed of stone so soft, that by 1888, it needed major repairs and in 1951, was declared unsafe and too expensive to restore, so the church was demolished and Treyford was to have two ruined churches. There are indications that Treyford had been a place of spiritual significance since ancient times. Nearby there is a group of circular mounds, known as the 'Devil's Jumps'. These are Bronze Age burial mounds thought to be about three to four thousand years old.

The 'picturesque ruin' of Cowdray castle still stands a few miles outside Midhurst on the banks of the river Rother. It was originally built as a fortified manor house in the thirteenth century, when it was known as Coudreye house. It was to be enlarged into a grand Tudor mansion in the sixteenth century when it was owned by one of Henry Vll's uncles. Unfortunately the house was burned down in 1793, leaving only the stone walls standing. When Mary viewed the castle, it would have been shrouded in ivy, but since it was damaging the structure, this was removed in 1917, so modern visitors now see the walls free of greenery.

Old postcard of Midhurst and Cowdray Castle ruins.

c/o Mrs Walton
Cyclists Rest
Midhurst
Aug. 21st 1898

My dearest boy,
I got your letter this morning, which was rather quick, if you did not write it till yesterday evening.

I expect it is hot cycling, for I find it very hot walking. Our beverage is stone bottle ginger beer. Lily drank enormous quantities and when her bill was brought, it was found to be mostly ginger beer, every other item in fact. The old landlady here caters for us entirely, so we don't have any of Loulou's accounts, no debiting or anything else of the sort, which is rather a relief.

We did not go to Church today; Phil and I went for a very hot walk. We tried to get to the Downs, which look quite close, but are really 5 miles off. We got as far as the foot, but then found there was only just time to get back to lunch, so had to return. There was no shade the whole way, and it was roasting hot, so I am sure I ought to have caught a little.

Tomorrow, we are going again and shall take our lunch with us in my little basket, so that we can have a nice long day.

I wish you were here, I am sure you would like it. There is such lovely country all round, and *such variety too – In one direction there are moors covered in heather and low bushes, and pine copses, then in another there is rolling park land and woods, then again there are pastures, the river Rother winding through them, and cattle lying on the banks and beautiful corn-fields with harvest in full swing.*

I wonder if I shall do any sketching. I ought to, but the heat makes me feel lazy.

This afternoon we went and had tea with the doctor and his wife; Mrs Peters (that is her name) left a card yesterday and asked us in to tea. They are very kind pleasant people.

The doctor has been a sort of Good Samaritan to Phil, and has healed up his wounds most wonderfully. He is a Norwegian, and a good looking man. I should have liked him better if he had not contradicted his wife flatly on several occasions, but I am bound to say she was just as bad and contradicted him, and over such stupid things too, such as vaccination. She argued on one side and he on the other, and he said 'If you would only listen to what I say', then she interrupted and gave her views.

I am very critical now of the manners of husbands and wives. I think they should be just as polite to one another after they are married, as they are before, don't you?

I shall never contradict you, at any rate before strangers and I am sure you won't will you dearest? No, of course you won't.

Goodbye darling   Ever your loving,   Tom

The principles of this loving, but quite stern little letter must have been taken quite seriously by both of them, because it was well known by the whole family that they were a totally devoted couple throughout their lives and lived together in splendid accord.

Their marriage took place at the Apostolic Catholic Church in Camberwell attended by their many family members. In Mary's case, she did not have the support of either of her late parents, but she had eight brothers and sisters to rally round and encourage her.

It is not recorded where they went for their honeymoon, but soon after, they were living in the little Surrey village of Stoke D'Abernon, where they remained for the rest of their lives. This place was mentioned in the Doomsday Book in 1086 and its seventh century church is one of the oldest in Surrey. It contains several magnificent memorial brasses, dating from Norman times.

Bertie purchased a house they named 'The Cottage', which was to be their home for the first eighteen years of their married life. This was in a delightfully rural setting which was ideal for Bertie's interests in natural history It was close to the Cobham and Stoke D'Abernon railway station, so Bertie could commute up to London each day. Their house had a large garden with plenty of space for the children to play in. There was also

The Cottage at harvest time. Watercolour painting by Bertie Bristowe

a meadow where they kept two ponies which were used to pull the trap into the village of Cobham, for shopping expeditions. Their son Bill wrote later of his happy childhood there.

Bertie was never an extremely rich man. Besides various investments, he earned a salary of between 1,000 and 1,500 pounds per year, but the young couple could afford to employ a cook, parlour maid and housemaid, as well as a gardener and gardener's boy. In addition, when they had babies, a nurse maid was added to the household, and later a governess, Miss Chapman who was always known as 'Chappie.' She became a good friend of the family and stayed with them for three generations.

Within a year of their marriage, in 1899, their first child, Evelyn, was born, and though as devoted as ever, Bertie felt able to leave his little family for a week to join his parents and family members at Tenby. This is a small coastal town in Pembrokeshire in South Wales. It had a long and at times, turbulent history. In ancient times it was a fishing community, but was taken over by the Normans and ruled by the Duke of Pembroke, who built a great castle to protect him from the wild Welsh men. They attacked it several times and in the thirteenth century city walls were built, to provide additional protection from invaders. In the middle ages it became a prosperous trading port, but this declined during the Civil War years. Another blow fell when the town was struck by plague in 1650 and the population was decimated.

Stoke d'Abernon Church, old postcard

Tenby's recovery began in the eighteenth Century, but it was during the Victorian era that the town really became prosperous again, particularly when the railway arrived in 1863. Hotels were built and attractive pathways constructed to allow people to take scenic walks. It became a centre for those interested in Geology and Natural History and venues for concerts and theatrical productions were provided. Also visitors could indulge in the healthy activity of sea bathing.

In 1897 the Royal Victoria Pier was built at Tenby, and extended in 1899, when it was officially opened by the Duchess of York. Fishing and pleasure boats used to moor there, and band concerts were given regularly.

> *8 Esplanade*
> *Tenby*
> *Sunday*

Darling Tom,
I arrived here safely. I had plenty of time at Paddington as I was there at 10.30.
The drive from Vauxhall recalled to me pleasant recollections of school days, that was the way we used to come, and also on the railway we were on the same line as far as Didcot, but there we took the Bath line which was new to me.
I had nothing to drink all day, and to eat I only had two current buns and two Banbury cakes, how would that suit you darling? The train was very late, in fact we did not arrive till 7.30, the Governor met me at the station; he is looking very brown and well, as do all the others. I gave your note to Ethel.

Tenby, showing the Victoria Pier, old postcard

Tenby is a charming little place and I wish you were here too, sweet Mary. I think that No. 8 Esplanade has the best situation in the place. The house is well up on the cliff and from the front you look straight across the Bristol Channel to Devonshire, which you can see on a clear day. I had a jolly swim in the sea this morning before breakfast with Claud. There are no bathing machines just here but both sexes undress at the foot of the cliffs in recesses and then run down to the sea.

After breakfast I went for a long walk with Claud & the Governor. The sea is a beautiful colour. We saw lots of 'hummingbird hawk moths'." Some stupid old Tosser wrote to the local paper to say that he had seen a humming bird and that they were seldom seen in this country. I also saw three magpies, that is lucky is it not?

The Mater thinks it would be rather a good plan, and I agree, that if Nurse Ransome is not engaged during Sept. and the beginning of October, she might come away with us to Bournemouth or Swanage and you could then see about a nurse later, of course, darling you must make terms with her if you like the idea.

Tomorrow, if fine, we are all going prawning, we sail along the coast till we get to a place where they are plentiful. We shall take our lunch with us and make a day of it.

I hope you are getting on well Darling, mind you are to be down next Sunday; and our sweet baby. How is she? Give her a kiss for me.

Best love Sweet Mary to you the baby and Nettie, Yours for ever, Bertie

Nettie was Mary's older sister who was married to James Henderson.

TENBY. ESPLANADE FROM SOUTH SANDS   54041

Tenby Esplanade where the Bristowe family stayed at number 8, old postcard

Two days later Bertie wrote another letter with more news of the holiday, but he was obviously missing Mary and impatient to hear from her.

8 Esplanade, Tenby
Tuesday Night

My sweet Wife.
I am anxious for news of you and our little one, and expect a letter tomorrow morning.

We are having glorious weather: Yesterday Claud and I went for a bicycle ride. We intended to go to a place called 'Stack Rocks', about 20 miles from here, but after we had gone about 8 miles Claud's bicycle broke down, the front wheel came clean off; it was lucky it did not happen a few minutes earlier as we had just coasted down a hill.

Today we all went in a boat about a mile along the coast to a pretty little cove where we had lunch, we caught 400 beauties and a lobster. I should have sent you some but thought they would probably go bad before they reached you. Tomorrow I am going in the coach with the Governor and Claud to Carew Castle.

I have tried sugar two nights and only caught one moth so I shall give it up as a bad job. We are all coming home together on Saturday by the train that should get to Paddington about 6 o'clock;

245

It will probably be late so I shall dine in town and come down to Stoke D'Abernon by the 9.50 from Waterloo.

How I long to see my two little girls again! I know darling Tom that you would like Tenby and hope to bring you here someday. I am at home alone this evening, I have been sugaring and caught nothing. Claud has gone to listen to the band on Castle Hill, and the other four have gone to a concert. I have a swim every morning before breakfast. I feel much better for my change but have got rather a 'guinea' nose.

The Miss Martin who married the rich German just before we were married has just got a little boy. It was in the paper.

I am just going out to smoke a quiet pipe on a nice seat in front of the house, where I shall sit and think of my darlings far away.

Goodbye sweet Tom. I shall probably write again before Saturday.
Yours for ever,
Bertie
Wednesday 9.30   One post and still no letter from you? You little brat!

Sugaring for moths involves making up a mixture of fermenting fruit, sugar and alcohol. This is smeared on the surface of trees, posts etc. at dusk. If the mixture is right, all the moths in the neighbourhood will be attracted to the enticing aroma of the bait at night time, making them easy to catch or observe. Bertie may have hoped to catch some of those handsome humming bird hawk moths (Macroglossum stellatarum) using this method, though they are often seen feeding on flowers during the day, so perhaps he pursued them with his butterfly net. These are one of the largest moths found in the British Isles and may be seen over Europe and Asia. They look and sound remarkably like small hummingbirds as they hover over flowers feeding through their long proboscis, while their wings beat so fast, they hum.

Life settled down at 'The Cottage', and soon Mary was to have her second child, William Syer, (known as Billie as a child and Bill later). He was born in September 1901, then some years later in 1906, came Margaret, always known as Peggy.

In May 1902 Bertie and Mary were once more apart. This time it was Mary who went for a holiday to Naples with her sister-in-law, Ethel, when they stayed at the 'Parkers Hotel'. Bertie remained at home, while the children were by the seaside at Littlehampton with their nannie. On the 12th May he wrote an affectionate letter addressed to 'Darling Wifie' in which he reported enthusiastically about a cricket match which his team won and he made 41, not so enthusiastically about dining alone with the Canon, 'rather an ordeal' when they discussed dry church business and a he added a bit of gossip about a rumour of an engagement. He then wrote:

I went down to Littlehampton yesterday. Mr Hodgeson went with me as far as Arundel, he was going to see his grandmother. He came back with me in the evening.

I found the kids in splendid health & looking so sweet, you will see a great change in Billie when you come home. I am so proud of him, darling Tom; I took dear little Evelyn out in the afternoon for a walk and we found some shells, she talks so much now. I bought a little garden chair for her the other day from a woman who came round to our house.

We had a meeting about the coronation festivities this evening at Oxshot, Mr F. Phillips in the chair as stupid as ever … Darling I am looking forward to having you back again. The garden is looking very pretty just now.

The Goodenoughs are going to Bognor for their holiday. I think the Durlstone party will probably go to Tenby. I go on Friday with Mr Hughes & your friend Richardson to Silchester after butterflies.

Darling I have no more news to tell you, I am now off to my lonely little bed.
Yours for ever
Bertie

The coronation Bertie referred to was that of King Edward Vll. His mother Queen Victoria had died on 22 January 1901 after being on the throne for over sixty-three years. The coronation was scheduled to be held on 26 June 1902, but things did not go according to plan.

King Edward was fifty nine years old when he acceded to the throne and was not a fit man. Only three days before the coronation day, he became ill and it was announced that he had been diagnosed as having perityphlitis.[abdominal abscess] Telegrams were sent throughout the Empire with the news that the coronation had to be postponed. The urgent operation to drain the abscess was undertaken at Buckingham Palace where it took place on a table in the music room.

The postponement of the coronation at such short notice caused enormous concern and confusion as plans for celebrations were all in place everywhere in the Empire. The King himself insisted that these should all go ahead as planned. He personally contributed 30,000 pounds towards a 'Coronation Dinner' for 5000,000 poor Londoners, which took place on 5 July.

The coronation of King Edward Vll and Queen Alexandra finally took place on 9 August 1902 at Westminster Abbey. Many of the foreign dignitaries who would have attended the ceremony in June had gone home, but there were still 8,000 guests in the Abbey from many parts of the Empire and it was a glittering affair with magnificent music. The service was kept as short as possible, since the King was still convalescing from his operation. It was conducted by the very elderly Arch Bishop of Canterbury, who was also not in very good health. This venerable cleric needed to be supported by two Bishops through the service and ran into trouble when he kneeled in homage to the King. he was then quite unable to rise to his feet without assistance from the King and several Bishops. He also placed the Imperial State Crown on the King's head backwards. Apart from a few mishaps, the coronation was deemed a splendid ceremony and was followed by a procession through London streets which were lined with thousands of cheering people happy to see their king in improved health.

In addition to being a devoted husband, Bertie was always a very kind and loving father and very proud of all three of his children.

Evelyn was a brilliant tennis player and even competed at Wimbledon. When young she fell in love with her cousin William Bristowe, but this liaison was frowned on by the family and William migrated to Canada. Later they both married other people and Evelyn had a son, but then was widowed. During the Second World War her cousin, William returned as a Canadian army officer. Their relationship was resumed and they remained together as a loving couple living at Cooden, a little Sussex seaside town for the rest of their lives.

Bill also excelled at sport. He and Evelyn made a formidable team in tennis mixed doubles matches. He was very active in athletics as a school boy, and later when he went to Cambridge in 1920. to study science. He was also awarded a 'Blue' for athletics. Like his father, Bill was a naturalist. From an early age, he became fascinated by spiders and their habits and was to become a world authority in that field, respected to this day by arachnology enthusiasts. He did not follow his father into the Stock Exchange, but took up a career in Imperial Chemical Industries (ICI). He married and had three children.

Peggy's interests lay in history and antiques. She had several books and articles published about Silhouettes and Jane Austen. She had two children. All Bertie's children inherited some characteristics from their father: his sporting prowess, interest in natural history, love of beautiful art objects and travel.

Bertie had returned from his journey around the world to live a very contented and largely uneventful life at Stoke D'Abernon with his wife and three children. He continued as a partner in the family firm at the Stock Exchange. Perhaps his foreign travel proved useful to him, since Ranald Michie in his book about the London Stock Exchange, while referring to trading after World War One wrote:

The jobbers, Bristowe Brothers …who had always been major players in dealings between London and Paris, resumed that activity as early as 1921 and there was also much jobbing activity in both rubber plantation company shares and South African gold-mining shares.

Bertie persisted in his study and collection of butterflies, moths and beetles which were stored in two large and beautifully constructed cabinets with many drawers. These, many years later, became objects of awe and delight to his grandchildren. He published articles in scientific journals, and gave talks to Entomology clubs about his findings.

He was an accomplished artist and produced some beautiful landscape paintings, some of which won awards. Like his father, he used to amuse his children by drawing cartoons about their activities. Bertie was an active member of the local cricket club and other community organizations, and judging by the in-depth conversation about Church matters he had with the Canon during their solitary dinner, he was a respected member of the Stoke D'Abernon Church Congregation.

All his early life, Bertie had dutifully done what was expected of him by his family and society at large. He had attended the schools chosen by his parents; he joined the family firm and worked alongside his father and brothers. He lived in a suburban family home and took part in social and sporting activities expected of a young man in his position. So in what way would his life been enriched and changed by his eight month journey around the world?

In all probability, this was the first time he had ever been totally independent of his family for any length of time. While on his travels, he had to look after himself and make his own decisions without the guidance of his parents. Previously, his life experiences had been very limited to England, with minor excursions to the European continent. He had mainly eaten English food, seen English countryside and associated with English people. On his world trip, he visited countries which were totally different to anything he had seen before, and met many people who looked, spoke and dressed differently to anyone he would have encountered previously. These ranged from the 'coolies' and trades people of the Orient, his fellow passengers who were of many different nationalities, and the Americans he befriended in Japan, on board the SS Gaelic and in their own country. In addition, he sampled some foods which certainly would never have been found in Camberwell, and was willing to try everything even though he may not have enjoyed the experience.

Of course another achievement was the addition of some spectacular butterflies to his collection, the like of which were never to be found in the home counties of England, which would have given him great satisfaction.

It is said that 'travel broadens the mind' and this seems to have been so in Bertie's case. He returned as a more confident and well-informed person and this led to what was to be the most important element to his future happiness. Previously he had been an upstanding and worthy young man, kind but predictable, so possibly a little boring. Now, for the first time in his life he had done something totally unpredictable and out of character. He embarked on a great adventure and returned full of enthusiasm, with new ideas and tales to tell. He became infinitely more interesting to a young lady such as Miss Mary Johnston.

Their son wrote of his mother that:

Although she had previously recognised Bertie's sterling qualities she now found him full of interests in which she could share.

The fact that at last Bertie was able to persuade Mary Johnston to marry him was to have a profound effect on his journey through the rest of his life. When they married, Mary proved to be a loving and ideal wife and they lived happily together until his death on 2nd December in 1926. In maturity, Bertie may have continued to be kind and predictable, but there is no indication that either of them found life boring.

The memories of his journey around the world may, in time, have become but a distant dream. However, he had only to let his eyes range around their house to observe the beautiful oriental works of art and colourful butterflies which he had collected, to be once more transported to the faraway places of their origin. Then, he could relive again the exhilaration of his life-changing travels 'in the realms of gold'.

Photo of Bertie and Mary dated 1926, the year of his death. Bristowe family album

Paintings on silk collected by Bertie in Japan, now in the
possession of his granddaughters

SIR SAMUEL WHITE BAKER, KCB 1821-1893

All of the photographs of Samuel Baker show him as an imposing man with a bushy beard and a stern expression. Frequently, he is standing next to the bodies of large animals he has just killed. One of his major passions in life was the pursuit of 'Big Game' to shoot, or hunt with hounds. He mainly travelled to places which had an abundance of large and preferably dangerous animals to be added to his trophies.

Baker was born in London in 1821. He had three brothers and three sisters, and his father, also called Samuel, was a well-to-do sugar merchant, banker, and ship-owner, with business interests overseas in sugar plantations. Baker was educated privately in England and then Frankfurt where he obtained a degree in Civil Engineering.

In 1843 he married Henrietta Martin, a vicar's daughter. It was a joint wedding ceremony with his brother, John, who married Henrietta's sister. Shortly afterwards, the two couples travelled to Mauritius to manage the family's sugar plantations.

In 1846 Baker was tempted by the promise of big game on the island of Ceylon. He resolved to spend twelve months there with his guns. After some months in the jungle, he contracted malaria and nearly died, so he was sent to the cool hills to recuperate and stayed at Newara Eliya, which was an insignificant settlement at that time. He did, however, make a rapid recovery from his illness.

He returned to England, but longed for the wilds of Ceylon, so with his brother John and their families, he went back to Ceylon to form a farming settlement at Newara Eliya. This was successful, but after eight years, Baker returned to England, where his wife died. He had previously lost two sons and a daughter, but had four remaining daughters whom he left with his sister in England, while he continued on his travels.

 In 1858, while travelling in Eastern Europe, Baker visited the slave market at Vidin in Bulgaria. He saw and fell instantly in love with a beautiful girl who was destined to be sold to the Pasha of Vidin for his harem and with a combination of bribery and bravado, managed to spirit her away to Bucharest. Florence Barbara Maria Finnian von Szasz was some twenty years younger than Baker. She had been orphaned and had a turbulent childhood, but she was well educated and could speak several languages. They were married in Bulgaria and had a second ceremony in England with the family.

Baker then spent several years travelling through the continent of Africa, accompanied by his wife, who wore more convenient male attire, when travelling in the wilds. They embarked on several expeditions exploring the Upper Nile region seeking its source, during which time they made several important discoveries, including Lake Albert and

Murchison Falls. He was also employed in attempts to suppress the slave trade in Africa.

Baker joined the ranks of famous African explorers and was knighted by Queen Victoria in 1866. He was awarded gold medals by the Royal Geographical Society and the Paris Geographical Society and was a member of the Royal Society. He became famous through the many books he wrote about his thrilling adventures in Ceylon and Africa. Finally in 1872, Sir Samuel and Lady Baker retired to an estate he had purchased in Devon, which was their home until his death in 1893. Lady Baker lived until 1916.

GERTRUDE COLVILLE BINDLOSS   1856-1944

Records indicate that Gertrude Bindloss was born in 1856 in Cheshire, and her early life was spent in the north of England. Her father, Richard Bindloss, was a cabinet maker and her mother was named Mary Anne. She had a brother, Thomas and also two sisters. Family circumstances made it necessary for Bindloss to earn a living, so having had a good education, she became a governess. She consistently kept a diary and sections of the unpublished account she wrote of her journey to 'Siam' in 1889 are included in this book.

She wrote that she decided to fulfil her desire to see something of the world and try to find employment on the continent. In 1881, while in the village of Chideock in Dorset, she was offered a position of English governess by Baroness Fanny Preecha Kolakan who was living in Biarritz. Her pupils were to be Baroness Preecha's two step children Kra Koon (Olivia) aged nine, and six-year-old Aron-y-Wung (Aron). She was to teach them for two years, before returning to England. Several years later, while living in Dorset, she was contacted by Thai authorities with a request to escort her old pupils back to their late father's relatives in Bangkok. Bindloss's employer Madame Fanny Preecha was the daughter of the British Consul General in Thailand, Sir Thomas Knox and his Thai wife. She lived an extremely adventurous life and when Bindloss first met her, she was only twenty-four and newly widowed under tragic circumstances. She had unfortunately fallen in love with a Thai nobleman Phra Preecha; they ran away and got married in spite of intense opposition from Fanny's father and the Thai Royal Court. Only a few weeks after their marriage Phra Preecha was arrested, imprisoned and later beheaded. Madame Preecha fled to France with all her jewels, her late husband's two children, by a previous marriage and her little son, Spencer who was born while his father was in prison. She lived an eventful life, which included much political intrigue and had a short-lived marriage with the Crown Prince of Cambodia, but she was not a very reliable mother. In 1889, Bindloss was employed to escort these children back to Thailand, because they had been more or less abandoned by their mother in France, where they might have become destitute but for the care of the Thai Legation staff.

It was an exciting journey, both for Bindloss and the children and when they had been safely delivered in Bangkok, she returned to England. Obviously, her ex-pupils retained a genuine regard for her, as she still received affectionate letters from them, written in perfect English many years later, when Olivia had married a Thai Prince and Aron had risen to a position of high office.

At some stage during her teaching career, one of her employers was the well-known actor Ellen Terry. They became life-long friends and maintained an affectionate correspondence for many years. When she retired from work, Bindloss returned to Dorset, to live with her mother and sister at Chideock. In 1912, at the age of fifty-six, she married Mr John Wheaton Tapper, who was a retired teacher from London. She was to continue to live in Chideock and the nearby town of Bridport until her death in 1944 at the age of eighty-eight.

ISABELLA LUCY BIRD   1831-1904

For a delicate lady who was recommended travel to improve her poor health, Isabella Bird's solo trips were extraordinary, especially since her travelling career only started in her forties. Her books made her famous and were avidly read by the Victorian travel-hungry public.

Bird's father was a clergyman and she had one sister, Henrietta. Bird suffered from 'nervous complaints' which included insomnia, depression and back pain. Eventually, when she was forty-years-old, her doctor suggested that travel might help her condition. Bird was invited to accompany a cousin to the United States. Her father gave her one hundred pounds and told her to come back when it was spent. Bird travelled along the east coast of the USA and Canada and the lively letters she wrote to her sister, Henrietta were published as a book: *The English Woman in America*.

In 1872, Bird travelled to Australia, which she did not like and on to the Sandwich Islands (Hawaii). She spent six months there. She climbed volcanoes and learned to ride astride, which she found better for her back. She wrote another book. Bird's next journey took her to the Rocky Mountains of America and especially in Colorado, still very much a 'wild west'. She rode alone through bad weather and rough terrain and met a one-eyed outlaw known as 'Rocky Mountain Jim'. It was not revealed in her book, A Lady's Life in the *Rocky Mountains*, precisely how close their relationship was, but she certainly was very fond of him.

Bird's next book, *Unbeaten Tracks in Japan*, resulted from her trip to Japan, when she travelled with her eighteen-year-old guide, into the north of Japan. She wished to get away from the areas frequented by the mindless 'globetrotters'. For a single white woman to venture into rural Japan was courageous in the extreme. After Japan, Bird travelled on to other South-East Asian countries. Bird returned home when her beloved sister, Henrietta, became ill and later died of typhoid. She then married Dr Bishop who had been a long-time friend and had cared for Henrietta. Five years later, Dr Bishop died.

Soon after her husband's death, Bird resumed her travels, resolving this time to become a missionary. At the age of fifty-eight, she went to India and Kashmir and the countries high in the Himalayas. She founded a hospital as a memorial to her late husband, and continued her journey in company with some military surveyors to Tehran. She then rode alone on her mule through Iran, Kurdistan and Turkey. Her book *Journeys in Persia and Kurdistan*, was published in 1891.

By 1894, Bird's health was failing. Even so she travelled back to Japan, Korea and Manchuria.

These were dangerous territories then as the Sino-Japanese War was in progress. She decided to visit China and nearly lost her life there when she was attacked by mobs calling her a 'foreign devil'. Nevertheless, she continued to explore the Far East until 1898.

Bird's last foray into the wilds was when she was nearly seventy. This time she rode around Morocco on a large black stallion that she needed a ladder to mount, where she visited the Berber Arabs in the Atlas Mountains. She and her trusty steed travelled about a thousand miles.

Bird was to remain at home until her death in 1904. Her remarkable travels were recognised when she was elected as the first woman to be a Fellow of the Royal Geographical Society.

ELIZABETH BISLAND   1861-1926

Elizabeth Bisland was born in Louisiana where her family had owned a plantation, however, during the Civil War they lost money and had to move into town. She was tall, beautiful and highly intelligent.

Bisland started her literary career by submitting poetry to the New Orleans Times Democrat. This led to an offer of a job at the newspaper. Later she moved to New York City where she wrote for several publications, including the new monthly, Cosmopolitan Magazine, where, she worked as Literary Editor reviewing books.

The new owner of Cosmopolitan, John Brisben Walker, read of Nellie Bly's projected race around the world in 1889 and decided it would be good publicity for his magazine to launch a rival attempt. Bisland was only given six hours' notice before departure. She protested she had people coming to dinner that night, but was put on a train, so as to leave on the same day to travel in the opposite direction. Her instructions were to send progress reports to be published in the magazine. Her literary style of writing was very different to Bly's, being lyrical and poetic dwelling on the beauty of the scene rather than the sordid and sensational. She wrote seven 'stages' for the magazine and these were published as a book in 1891, In Seven Stages: A Flying Trip Around the World.

The circulation of the magazine was increased significantly as people wanted to read her dispatches, but since it only came out monthly, Bisland received far less publicity than did Bly. Though she did her best to complete the journey as quickly as possible, she always denied it was a race or competition. She also shunned any attempts to become a celebrity on her return, considering the adulation to be in bad taste.

Bisland might have equalled, or even beaten Bly's time, but for the serious delays in the last stage of her journey, when she was misinformed that the fast ship she could have taken across the Atlantic, had left, when in fact it had not. She then had to travel by train and ferry from Dover to Ireland. The ship she boarded in Ireland was old and slow, battling westerly storms, so she finally arrived after travelling seventy-six days, four days longer than her rival.

Soon after her return to the United States, Bisland travelled to England for a year where she continued writing and met many of the English literary figures of the day. On her return to New York, she married a corporate lawyer, Charles Whitman Wetmore in 1891. Together they had built a grand mansion in the Tudor style on Long Island, which they called Applegarth. After her marriage, Bisland continued to write under her maiden name. She published several books and wrote articles and essays until shortly before her death from pneumonia in 1929.

NELLIE BLY (Elizabeth Jane Cochran)   1864-1922

Elizabeth Cochran was born near Pittsburgh where her father was the owner of a mill. She was one of ten children. Her father died when she was very young, leaving the family in poverty.

In 1880 an article was written in the Pittsburgh Dispatch entitled, *'What are Girls Good for?'* This suggested that girls should be confined to domestic duties and denigrated working women. Elizabeth was inspired to write an angry, but well-constructed response. This impressed the editor so much that he offered young Elizabeth a job, but suggested she should write under the name of Nellie Bly.

She continued to write for the paper, but found she was increasingly pushed into the fashion and social pages while she wanted to write gritty stories about the poor treatment of women in the work-place. Eventually she left Pittsburgh and travelled to Mexico. She sent back articles about Mexican life and politics, but ran into trouble when she became too critical of the Mexican government and had to make a speedy exit from the country.

In 1887, Bly decided to try and break into the male dominated New York newspaper world. She found this extremely difficult, but after four months, by which time she was nearly starving, she managed to get a position on the staff of the New York World under editor Joseph Pulitzer. One of her first assignments was to feign madness and get herself admitted as an inmate in Blackwell Island Insane Asylum. Her report caused a sensation by uncovering the inhumane treatment and sub-standard conditions within the asylum, and led to changes in government policies for the treatment of the insane.

In 1888, Bly suggested to her editor that she should attempt to travel around the world in under eighty days, to beat the fictitious record held by Phileas Fogg in Jules Verne's book. Though initially reluctant, Pulitzer could visualise the publicity potential in such a story, so taking one dress, a warm coat and several changes of underwear in a small valise, she sailed on the steamer, *Augusta Victoria* to England. She then travelled to France to interview Jules Verne. She carried on around the world by way of steam ships and trains, all the while sending sensational stories back via electric telegraph. In these, she wrote in a racy style, dwelling on the dramas of delays, bad weather and the 'primitiveness' of the people and their outlandish customs. The journey ended with a dash across the USA from San Francisco to New York in a specially chartered train. She was met by a ten-gun salute and huge crowds of people. She arrived as a famous woman and soon after, she set off on a forty-city lecture tour to tell the world about her trip.

Additional publicity was generated by the newspaper offering a prize of a free trip to

Europe to the person who could guess the exact time taken to complete the journey (seventy-two days, six hours and eleven minutes). They also introduced a board game based on her journey.

After her epic journey, Bly returned to investigative journalism, focusing on women's issues, until 1895, when she married an industrialist forty years her senior. She then reinvented herself as a business woman, assisting him and continuing to run the factory after his death.

Later she was to return to journalism and in the First World War, became a war correspondent reporting from the Eastern Front. After the war, she ended her career as an 'Advice Columnist' and died in New York in 1922. She is remembered as a significant advocate for equal rights for women.

F. W. BURBIDGE   1847-1905

Frederick William Burbidge was the son of a Leicestershire farmer and fruit grower, who trained as a young man at the Royal Horticultural Society gardens at Chiswick. He continued his studies at Kew Royal Botanical Gardens, where he became an expert draftsman and botanical artist.

In 1876 he married Mary Wade, but a year later he left her in England to embark on an expedition to Borneo, and was away for two years. He was employed as a plant collector by Messrs Veitch, one of the largest nursery gardens in Europe. They specialised in exotic and unusual plants and he managed to bring back around one thousand species, many new to botanists. On his return he wrote a book called *The Gardens of the Sun: or A naturalist's Journal on the mountains and in the forests and swamps of Borneo and the Sulu Archipelago*. He dedicated it to his wife: 'I dedicate this book to My Wife, because while I worked abroad she waited at home. Most of us know how easy it is to labour – All of us know how hard it is to wait.'

In 1880, Burbidge was appointed as Curator at Trinity College botanical gardens in Dublin where he continued for the rest of his career. During this time he wrote many books on botany and horticulture and became highly respected in his field. He had an honorary degree (MA) bestowed on him by Dublin University and was awarded the Victoria Medal of Honour by the Royal Horticultural Society. In addition he had many new plant species named after him. Burbidge died of heart failure in 1905.

SIR WILLIAM HENRY GREGORY, KCMG   1816-1892

Sir William Gregory was a member of a well-to-do family in Ireland. He was born in Dublin Castle and was educated at Harrow and Christ Church College, Oxford. He inherited a large fortune from his grandfather, but he spent most of it on his passion for horse racing.

In 1842 he became a Conservative MP representing Dublin, but lost the seat at the next election, so he decided to travel. In 1855, he explored Egypt, Tunisia and other countries in the Middle East, and wrote a two-volume book of his experiences which became popular with the Victorian travelling public.

In 1857, he once more became a Member of Parliament, this time standing as a Liberal-Conservative, when Sir Robert Peel was Prime Minister. While travelling in the United States he was befriended by some politicians, who supported the Confederate side in the American Civil War. He also supported the Greeks in their struggle for independence from the Ottoman Empire. Another issue he tried to resolve was better housing and security for Irish tenant farmers. After serving for fourteen years, he retired from Parliament in 1871, and was invited to become Governor of Ceylon.

In 1872 Gregory married Elizabeth, who was the daughter of a fellow MP and had recently been widowed. Soon after the wedding, they travelled to Ceylon for him to take up his duties. In his autobiography, he writes of their enchantment with the country and his plans for various improvements that he saw were needed. They enjoyed travelling around the island and meeting the local rulers and people generally. He was an energetic and determined man and during his tenure, achieved much progress. He persuaded the Colonial Office to release funds for improvements to government buildings, hospitals, prisons, Colombo Port and the roads. Another area of improvement was the restoration of the irrigation system in the centre of the island which allow resulted in much better crops of rice and greatly improved the health of the communities. He took a keen interest in the archaeology and natural history of the island and encouraged scientific studies and publication of books on the subjects.

Sadly, Gregory was to lose his beloved wife to sun-stroke in 1875 and for a while, he found it impossible to undertake his work with enthusiasm. He took leave of absence for a few months, but returned to Ceylon to complete his term of office. One notable event during this time was the visit of Edward, Prince of Wales. This involved much pomp and ceremony at official functions and balls, but the Prince was keen to shoot elephants, so a chaotic hunt in torrential rain occurred. The Prince got his elephants, but one of them that he had just 'killed' (and was climbing on for a triumphant photo), then rose to its feet and lumbered off, back into the jungle. Luckly, without pausing to exact revenge on the heir to the British Empire's throne.

In 1877 Gregory resigned as Governor of Ceylon and returned home, visiting Australia on the way. In 1880 he married Isabella Augusta Persse who was thirty-five years his junior and together they spent some of their time in England and his estates in Ireland. They also travelled widely, including two return trips to Ceylon. He died of respiratory failure in 1892. His autobiography was edited and published after his death by his widow in 1894. Lady Augusta survived him by nearly forty years, dying in 1932. She became well known as a poet and playwright and was one of the leading figures in the Irish literary revival.

RUDYARD KIPLING   1865 – 1936

Joseph Rudyard Kipling, in his day, was probably the best known and most popular writer of prose and poetry for adults and children in England. When he was awarded the Noble Prize for literature in 1907, he was described as: 'The greatest genius in the realm of narrative that that country [Britain] has produced in our time.'

Kipling was born in 1865 in Bombay [Mumbai] and spent his early childhood in British India, which had a profound influence on his future life. At the age of six, he and his three-year-old sister, Alice were sent back to England to attend school and lodge with a couple who treated young Kipling very harshly. He spent five very unhappy years there, until his mother removed them in 1877 and he was sent to the United Services College at Westward Ho in Devon.

On leaving school in 1882, Kipling returned to India. He worked there until 1889, as a journalist with various newspapers, and published his first collections of poems and short stories, but in 1889, following a dispute with his editor, Kipling decided to return to England and travelled there via Japan and the USA, where he met Mark Twain.

Kipling lived in London and continued his literary career, including the production of his first novel, *The Light that Failed*, but became mentally unwell and in 1891, his doctor advised him to take a sea voyage. He travelled to South Africa, Australia and New Zealand and back to India to spend time with his parents.

In 1892 he married Caroline Balestier, having proposed to her by telegram and they took their honeymoon in the USA, where Caroline came from and then to Japan. Whilst in Japan, they discovered their bank had failed, so they had no money. They returned to Caroline's family in Vermont. Kipling and his wife settled in Vermont, during this time he continued to write books and poems, including the *Jungle Books*. This was a happy and productive time and they had their first daughter, but in 1896, the family returned to England where they settled first in Torquay. The following year they moved to Rottingdean in Sussex and in 1902, Kipling purchased 'Batemans', a house built in 1634, where he stayed until his death in 1937.

By this time his writings had made Kipling extremely famous. Besides the Nobel Prize, he received many other medals and awards. His poetry and books were much loved by young and old and he was regarded as the poet of the Empire. Some of his works had political content, supporting the British Empire, and the British against the Boers in South Africa, and later, he was strongly against the German Kaiser's aggression before and during the First World War. During the war he wrote to support the war effort, but he was deeply concerned about the way it was fought and the huge loss of life. His nineteen-year-old son was one of the soldiers killed.

Kipling continued to write after the war, but he produced less and people began to regard some of his work as being too jingoistic and dated. As peoples' attitudes changed, his fervent support of the Empire became less popular. Even so, many of his poems and stories have survived the test of time and are still loved by people several generations after they were written. In 1995, his inspiring poem, *If*, was voted by the British public as their most favourite poem, and many of his books have been turned into extremely successful movies. Rudyard Kipling lives on through his works to this day.

WILLIAM MAWSON   1866-1947

William Mawson was a man with a strong Christian faith. He was born in Yorkshire and lived in the Pontefract and Castleford area, where he worked as a wheelwright and joiner. He also became a Lay Preacher in the Methodist Church. In 1888 at the age of twenty two, he married Esther Milner, who was nineteen years old, and in the same year, the young couple left their home for Western Australia. They sailed from Tilbury with the Orient Line, on the mail ship *Liguria*.

The journey took five weeks and Mawson recorded his experiences of the voyage in an exercise book. The diary was stored in a chest and not discovered by the family until 1988 and has since been transcribed. On arrival at the town of Albany, on the south coast of Western Australia, Esther was very unwell for some time, but William found employment and rose to become a master builder and carpenter. Later they were to buy a farm where Esther ran a dairy.

In 1893, Mawson was offered the position of Home Missioner (a lay man who is commissioned by a bishop to share faith in Jesus Christ through ministries of love, justice and service) based at the town of Beverley, but covering many small settlements between Beverley and Mount Barker. He travelled by train, or a hand operated tricycle, if the train was not scheduled. Over the three years he held this position, it was estimated he travelled 70,000 kilometres.

In 1896, they returned to Albany, where Mawson resumed his building activities and was responsible for the construction of many substantial houses and churches in the district. They also bought a larger farm, which was needed to house Esther's expanding dairy business. This was twenty-five kilometres north of Albany at King River.

Mawson served time as an Albany Town Councillor for many years, and later as Mayor. During his tenure several significant public works were completed. One, of vital importance, was to ensure the growing town of Albany had a reliable supply of clean water. The town surveyor informed the Council about a stream high up in the mountains. They resolved that nearly all the town councillors would mount an expedition to inspect and assess this water source. It was going to take several days to get there and back, so essential supplies and camping gear were loaded into two horse carts and at 7am the party set off. It took an hour to reach Mawson's farm where Esther supplied them with a cooked breakfast. When refreshed, the expeditioners set off into the bush in the Mount Many Peaks area. It was hot steep climbing, particularly the last hour, which had to be accomplished on foot, but they found the beautiful crystal-clear stream. It was reported that Mawson was so uplifted by the sight of it, he sang a spirited rendering of the hymn, 'Let us gather at the River', and later said, 'I drank and drank again at that life-giving stream.' The other councillors, who were not teetotal like Mawson, toasted their discovery with bottles of beer from the Albany Brewing Company, which were part of the essential supplies they had brought with them.

Mawson was a pillar of society around Albany and served his community tirelessly in many capacities. Esther continued to run her thriving dairy farm and they had three sons, having lost one daughter in infancy. They died in their eighty-first years, William in 1947 and Esther in 1949. They were both much loved and respected members of their community.

MARIANNE NORTH   1830-1890

Marianne North's name is remembered by the many people who visit the pavilion at Kew Royal Botanical Gardens that bears her name and contains an assembly of wonderful flower paintings that she created.

She was born in Hastings, with one younger brother and sister. Her father, Frederick North, was a wealthy land owner and Member of Parliament. North loved singing and painting, both of which were considered suitable occupations for a young lady of her status. Whenever travelling with her family in Europe, she kept a beautifully illustrated journal. After North's mother died in 1855, as the oldest daughter in her family, she was expected to run the household and act as hostess for her father. She continued to travel with her father, particularly after he ceased to be an MP and they had more time to venture further. North took up oil painting and also became more interested in botany. She became a good friend of Sir Joseph Hooker, a leading botanist of the day and Director of Kew Royal Botanical Gardens.

North became very close to her father, so she was devastated by his death in 1869. To help overcome her grief, she resolved to keep travelling. She firstly went to Europe with her maid, but then, sold the house in Hastings and in 1871, set off for Jamaica, via the United States and Canada. Everywhere she went she painted flowers, trees and landscapes. Her paintings were not formal botanical records, but painted as they grew in their natural habitat. The next year she continued on to Brazil where she travelled alone and painted the beautiful tropical flowers she saw everywhere.

To escape the winter of 1875, North set sail for Tenerife and did not return to England until May. In August of the same year, she was off again for the United States and travelled by train to the west coast. There she visited San Francisco, Yosemite National Park and other beautiful areas: everywhere painting lovely pictures. In October she journeyed on to Japan, intending to stay for several months, but found the winter too cold for her health, so fled to warmer climes and spent most of the next year in Singapore, Borneo, Java and Ceylon before returning to England, where she spent six months. Her next expedition was to India.

When she returned to England in March 1879, she hired a gallery to exhibit her paintings because so many people had come flocking to her home wanting to see them. They caused a sensation and the Pall Mall Gazette first made the suggestion that such a collection should be housed at Kew. During 1880 and 1881 North painted in Borneo again, then, at the suggestion of Charles Darwin, visited Australia and New Zealand where she marvelled at the strange antipodean flora. On her way home, she re-visited the United States.

North was determined that her collection should contain flora from all the continents, so her last major journeys were to South Africa, the Seychelles and Chile. Then, at last her task was complete and all 832 paintings could be displayed in the Marianne North Pavilion at Kew Gardens, which she had designed and paid for herself.

North's achievements were remarkable. She had travelled the world alone, often under difficult circumstances, but by the end, her health was beginning to fail and all she desired was a quiet life in the country in her house in Gloucestershire. She created a garden full of rare plants, where she enjoyed welcoming her friends and family to visit her. She died in 1890, at the age of fifty-nine.

SIR THOMAS STAMFORD RAFFLES   1781-1826

Most people know of Sir Stamford Raffles as the founder of the great city of Singapore, with a grand hotel there named after him, but few know of the disappointments, disasters and sad events he endured during his comparatively short life.

Thomas Stamford Raffles was born on a ship off the coast of Jamaica. His father was a sea captain who was to fall on hard times, so young Raffles had to leave school at the age of fourteen. He was put to work as a clerk at the London office of the British East India Company. People were impressed by his brightness and diligence, so in 1805 he was sent to the new Port of Penang, on what was then called Prince of Wales Island.

Stamford did well in Penang. He studied the local culture and natural history and learned to speak Malay. He married Olivia, the widow of a doctor. She was some years older than him, but they were a very devoted couple. He was a protégé and assistant secretary of Lord Minto, the Governor-General of India, who was impressed by Raffles' abilities.

In 1811 during the Napoleonic Wars France conquered Holland, so Dutch colonies became French possessions. It was decided to invade the Dutch ruled island of Java and establish British rule there. Raffles was appointed Lieutenant-Governor. During his tenure, he tried to rescind some of the harsher Dutch practices, and instigated studies into the natural history, archaeology and history of the island. In 1814 Raffles' wife Olivia died, which completely shattered him. To add to his woes, he was accused of mismanagement, resulting in poor financial returns and ordered back to England in disgrace. There, he was able to clear his name and the Prince Regent knighted him. He married his second wife, Sophia in 1817.

Sir Stamford and his wife returned to the East, where he was appointed Resident of the British post at Bencoolen (Bengkulu). This was on the west coast of Sumatra and was known as a hell hole. It had a wet and unhealthy climate, little agricultural possibilities and a miserable population. It was obvious this was not suitable as a centre for British traders, so Raffles looked elsewhere.

In 1819, Raffles picked Singapore, a small fishing village with a magnificently sheltered harbour. He negotiated with local rulers to allow the British to set up a trading post there. Needless to say, the Dutch were furious, but Singapore quickly became the great success story of the region. As a free trade port, there were soon more ships arriving there, than all the other local ports put together.

Raffles only lived in Singapore for eight months in all; he stayed just long enough to set things up and make arrangements for essential services to be established. An administrator was appointed, but Raffles had to return later on to deal with his bungles and write a constitution.

While Singapore thrived, Raffles and his family were sent back in Bencoolen. All were in bad health and four of his young children died. In 1823, Raffles, his wife and one remaining daughter, set off for England, but their ship burned, and with it, all their possessions. Eventually, they reached England, and Raffles was honoured by being made the first President of the Royal Zoological Society; however, The East India Company claimed he owed them £22,000 for losses he caused them. While the dispute went on, Raffles died suddenly of a cerebral haemorrhage. He was only forty-four years old. The Company then demanded all the money in his estate, which amounted to £10,000. This left his widow and child with very little.

ELIZA RUHAMAH SCIDMORE   1856-1928

Eliza Scidmore was a fiercely independent lady with a passion for travel, writing and photography. She achieved many 'firsts' throughout her career.

Scidmore (pronounced Sidmore) was born in Iowa, USA, and her parents separated during the Civil War. She lived with her mother in Washington. Eliza attended college for two years then, at nineteen, started writing the social pages for a local newspaper. As soon as she saved enough money she travelled to Alaska, firstly in 1883, when she was on the first ship to penetrate Glacier Bay. She wrote articles about her experiences for newspapers and magazines, including the National Geographic Magazine. She made other excursions there and in 1885, her articles were collected to form the first guide book of Alaska.

In 1885, Scidmore and her mother travelled to Japan to visit her brother who was a member of the consular staff. This was to be the first of many visits, as she fell in love with the country and its people. This resulted in her book: *Jinricksha Days in Japan,* published in 1891. She was to write another book about Japan later.

In 1890 Scidmore became a member of the National Geographic Society and contributed articles about the places she visited, with her own photographs to illustrate them. She was the first female photographer used by the Society and later was to become the first woman to be a member of their board.

Throughout the 1890s, Scidmore travelled in China, India, Philippines, and Java, as well as several return trips to Japan. She wrote popular books about all the countries she visited. In 1896, while reporting on the effects of an earthquake in Japan, she introduced the word, 'Tsunami' into the English lexicon.

When she saw how beautiful the spring cherry blossom was in Japan, she was inspired to suggest that Washington should grow cherry trees in the parks there, but her idea was resisted for years. Finally Helen Taft, the President's wife, supported the concept. In 1910 Japan donated 3,000 cherry trees that were planted along the Potomac River in the newly created Potomac Park, near the Washington Monument. These made a wonderful display in the spring and are still admired today.

Scidmore continued to write for the National Geographic for many years, until her death in 1928. She was an intensely private person and stipulated in her will that her papers were to be destroyed at the time of her death and her ashes were to be interred at the place she loved the best in the world: Yokohama.

HIS HIGHNESS RAJA-i-RAJGAN JAGATJIT SINGH OF KAPURTHALA, GLSI, GCIE, GBE 1872 -1949

This noble Sikh prince was the ruling Maharaja of the princely state of Kapurthala in India, who came into his inheritance at the age of five and was to rule for sixty-seven years. He was intensely loyal to Britain, a lover of French culture, and was a gifted linguist. Portraits show him looking extremely regal, with a large turban, magnificent traditional garments and many jewels.

He was recognised world-wide as a great ruler, and numbered among his friends most of the ruling heads of the world whom he met during his travels. He stayed three times at Windsor castle as a guest of Queen Victoria and was friends with several Presidents of the United States. In later life, he was to serve as India's representative on the League of Nations in 1926, 1927 and 1929. He was awarded countless decorations and medals throughout his life.

During his rule, he embarked on some major building programs in Kapurthala: several magnificent palaces (his main palace was modelled on the Palace of Versailles), religious temples and lovely gardens. He was much loved and respected by his subjects.

He enjoyed travelling and visited many countries. He was to go around the world twice. He travelled in style with a retinue of servants and as a matter of course, was invited to stay at royal palaces, government houses, or the very best hotels wherever he went. The fact that he was a man of immense charm and could speak many languages also helped to make him a very welcome guest.

He wrote several books about his journeys. They were published as limited additions, which he said he wrote mainly for the benefit of his family. Now, copies of his books are collectors' items and are worth many hundreds of dollars. A copy of *My Travels in Europe and America* was presented to Queen Victoria in 1896 and is still held in the Royal collection of books at Windsor.

Maharaja Jagatjit Singh had several wives during his lifetime and he insisted that his children should receive the best education available. Many were sent to elite schools and colleges in England and France, so they could take their place, as he did, as cosmopolitan citizens of the world. He died in 1949 at the age of 76, much loved and mourned by all who had known him.

MAJOR THOMAS SKINNER, CMG 1804-1877

Major Skinner was one of the key figures in the development of the roads system throughout the island of Ceylon. He served there for nearly fifty years, which says a lot for his tenacity and strong constitution. This enabled him to survive the myriad of tropical diseases that killed so many of his contemporaries. During an extremely busy life, he married Georgina Burrell and they had six children.

Skinner was born in St John's, on the island of Newfoundland. His father, a British Army officer, was stationed there. His mother died when he was very young. Later the family returned to England, but when his father was posted to Ceylon, Skinner and his sister were placed in a school in Britain, where they remained as permanent boarders for six years.

At the age of fifteen, Skinner travelled out to Ceylon to join his father who was stationed at the port of Trincomalee. He joined the army and found himself, as Second Lieutenant, in charge of a detachment of Ceylon Rifles soldiers. He had to lead a march all the way from Trincomalee across the island to Colombo. Since he was small for his age, they could not find a uniform to fit him, so he had to wear his old school jacket for his first military duty. This journey was quite a feat, considering his age, as there were no proper roads and the route passed through countryside which had recently been in a state of rebellion.

Life in the army was tough for a small boy of fifteen. He had to contend with sadistic officers, constant drilling and parades. On the first occasion he was invited to dine with the Governor, wearing full dress uniform and a huge sword, he disgraced himself by falling asleep at the table, but Lady Brownrigg took pity on him and let him sleep on her bed until the other officers were ready to return to barracks. He also became very ill with dysentery, which continued until he was transferred to the high country where his commanding officer dosed him with laudanum and port. When he recovered, he was left in charge of the post and at this time, shot his first elephant. This was to be the first of many he shot whilst in Ceylon. He nearly died of malaria when out hunting in the jungle, but he was cured by being bled, dosed with forty grains of calomel (mercurous chloride) and doused with cold water.

In 1820, Governor Sir Edwards Barnes decided that an effective network of roads must be built and invited Skinner to take charge of some sections. In spite of a complete lack of experience, Skinner commanded a road gang and found that he enjoyed the work. He continued building roads throughout the island and was ordered to make a survey of the mountainous region around Kandy. Ten years later, in 1830, he was sent on a recruitment drive for soldiers from the Malay Archipelago.

In 1841, Skinner was appointed Commissioner of Roads, a position he held until his retirement in 1867, by which time the post was enlarged to be Commissioner of Public Works. Skinner was the main advocate of the need for railways, and subsequently construction started in the 1850s. In addition, he acted as Auditor General and served on the Legislative Council between 1854 and 1861.

Skinner's wife died in 1866 and he retired, returning to England in 1867. He was awarded a CMG and a generous pension in recognition of his long and distinguished service. He had a happy retirement with his family and spent time fishing, and looking at his magnificent collection of sea shells, which he eventually presented to the British Museum. Skinner wrote his autobiography, *Fifty Years in Ceylon*, which was edited by his daughter, Annie and published after his death.

MARY STEUART

Mary Steuart wrote a charming, beautifully written book, entitled *Everyday Life on a Ceylon Cocoa Estate* which was published in 1905.

Steuart wrote the book during the months she spent in Ceylon visiting her son, Rob, who was a trainee planter of cocoa. He had invited her to stay with him for the winter months, telling her he lived in a charming bungalow, not far from Kandy, with a tennis court and rose-garden, with plenty of nice neighbours nearby. On her arrival, she was disconcerted to find he had been transferred to an extremely isolated place, miles from any neighbours or shops for provisions. The simple accommodation was designed for one bachelor only, so the first thing they needed to do was to get permission to build on an extra room for her to sleep in.

Steuart realised she would be spending many hours on her own while her son was out working on the plantation, so she decided to while away the time by writing of her experiences. The result is a book which conveys a vivid picture of what life was like for a young, single man on a plantation, at the beginning of the twentieth century. She writes of dealings and dramas with the domestic staff and the Tamil 'coolies', encounters with wild animals and occasional social occasions with other planters. She speculates on how the average young Englishman, often straight from school, would cope with the isolation and responsibilities; all for a salary less than that of a junior clerk in England.

There is nothing in the book which reveals much about the Steuart family circumstances, or what happened after the book was written. One wonders if Rob, like so many young men of his age enlisted in the First World War and if so, whether he survived.

JOHN STILL   1880-1941

John Still was a man who had an intense love for Ceylon, but suffered from bad health mainly caused by the tropical climate and attendant diseases. He wrote several scholarly books about the island and its history, but sadly destroyed many of them, judging them not worthy of publication.

John was born in England and educated at Winchester College. At the age of seventeen he started life as a trainee tea planter in Ceylon, but he soon found he was more interested in the wild life and jungles of the country than in tea, so in 1902, he joined the Ceylon Department of Archaeology, to work as an assistant to H. C. P. Bell. This enabled him to spend time in the jungle and he made several important archaeological discoveries in Anuradhapura, Mihintale, Sigiriya and the ruins of Polonnaruwa. Unfortunately, although he loved the work, he only continued for five years because he became so ill with malaria that he was invalided back to England.

However, he returned to Ceylon in 1908 and worked in the Land Settlement Department and then in 1911, at the Ceylon Labour Commission. He became Secretary of the Ceylon Planters Society and married in 1914.

At the outbreak of the First World War, Still enlisted in the Ceylon Contingent and was posted to the Middle East. He was captured by the Turks who imprisoned him for several years. During this time, in spite of being in very poor health, he wrote two books, *Poems in Captivity* and *A Prisoner in Turkey*. These had to be concealed in a hollow walking stick. He sent coded letters to England to alert the authorities to the sufferings of the prisoners of war in Turkey, so steps could be taken to alleviate the conditions.

After the war, Still returned to Ceylon and resumed his employment with the Planters Association, but again his increasing ill health forced him to return to Britain in 1926. He and his wife went to live in Wales where he wrote books: *Jungle Tide* was published and received critical acclaim. He wrote several other books which he destroyed. Still's wife died during this time, leaving him with his only son, John.

Now suffering from diabetes and arthritis, Still moved to Rhodesia in 1939 where he was cared for by the daughter of an old friend from Ceylon. As a final tragedy in his life, Still's son was killed while serving in the RAF in 1940. This was a blow from which he never recovered, and he died in 1941.

MARK TWAIN   1835-1910

Samuel Clemens, or Mark Twain his pen name, was born in Florida, Missouri, at the time of an astral appearance of Halley's Comet. His family moved to Hannibal, Missouri. This environment provided material for later literary works, such as *The Adventures of Huckleberry Finn* and *Tom Sawyer*.

Twain started his working life at a young age; primarily as an apprentice to a printer, but he also started writing articles for his brother's newspaper. He then worked as a river boat pilot on the Mississippi River. He next travelled to Nevada, partly to avoid having to fight in the American Civil war. There he tried mining with lamentable lack of success, but these experiences were things he wrote about when he branched into satirical writing for the local newspapers. In 1866 he travelled to the 'Sandwich Islands' as Hawaii was known then and wrote for papers there.

By 1867, he was in New York where he heard of a planned excursion to Europe and the Holy Land, and managed to get himself sponsored by several New York newspapers, which would pay for his trip in exchange for articles about the journey. These very funny accounts were extremely popular and were later published as a book named Innocents Abroad. It was during this trip that one of the other passengers showed him a photo of his sister. Twain decided instantly this was the girl for him, and so she was. He and Olivia Langdon were married in 1868, and had three daughters and one son, who died as a boy. They had a very happy marriage.

The family first lived in Buffalo, New York and then in Hartford Connecticut, during which time Twain wrote hugely successful books, short stories and articles for the press. He was much in demand as a public speaker and he could charge substantial speaker's fees. He travelled widely, sometimes with his wife, sometimes alone, including journeys to Europe and throughout the world, where he was nearly as well-known as in his own country.

The revenue from his writings and public speaking made Twain a rich man, but at the same time, he made some unwise investments. By the 1890s he was deeply in debt, so he and his wife embarked on a round-the-world lecture tour, visiting countries including New Zealand, Australia, South Africa, India, and many more. People flocked to hear his witty talks and on their return to New York, he was able to repay all money he owed. Twain wrote about this journey in the book, *Following the Equator*, which is a wonderful travelogue written in his unique satirical style.

Twain continued writing and also visiting Europe, but in 1904, his beloved wife, Olivia, passed away, also several close friends and family members died This caused him to sink into a deep depression, so the last years of his life were not happy ones. He died at the age of seventy-four in 1910, coincidentally just as Halley's Comet visited the earth once more.

Mark Twain has been recognised as one of America's greatest National Treasures. His writings have given pleasure to people all over the world and he was awarded honorary doctorates by universities in the United States and other counties. His name is still well-remembered today and his works gain new devotees when they are presented in the form of films and TV programs.

ALFRED RUSSEL WALLACE   1823-1913

Alfred Russel Wallace, known as the 'father of biogeography', was a naturalist and explorer, who rose to great fame from humble beginnings. His family were respectable, but poor, his father having lost almost all his money to a swindler. Alfred, who was the second youngest in a family of ten, left school at fourteen, due to a lack of funds. He went to work with his older brother as a surveyor. They travelled around the countryside and Alfred became extremely interested in the flowers that he saw. He bought a book to help identify them and started a collection of dried flowers.

He next went to Leicester where he obtained a post at a school, teaching surveying and other subjects, but he also continued to pursue his study of natural history, particularly beetles. He was amazed at their colours and complexity and he collected about one thousand species around Leicester.

At the age of twenty-five, Wallace and his naturalist friend, Henry Bates, embarked on an expedition to Brazil. They explored and collected specimens in the wild country around the Amazon. These were sent back to museums and collectors. It was here that Wallace first became interested in the theory of evolution.

By 1852, Wallace was in bad health, so he returned to England. Disaster struck when the ship caught fire and sank, taking most of his precious scientific notes and specimens. Wallace and the ship's crew were adrift in two leaky life boats for some time, but fortunately were picked up by a cargo boat and taken to England.

Wallace's next expedition, which was to last eight years, was to the Malay Archipelago and Borneo. During this time he collected thousands of specimens, about five thousand of which were new to science. These were sold to finance the trip. It was at this time that Wallace firmed up his ideas on evolutionary theory and natural selection. He also discovered the biogeographical line between Bali and Lombok, islands of the Indonesian archipelago, which divided the flora and fauna into those that originated in Asia (west of the line) from those of Australasia (east of the line). This came to be known as the 'Wallace Line'. He wrote a paper on his theory of evolution and sent it to Charles Darwin, for his opinion. This caused great embarrassment to Darwin because he had come to the same conclusions himself some time before, but had never published them officially. It was decided to solve the problem of precedence; both papers should be presented at the Linnaean Society at the same time. Wallace was away in Borneo, so inevitably Darwin received the lion's share of credit and fame.

Wallace returned to England in 1862 with his many thousands of specimens. These were sold to generate some income, because, unlike Darwin, he had no independent means. He married Annie Mitten in 1866 and then settled down to write his book, *The Malay Archipelago*. This is recognised as one of the best nineteenth century books on scientific travel. He also wrote about a thousand papers on his findings and twenty-two other books. He received many awards and medals for his contributions to natural history and was revered as one of the most respected scientists of his day. He died at the age of ninety in 1913.

References

Aoki, Eiichi, Japanese Railway History: Dawn of Japanese Railways (Japan Railway and Transport Review; 1, pp 28-30, March 1994)

Anderson, Roy, White Star (Prescott, Lancashire: T Stephenson & Sons Ltd., 1964)

Baker, Sir Samuel White, Eight Years Wandering in Ceylon (UK: Dodo Press, 2015)

Barley, Nigel, The Duke of Puddle Dock. Travels in the Footsteps of Stamford Raffles (Penguin Books, 1993)

Bindloss, Gertrude, My Trip to Siam (unpublished memoir, 1887)

Bird, Isabella, Unbeaten Tracks in Japan (London: John Murray, 1879)

Bisland, Elizabeth, In Seven Stages: A Flying trip Round the World (New York: Harper and Bros., 1891)

Bly, Nellie, Round the World in Seventy-two Days and Other Writings (New York: Penguin Classics, 2014)

Bristowe, Bertie A. Notes Taken During my Journey Round the World (unpublished memoir, 1897)

Bristowe, W.S., An Outline of his Life and a List of his Publications (unpublished memoirs, 1976)

Bristowe, W.S., The Bristowes, After and Before the Norman Conquest (unpublished memoirs, 1976)

Burbidge, Frederick William, The Gardens of the Sun: or a Naturalist's Journal on the mountains and forests and swamps of Borneo and the Sulu Archipelago (London: John Murray, 1880)

Burk, Kathleen, The Grand Tour of Europe (Lecture transcript at Gresham College, 2005)

Carol Belanger Grafton (ed), Humorous Victorian Spot Illustrations. Dover Publication, 1985

Chamberlain, Basil Hall, Mason, W.B., Handbook for Travellers in Japan (London: John Murray, 1885)

De Kerbrech, Richard, Ships of the White Star Line (London: Allen Ltd., 2009)

Dick, H.W., Kentwell, S.A., Beancakes to Boxboats: Steamship Companies in Chinese Waters (Canberra: The Nautical Association of Australia Inc., 1988)

Gamage, Rajika, An Illustrated Field Guide to the Fauna of Sri Lanka Volume 1: Butterflies (Baddegama, Sri Lanka: Rajika Gamage, 2013)

Gregory, Sir William, An Autobiography (London: John Murray, 1894)

Grossmith, George and Grossmith, Weedon, The Diary of a Nobody (London: J.M. Dent & Co., 1948)

Haputhanthri, Kumudini Dias, History Supplementary Reader (Nugegoda: Sarasavi Publishers, 2013)

Higgs, Michelle, A Visitor's Guide to Victorian England (Barnsley: Pen and Sword Books Ltd., 2014)

Horn, Pamela, Pleasures and Pastimes in Victorian Britain (Stroud: Sutton Publishing 1999)

Howarth, David & Howarth, Stephen, The Story of P&O (London: George Weidenfeld & Nicholson Ltd., 1994)

Jagatjit Singh, Rajgan, Maharaja of Kapurthala, My Travels in China, Japan and Java (London: Hutcheson, 1903)

Johnston, Sir Harry, The Story of My Life (Indianapolis: Bobbs Merrill Company, 1923)

Kipling, Rudyard, Kipling's Japan: Collected Writings (London: Bloomsbury Academic Collection, 1988)

Kipling, Rudyard, The Five Nations (New York: Caxton Press, 1903)

Lloyd, W.W., P&O Pencillings (London: George Weidenfeld & Nicholson Ltd., 1892)

Louis, William, R., Sir Percy Anderson's Grand African Strategy 1883-1889 (English Historical Review, Vol. 81, 1966)

McCart, Neil, Passenger Ships of the Orient Line (Wellingborough: Patrick Stephens Ltd., 1987)

McDougal, Robert, & Gardiner, Robin, White Star Line in Picture Postcards (London: Ian Allen Ltd., 2003)

Macy, Sue, Wheels of Change: How Women Rode the Bicycle to Freedom (With a Few Flat Tires Along the Way) (Washington: National Geographic Publications, 2011)

Mawson, William, An Account of the Journey to Western Australia (unpublished memoir, 1888)

May, Trevor, Victorian and Edwardian Horse Cabs (Oxford: Shire Publications, 2010)

Michie, Ranald C., The London Stock Exchange: a History (Oxford: Oxford University Press, 1999)

Morgan, Kenneth. J., The Oxford Illustrated History of Britain (Oxford: Oxford University Press, 2008)

Morris, Neil, Life in Victorian Times: Travel and Transport (London: Belitha Press, 2013)

Morris, Neil, Life in Victorian Times: Home School (London: Belitha Press, 2000)

Morris, Neil, Life in Victorian Times: Sport Leisure (London: Belitha Press, 1999)

Morris, Neil, Ships Past and Present (London: Belitha Press, 1999)

Nappo, Salvatore Ciro, Pompeii (Vercelli, Italy: White Star Publisher, 2011)

Peebles, Patrick, The History of Sri Lanka (London: Greenwood Press, 2005)

Raffles, Sir T Stamford, History of Java (London: John Murray, 1832)

Ridley, Jane, Bertie: A Life of Edward Vll (London: Chatto and Windus, 2012)

Royal Botanic Gardens, Kew, A Vision of Eden: The Life and Work of Marianne North (Exeter: Webb & Bower, 1980)

Scidmore, Eliza Ruhamah, Jinricksha Days in Japan (New York: Harper & Brothers, 1891)

Scidmore, Eliza Ruhamah, Java, the Garden of the East (New York: Century, 1897)

Scott-Pagett, Rupert, A P & O Passage to india – P & O Steam Navigation Company (www.pandosnco.uk/a_passage_to_india.html)

Skinner, Major Thomas, Fifty Years in Ceylon (Dehiwala, Sri Lanka: Tisara Prakaskayo Ltd., 2010)

Steuart, Mary E. Everyday Life on a Ceylon Cocoa Estate (London: Henry J. Drane, 1905)

Still, John, The Jungle Tide (Dhiwala, Sri Lanka: Thisara Prakashakayo Ltd., 2002)

Swinglehurst, Edmund, The Romantic Journey: The Story of Thomas Cook and Victorian Travel (London: Pica Editions, 1974)

The Young ladies' Treasure Book: A Complete Cyclopaedia of Practical Instruction for All Indoor and Outdoor Occupations and Amusements Suitable for Young Ladies (London: Ward, Lock and Co., 1890)

Turner, David, Victorian and Edwardian Railway Travel (Botley, Oxford: Shire Publications, 2013)

Twain, Mark, Following the Equator (Hartford, Connecticut: The American Publishing Company, 1897)

Twain, Mark, Innocents Abroad or the New Pilgrim's Progress (Hartford, Connecticut: The American Publishing Company, 1869)

Ver Berkmoes, Ryan, Butler, Stuart, Karafin, Amy, Sri Lanka (Lonely Planet Publications, 2012)

Wallace, Alfred Russel, The Malay Archipelago: The Land of the Orang-Utan and the Bird of Paradise, A Narrative of Travel with Studies of Man and Nature (London: MacMillan and Co., 1890)

Williams, Harold S., Shades of the Past: Indiscreet Tales of Japan (Tokyo: Charles Tuttle, 1959)

Wright, Arnold, Twentieth Century Impressions of British Malaya: Its History, People, Commerce, Industries and Resources (London: Lloyds Publishing, 1908)

Acknowledgements

I am so grateful to the many people who have given generously of their time and knowledge to help me in the creation of Travels in the Realms of Gold.

Firstly I would like to thank my two sisters who have both been invaluable in their encouragement and support throughout the venture. It was in Belinda's house that I first discovered Bertie's journal and also where most of the Bristowe memorabilia and photos are kept. Without her kind and generous hospitality and wise advice, this book would never have happened. Richenda has also been endlessly encouraging and as an experienced writer of books, was able to guide me in so many ways and assist with editing, formatting and other practical matters: All done with endless good humour and patience.

I am also grateful for the editing and advice from Alison Fox and Mary Edgar who assisted me in the earlier stages.

I want to thank my cousins, Susan Horner, John Henderson and Sophie MacCaulay, who kindly contributed family papers or images which helped me to present a fuller picture of Bertie and the family as it was in the 19th century. I am also grateful to Margaret Davies and her family for granting me permission to use sections of William Mawson's vivid account of his sea voyage.

As the writing of the book progressed, I became increasingly fascinated by the magnificent old steam ships, about which I knew very little. I have learned so much about shipping, and in particular P&O from Michael Vale, who has assisted with advice, documents, encouragement and in correcting my more glaring inaccuracies and mistakes about maritime matters. I also received some invaluable assistance with facts about the White Star Line from Roy Anderson, some information about early shipping from Colin Elwood and Eddie Valentine, whose grandfather had been captain of Fatshan early in the 20th century.

I would like to thank Ian Farquhar for giving permission to use his images of ships. Also Stanford University Library for granting permission to reproduce their images of O&O ships.

Over the time I have been writing this book, I gained useful insights from the advice and inspiration I received from Des Cox and other Maritime Memories members. I travelled with them on many sea voyages and their collective expertise in shipping history is awesome.

I would like to thank Julianne Waldock of the WA Museum, who photographed specimens of Sri Lankan butterflies from their collection and gave me permission to reproduce them. Also Sally Birch, a gifted artist, who painted the beautiful image of Kallima butterfly especially for this publication.

There are some people I have only met via the internet, but have been able to make valuable contributions to this book. One is Beth Ellis at P&O Heritage who assisted me with images and information. Another is Pat Sabin who gave me permission to use her beautifully restored vintage postcards of various US scenes.

I obtained good advice from the Federation of Australian Writers WA writers' group meetings. These were led by Louise Allen, who was most inspiring and motivating. It was exciting to hear of other members' endeavours and receive their encouragement with mine. I must also pay tribute to the role of the University of the Third Age members who urged me to start this book in the first place.

I have to confess that computer technology and I do not always agree, so I have really appreciated the support and practical assistance in technical matters kindly given by Sinisa Veselinovic and Stefano Cappelini.

And thank you to Helen Isles, Linellen Press, for taking on the publication of this book.

Finally, as writing can be a solitary occupation, I have always valued the companionship I received from Amy, my cat. She invariably insisted on sitting on my desk in front of the computer screen and supervising my work as I typed. She just occasionally would step on the keys, with some interesting results.

Virginia Bristowe

Co-writer, Amy

www.ingramcontent.com/pod-product-compliance
Lightning Source LLC
Chambersburg PA
CBHW062022090426
42811CB00005B/930